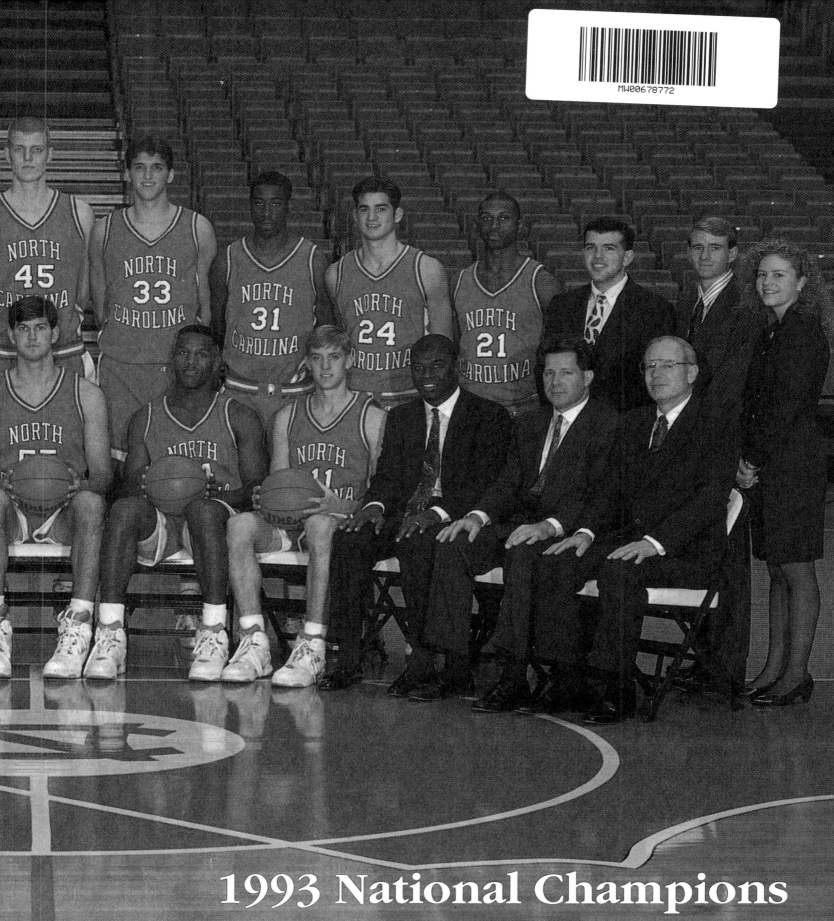

1993 National Champions Of College Basketball

ACC BASKETBALL HANDBOOK'S

NORTH CAROLINA

NATIONAL CHAMPIONSHIP

1993

Season Of Dreams

ACKNOWLEDGMENTS

We're proud to present what we think is the best and most comprehensive book on North Carolina's 1992-93 NCAA basketball championship season. Our goal was to make this a book about the coaches and the players who made it all happen, and then put it together in story form so that you can relive the thrills of the season, all the way from the start of practice on Nov.1 to the celebration on the Superdome court on the night of April 5, 1993.

Our most special thanks go to the North Carolina players. They shared with us their private thoughts, gave us their insights and best wishes. These young men are champions in every way.

Coach Dean Smith and assistants Bill Guthridge, Phil Ford and Randy Wiel were generous with their time and remarks.

Basketball office secretaries Linda Woods, Kay Thomas and Ruth Kirkendall have put up with us for many seasons. The first face you see when you walk into UNC's basketball office is that of Angela Lee. She is as good at her job as George Lynch was at his, and we couldn't get along without her.

Bobby Jones, one of the greatest players in Carolina basketball history, wrote the moving foreword for this book. He was nice to do this for us, and when he accepted the assignment, he carried it out with his customary brilliance.

My most special thanks go to Sherry Blythe, who labored long and hard over the book's layout and design; to reporters Mike Small and Bert Woodard for their excellent interviewing and proofing skills; to Scott Cooper and Gara Phillips and photographer Keith Worrell, and also to Brett Shippy of UMI Publications.

Our task was made easier by the friendship and encouragement of John Lotz, an assistant athletic director at Carolina, and also by good friend Dave Hanners, who served as an administrator last season but now goes back to his first love of coaching.

We were assisted by Martha Mills, Hazel Minor, Joan Pendergraph and Cathy Campbell in the records department of the UNC General Alumni Association.

This book is given a special and unique flavor because of contributions from former players, most of whom interrupted busy schedules to gladly participate.

We thank Eric Hutchinson, in the public relations department of the Boston Celtics; Bob Zink, assistant in public relations for the Cleveland Cavaliers; and the public relations department of the Los Angeles Clippers.

Reporter Chris McManes got us the quote from Michael Jordan and long-time friend Kevin Barris interviewed Kenny Smith in Houston.

Carolina's basketball season was a long and twisting journey to the championship. So was the writing and gathering of information and production of this book. It was a tedious assignment, often frustrating, but always done with love and care. In the process, we gained even a keener appreciation of the greatness of what Dean Smith has built at North Carolina. To be sure, it goes much deeper than winning basketball games and championships.

The project was undertaken for you, the Carolina basketball fan. We hope you enjoy the following stories and pictures. It was truly a "Season of Dreams," and we hope this book keeps your dream alive and fresh in your mind for years to come.

• • • • • • • • • • • • • • • •

North Carolina National Championship Staff:
Ivan Mothershead, Publisher; Charlie Keiger, Associate Publisher; Merry Schoonmaker, Associate Publisher; John Kilgo, Senior Editor; Mike Small, Bert Woodard, Scott Cooper, Gara Phillips, Interviewing-editing; Sherry Blythe, Brett Shippy, Design, layout and typesetting; Amy Vail, Mark Cantey, Terry McCorkle, Asst. Editors.

Contributing Photographers:

Michael E. Anderson	Beth McGorigal
Walter Beasley	Ross Obley
Drew Cline	Will Owens
Jim Crawford	Charlie Pack
Julian H. Gonzalez	Ed Pasley
Jim Hawkins	Steve Smith
Robert Hull	Vern Verna
Jeff Jacobsen	Wide World Photos
	Keith Worrell

*any ommissions purely unintentional

ISBN # 0-943860-07-5

Table of
CONTENTS

"This is for you,"
Dean Smith said to
his players.

FOREWORD

- **UNC '74**
- **Former NBA All-Star**
- **Currently Director of Development, Athletic Director, Head Men's Basketball Coach**
  Charlotte Christian School, Charlotte, N.C.

This was a special basketball team, even by Carolina basketball standards. Unfortunately, the way the college game has gotten, being a good team, even a great team, doesn't guarantee a national championship. I'm thankful that this Tar Heel team was able to weather some of the storms that it went through in the playoffs to achieve its goal of winning the national title. I'm very appreciative of this Carolina team, these players, for providing Dean Smith another national championship, something that I, and so many of his other former players, couldn't do for him.

Coach Smith deserves many national championships and it was fitting that this team was able to accomplish this goal. They may not have been as talented as some of Coach Smith's other teams, but look at the leadership. That was key. George Lynch, to me, was the key to the whole thing. His leadership, determination, refusal to lose, is hard to replace. As Coach Smith pointed out many times, George did a lot of good things on the court, but he also had the mentality that strengthened all of the other players.

My time in the Carolina basketball program with Coach Smith was more of a foundation for me, not only in athletics but also in life--discipline, being on time, submitting to authority, learning to work with others. All coaches want to teach these things. A lot of coaches will stress one thing and some other coaches will stress another, but Coach Smith's efficiency of winning games while at the same time instilling in his players character traits is the strength of Carolina's program.

People say that Coach Smith goes after good people, and he does, but there are a lot of good people in college athletics who get misguided and misdirected. Coach Smith has consistently over the years given the effort during a player's career, and then after that player's career, to make sure that person has a chance to be successful in our society. When you sign a letter-of-intent with Dean Smith, you sign on for life.

In basketball, I've been fortunate to have been successful at all levels of the sport. In high school, with my size, that was easy. But Coach Smith's program is the kind that gives you the opportunity to succeed at the college level and reach the next level. Sometimes, Coach Smith will sign a player and people say, "Why has this guy been signed?" I remember my high school senior year, there were four of us and the media called it a bad recruiting year. They picked Carolina, as they often do, to be third, fourth in the league my freshman year. But we never finished worse than second during my career.

Coach Smith has developed a system that is amazing. It's hard to do that in such a "me-oriented" society, but he has gotten people to understand the value of submitting and allowing somebody else's ability to come forward for the good of the team. As you become less, the team becomes more. He's convinced his players that, and it works. It's incredible how he's done that. He's a great basketball coach, he's a genius on the court as far as coaching, but more than that, as far as working with players, the mental attitudes that he develops with his teams, the toughness that they have, I don't know of another coach in the country who has been able to do that for the number of years that he has.

The mystique of the Carolina basketball family is very real. We are a family. It is an impressive fraternity and it stems from Coach Smith. I do things for people whom I don't even know, who played for Coach, maybe in the 1980s and didn't play much, and if I can help them in any way, I do, and it's mainly because of Coach Smith. I look at his influence on his players. He's planted all of these seeds and they have sprouted, and they are out there being good citizens and helping other people. His influence with his former players goes well beyond what he does personally on a day-to-day basis. He has impressed upon us, really as a second father, some values and motivations that he carries.

I'm a high school coach now, but Coach and I don't have the time to sit down with each other and talk strategy very often. He has made available to me, as he does all his former players who are now coaches, his film library and his film room, and I've been up to Chapel Hill a number of times to look at different defenses and offenses. But when we get together, we talk about other things besides Xs and Os. There is more to coaching than Xs and Os. When I talk to Coach Smith, I like to find out how he's doing, encourage him and share each other's lives.

What Coach Smith has done for 32 years at Carolina can't ever be duplicated anywhere. Most college coaches are motivated to win a bunch of games, make a good salary, and if they influence some kids the right way, fine. But Coach Smith has reversed that. His priority is to help kids, to make a difference in their lives. Then, he believes, once you've achieved that, the other things--the victories, the effort--are so much easier to accomplish. It all comes together. When you've shown your sincerity in people's lives like he has, anything is possible.

One of the things that stands out for me, as far as my career at Carolina, was when we lost in my junior year in the first round of the ACC tournament. That is something that doesn't happen very often at Carolina. Walking off the court to the locker room, Coach Smith stopped me and said, "Bobby, I really appreciate the effort you gave today." For him to say that at that time really meant a lot to me. It showed me what he really cared about. We were out, our season was over, because then only one team from the ACC went to the NCAAs. His concern was that I wasn't down or dejected.

You can tell when people are sincere, when people have their priorities in order and not, "if you don't win for me, then you're not a value to me." That's not Coach Smith. You are a value to him as a member of his extended family. He never gives up on a player, on an individual. If a kid has an emotional or personal problem, Coach Smith goes the extra mile for that individual. If the kid, confidence-wise, needs to play, and even though it might not help the team in the short term, that kid will play some. If it's for the best long-term for that player, he'll play.

Coach Smith values people much more than victories. He knows that those things, the victories, will take care of themselves down the road. I wrote him recently, and I used a scripture about blessings, and he wrote me back and said, "The Lord does bless." Coach Smith started off not very popular in Chapel Hill, but he stuck with his beliefs and his system and he worked harder than everybody else, and he worked his way to where he is today. He stuck with what he thought was right. He's been faithful and that's why he continues to be blessed, professionally and personally.

Both Coach Smith and I have deep religious beliefs. We're different as far as theological background goes, but that doesn't lessen my affection for him or his for me. Our bottom line is the same, trying to honor God with our lives. People come up to me all the time and ask me, "Is Dean Smith that wonderful, is he that good of a man?" Well, he really is. People have seen his success, but people today always expect a successful individual to be different behind the scenes than he is in the public eye. But Coach Smith is the same.

I was in his office visiting with him last year, and during that time, he had four or five telephone calls, one from Australia, one from somewhere else in the world, trying to get his players who were not going to be in the NBA a position to work somewhere. His life is devoted to his family, his extended Carolina basketball family. That family is extremely large now, after 32 years of coaching, and his staff is not that big. It is incredible what they continue to do for all of us.

I can't imagine how busy Coach Smith is on a daily basis, so I write more than I call. When I go up there, I always stop by to say hello or leave him a note. He always has time for his players, past and present. He always makes time. He has set his priorities and goals, and he follows them. He's a communicator, but the bottom line is that he's a good, sincere man. There are not that many who have reached the success level that he has who have not cut corners, or hurt somebody, or done something that's not appropriate. He's done it the right way.

When you play for Coach Smith, you're a little intimidated. He's a tough coach with a complicated system and he demands a lot. But you know as a player, because you've seen the results of the players who have come before you, that, "Hey, this is going to work out for the best. I need to be learning this and I need to be under his discipline." Very few players leave, and the few that have, it's their loss. But Coach Smith even stays involved with the few who have left his program. It's amazing.

> " ...I shudder when I think of what would have happened if I hadn't gone to Carolina and been with coach Smith. I wouldn't have been the athlete that I turned out to be and I wouldn't have been the person that I am. "

When I used to go to his office as a player, he would call you in to check on your grades or whatever, and I remember coming out a few inches shorter. I was always amazed how he did it--a little comment here and there. It was intended to keep my head from getting big, from getting an ego, and again, not being the center of attention on the team. It helped me and it helped the team. Just look at the Carolina players in the pros. There are so few problems. Who's holding out? Who's having problems? Very few. It goes back to what he instills in his players, that we're not the center of the universe.

In closing, when I think back to all the decisions I've made in my life, to me the number one decision was to become a Christian. The next important decision was getting married and easily the third most important decision in my life was choosing North Carolina. I shudder when I think of what would have happened if I hadn't gone to Carolina and been with Coach Smith. I wouldn't have been the athlete that I turned out to be and I wouldn't have been the person that I am. I thank Coach Smith for that.

We are indeed experiencing one of the greatest coaching eras in the history of sport and one of the finest men in the history of sport. Let's celebrate the 1993 NCAA championship, but let us all remember to stop and acknowledge the man who made it all possible.

Dean Smith's Big Year

SPECIAL TEAM WINS GRAND PRIZE

Dean Smith was vacationing at the beach with his family in the summer of 1992, when in a quiet moment he took a tape of Carolina's loss to Ohio State in the NCAA tournament the previous March and slipped it into a VCR.

Smith studied that tape closely, and he didn't like what he saw. The veteran coach had built his powerhouse basketball program on defense. For three decades his Carolina teams had played defense with a controlled fury. The Tar Heels were known to attack. They trapped and pressed and gambled and set a fast and reckless tempo. Opponents had a hard time running an offense against UNC's pressure, and those who analyzed the coach's philosophy put it simply: "If you don't play defense, you don't play basketball at North Carolina."

But when Smith looked at the UNC-Ohio State tape, he saw one of his players loaf on defense. He didn't see the defensive execution that his teams had made famous. "That is not North Carolina basketball," Smith said to himself, and he vowed right then and there to do something about it.

He returned to Chapel Hill, met with his staff, and assistant coach Bill Guthridge recalls that meeting. "Coach watches a lot of tape when he goes to the beach," Guthridge said. "He said our defense wasn't as good as it had been or should be, and he said it would be a lot better this season."

Carolina's players knew when they reported for preseason practice on Nov. 1, 1992 that defense would be a priority. Smith and his assistants never let the players forget that. The coaches found out quickly, however, that it wasn't necessary to hound the players about the importance of playing tough defense. This team, with five seniors on the roster, knew that defense was the cornerstone of Carolina basketball, and the players enjoyed that part of the game, considered it fun and exciting and challenging.

Opponents shot only 41.3 percent from the field against the Tar Heels in 1992-93, and from 3-point range Carolina held opponents to 32.8 percent. UNC also had 105 fewer turnovers than its opponents, yet another indication of an active and effective defense.

Nobody is going to get Smith to compare his teams or his players. "Do you have a favorite child?" he asks those who have tried. Nevertheless, the suspicion is that this team's personality was a perfect fit for Smith's teachings. The players were unselfish almost to a fault. "Shoot the ball or I'll take you out of the game," Smith told Henrik Rodl and Pat Sullivan.

Rodl, a senior, lost his starting job to sophomore Donald Williams midway through the ACC schedule. But instead of sulking, Rodl said to Williams: "You deserve it." Seniors Scott Cherry and Matt Wenstrom accepted reserve roles with enthusiasm. Senior walk-on Travis Stephenson was thrilled to be on the team and earned his spurs in practice.

The team's leader was George Lynch, 6-8, a senior, who competed with a champion's heart. Lynch would not back down from any challenge, was a leader-by-example. He never missed practice or games. He played when he didn't feel well, he played through injuries and he never made an excuse.

Lynch also presents an interesting paradox for those who mistakenly insist that Smith has a system that is unyielding. The coach knew that he had in Lynch a tremendous athlete who played the game by feel, almost by hunch. Put him in too much of a structured setting and it would negate his raw talent. Lynch roamed the court on defense, gambled, sometimes double-teamed when it wasn't in the scheme. He was such an intense rebounder that he sometimes went to the defensive boards without boxing out his man. Instead of asking Lynch to conform to a rigid system, Smith changed his plan to make best use of his player. Lynch is a rare talent and Smith wanted to nurture that talent, not stymie it. He gave Lynch tremendous freedom and in the process had other players cover for him. Lynch blossomed into such an effective player that Carolina's opponents had no answer for him.

Just as Lynch is impossible to peg as a player, so too is Smith as a coach. About the time people think they have him figured out, he surprises them. It is true that he has a basketball philosophy that is unbending. He believes in defense, he preaches that basketball is a team game, insists that his teams play hard, take good shots, thank the passer. Much of basketball's beauty in his eyes rests in the game's simplicity, which means he prefers the sure pass to a no-look, behind-the-back flip. You can throw one of those passes at Carolina, but you had better complete it.

If you consider those principles a conservative way to teach the game, then you have the other side of the man, the devilish side that makes him so unpredictable, and at a quick glance might even make his philosophy seem incongruous. His teams play high risk basketball. He throws the lob for dunks. He disdains the outside shot until he tries to get the ball inside with intricate screens and pinpoint passing. In no way does he subscribe to the "take-what-they-give-you" brand of basketball. "We'd rather take what we want," he says defiantly, "because we're pulling for North Carolina to win."

His defense is based on attack. Opponents are forced to spend much practice time preparing for Carolina's changing defenses, the traps and double-teams and gambles. Smith's teams have been known to give up some easy shots to create a fast tempo. With a two-point lead on the road against Big East champion Seton Hall, UNC had the ball out of bounds in the backcourt with 27 seconds left. Instead of settling for a safe inbounds pass and killing the clock, Smith went for it all. He got Derrick Phelps open behind screens to receive a long pass and score on an open layup to sew up the game.

A highly competitive man himself, Smith's nature is to take risks. With his team down 62-61 to Michigan in the NCAA championship game, Smith saw four players give the tired signal. He didn't hesitate. He substituted Rodl for Phelps, Scott Cherry for Donald Williams, Pat Sullivan for Brian Reese, and Eric Montross for Kevin Salvadori. That lineup did not get a shot off before the 45-second clock expired and Michigan scored a 3-pointer by Jalen Rose to lead, 65-61.

Smith would have been ripped by critics for those substitutions

if Carolina had lost the game, that is for sure. However, he refuses to worry about such things. He doesn't take a popularity poll before making key decisions. Maybe politicians could learn from him. He believes in using his bench and he teaches from the first day of practice that all players are important and should be ready to go into any game at any time. He does not change what he teaches and what he believes in just because the prize is the national championship. He saw four tired signals in the Michigan game, so he put in four fresh players. He would have done the same thing against Cornell. Maybe the substitutions had an effect down the stretch. After all, Carolina outscored Michigan 14-4 in the last 4:31. Also, Carolina's opponents usually talk about the team's great depth. The only way to build depth is for the head coach to have the courage to play his bench.

No less of a coaching genius than the late Paul (Bear) Bryant, who won five national championships coaching football at Alabama and was a closet basketball fan, admired Smith's coaching, especially his willingness to use his bench. Bryant was intrigued by Smith's use of a "Blue team," in which the Carolina coach inserted five reserves to play together for a couple of minutes. The two coaches, as different as they were in personalites, met at a neutral site for a couple of summer days and talked about their coaching beliefs. Bryant liked Carolina's "Blue team" so much that he created his own version of it for his Alabama football program, and with great success.

It didn't take Smith long to learn to enjoy his 1992-93 team. He knew after the first week of preseason practice in November that the players had worked hard in the offseason. Smith had told the players at their banquet the previous spring that he was going to be tough on them. "No more Mr. Nice Guy," is the way he put it.

He told friends about that time that he was going to coach the 1992-93 team "the way I did when I was afraid I would get fired." The players who worked hardest, who competed best, who did all of the little things that it takes to win would be the ones who would play.

Was Smith tougher on this team than he had been on recent ones?

"I don't think so," said senior Henrik Rodl. "It was hard for him to be tougher because we won so many games. I don't think he changed much in his approach."

Said senior Scott Cherry: "Coach was definitely intense this year, maybe a little more intense. But he was into it every year that I was here. He's always gotten his point across."

Freshman Larry Davis got his first look at Dean Smith the coach on Nov. 1. "I thought Coach Smith would take it easy on the freshmen the first day of practice," Davis said. "He didn't. He'd tell one of us to run drill No. 1 and we wouldn't have a clue. We sprinted everywhere. The whole thing was so organized. It was real different."

There is no doubt that Smith and this team communicated extremely well. He made some changes to accommodate the players. His "red light, yellow light, green light" rule for 3-point shooters was abolished. Still, the players had to recognize what a good shot was and were expected to exercise good judgment. Shot selection hit the skids in mid-December, but it improved after the team returned from Hawaii's Rainbow Classic in late December.

In studying his personnel the previous summer, Smith also saw that his point guard, Derrick Phelps, had excellent potential as an offensive rebounder. He changed his scheme to rotate either Henrik Rodl or Donald Williams back on defense, which freed Phelps to go to the offensive backboards. Phelps came up with many big rebounds during the season and averaged 4.4 rebounds a game, which was third on the team behind George Lynch and Eric Montross. Not bad for a point guard.

Game by game, you could see things come together for this

team. The players wanted to play the type of basketball that the coach taught. It was beautiful to watch. Smith knew he had a weapon on defense in the person of Phelps. Lynch, the athlete with freedom to do some free-lancing, disrupted opponents. Donald Williams, a big guard, was much improved on defense. So was forward Brian Reese. Then, on Dec. 22, in the second half against Ohio State, center Eric Montross followed Smith's instructions to front Buckeye star Lawrence Funderburke in the pivot, and it was on that night that UNC's defense became powerful and sometimes overwhelming. Pat Sullivan, Henrik Rodl and Kevin Salvadori were also reliable defenders.

Carolina's offense got a lot off its defense, that is true. But the team was also very effective in a half-court offense because it had so many different ways to score. When Phelps penetrated the defense, when Reese broke down defenses by slashing to the basket, and when Williams hit from outside, the Tar Heels were a juggernaut. Lynch and Montross were virtually unstoppable on the inside when those three other parts of the offense were in gear.

It seemed to those on the outside as if the coach had put together just about the perfect team. Smith, who is 62, coached his 32nd Carolina team in 1992-93. American society, for various reasons, likes to usher its veterans to the sidelines and replace them with younger people. But Smith seems to get better with age. He has lost none of his competitiveness or desire. You can walk up the steps beside him and he'll try to finish first. Sure, there are some parts of the job that he likes better than others, but he still loves the teaching and the competition. He enjoys the challenge of a full arena and a tough opponent with a lot at stake.

"Coach Smith showed this year that you don't have to have the most talented players in the nation to win a national championship," freshman Larry Davis said. "He takes what he has and wins. A smart coach and guys that bond together, who really love each other and play hard every day, can sometimes overcome greater talent. We proved it."

It was certainly a year of milestones for Smith. He now has 774 wins as Carolina's coach and is second on the major college list of all-time basketball victories to the late Adolph Rupp. Observers, trying to predict how much longer Smith will coach, put pencil to paper and guess how many more seasons it would take Smith to pass Rupp's 875 victories. As odd as it might seem to those who do not know the man, that record holds absolutely no fascination for Smith, nor will it have any bearing on how much longer he coaches. He genuinely dislikes coaching records and does his best not to talk about his.

While Smith disdains the personal spotlight, he is a proud man and protective of what his players have built over more than three decades of basketball masterpieces. He himself has done it all. He coached the USA team to an Olympic Gold Medal in basketball in 1976 after it lost to the Soviet Union in 1972. He has won more ACC regular season and tournament championships than any other school, let alone any other coach. He won the NIT when it was a special tournament. He has two NCAA championships to his credit, and had it not been for untimely injuries, he probably would have two or three more.

He and his Tar Heel program have been the target of other ACC schools for more than 25 years. N.C. State challenged in the early 1970s with David Thompson and Tommy Burleson. Virginia offered a stern test in the early 80s with Ralph Sampson. Duke, with a great run of its own, was the latest, but even in the Blue Devils' greatest era--the time of Christian Laettner--Carolina won the head-to-head competition, 6-5. Smith and Carolina remain the standard by which all others are measured.

Smith pulled all of the right strings in 1992-93. His courtside strategy in NCAA wins over Arkansas and Cincinnati was clinical. The most striking moment of the season, though, might have been the way he orchestrated the 21-point second-half comeback victory over Florida State. The way he used his timeouts, the manner in which he completely changed the game's momentum, the teasing of Florida State with some zone defense when he was way behind, and the confidence he gave his team represents a kaleidoscopic view of his coaching wizardry.

"I'm never worried when we're behind," said Carolina junior Brian Reese. "We know we can come back because we've done it since my freshman year. We come back from crazy deficits. That's Carolina basketball. That's Dean Smith."

As hard as Smith tries to remove himself from the center of attention, he was still one of the chief motivational sources for the 1992-93 Tar Heels. The players heard the criticism that he had won only one national championship, and they grew tired of it.

"We heard and heard that he hadn't won an NCAA championship in ll years," said Eric Montross. "So what? Most coaches never win one. It's funny that his critics don't look at the rest of his record and see all the things he's done. But now that we won this one, it'll be awfully hard for anybody to take a crack at him."

Derrick Phelps, the point guard who is the extension of Smith's philosophy on the court, said the players wanted to win the NCAA title for themselves first. "But we definitely wanted to win for Coach Smith, too," he said. "He does so much for us and teaches us so much. The man is too good to be judged on how many championships he's won."

In one of the player-only huddles on the Superdome court during the Michigan game, George Lynch looked at his four teammates and said: "Coach deserves this one."

As time ticked down in the championship game against Michigan, Smith pointed his finger at sophomore Donald Williams and told him to shoot two crucial technical foul shots with 11 seconds left. It was ironic, because the year before, when Smith saw that Williams would be helped by a year at point guard, rumors swirled that the player was unhappy and would transfer. A year later, there was Williams, in his team's biggest game, shooting the foul shots that could clinch the championship.

"It's hard to explain what I feel for him," Williams said of Smith. "It's right here in the heart. There were times in practice when I thought I despised him. But when it was all over and I saw him standing there on the court while we celebrated after beating Michigan, I wanted to go up to him and tell him I loved him and thank him for everything he did for us."

Smith watched his team enjoy the aftermath of the 77-71 win over Michigan for the national championship. He hugged his play-ers, snipped the last cord of the net and handed it to the team. As the players continued their celebration, Smith, who had taken teams to the Final Four in four decades, slipped quietly off the court and took the long walk to the Carolina locker room. A couple of hundred fans leaned over the railing located over the dressing room and cheered him wildly, called his name.

A shy man in some ways, Smith lowered his head, acknowledged the cheers with a slight wave of his left hand, and said softly, "Thank the players."

Then he went into the locker room and shut the door, alone with his thoughts, his place in basketball history assured. The spotlight was shining and the crowd stayed to cheer. It was a festive and emotional time and the coach wanted his players to be the center of attention.

That, too, is Dean Smith.

Number of ACC Regular Season Championships Won By A Head Coach

Coach	School	Titles
DEAN SMITH	NORTH CAROLINA	16
Frank McGuire	UNC, South Carolina	6
Vic Bubas	Duke	4
Everett Case	N.C. State	3
Terry Holland	Virginia	3
Mike Krzyzewski	Duke	3
Harold Bradley	Duke	2
Lefty Driesell	Maryland	2
Bones McKinney	Wake Forest	2
Norm Sloan	N.C. State	2
Jim Valvano	N.C. State	2
Bobby Cremins	Georgia Tech	1
Cliff Ellis	Clemson	1
Bill Foster	Duke	1

Number of ACC Tournament Championships Won By A Head Coach

Coach	School	Titles
DEAN SMITH	NORTH CAROLINA	11
Vic Bubas	Duke	4
Everett Case	N.C. State	4
Mike Krzyzewski	Duke	3
Norm Sloan	N.C. State	3
Bobby Cremins	Georgia Tech	3
Bill Foster	Duke	2
Frank McGuire	UNC, South Carolina	2
Bones McKinney	Wake Forest	2
Jim Valvano	N.C. State	2
Lefty Driesell	Maryland	1
Terry Holland	Virginia	1
Press Maravich	N.C. State	1
Bud Millikan	Maryland	1

DEAN SMITH'S ROAD RECORD IN THE ACC (1967-93)

Team	ACC Road Record	Pct.
Florida State	11-5	.686
North Carolina	122-62	.663
Duke	75-107	.412
N.C. State	73-108	.403
Virginia	61-124	.330
Maryland	58-127	.314
Georgia Tech	31-69	.310
Wake Forest	45-136	.249
Clemson	33-151	.179

Dean Smith's Record In The ACC (1967-93)

Team	Won	Lost	Pct.
NORTH CAROLINA	279	87	.762
Florida State	23	9	.676
Duke	199	165	.547
N.C. State	190	176	.519
Virginia	173	193	.473
Georgia Tech	87	113	.435
Maryland	158	208	.432
Wake Forest	139	227	.380
Clemson	130	236	.355

THE DEAN SMITH FILE

Winningest NCAA Division I Men's Basketball Coaches

Coach	College	No. Of Years	Total Victories
1. Adolph Rupp	Kentucky	41	875
2. DEAN SMITH	NORTH CAROLINA	32	774
3. Henry Iba	NW Missouri State, Colorado, Okl. State	41	767
4. Ed Diddle	Western Kentucky	42	759
5. Phog Allen	Baker, Haskell, Central Missouri State	48	746

• • •

Dean Smith By Decade

DECADE	Overall Record	ACC Record	ACC Regular Season Titles	ACC Tourney Titles	Final Fours
1960s	147-62	77-35	3	3	3
1970s	239-65	92-32	6	4	2
1980s	281-63	110-30	6	3	2
1990s	107-33	41-19	1	1	2
TOTAL	774-223	320-116	16	11	9

• • •

All-Time NCAA Tournament Victories By Head Coach

Coach	School	NCAA Win
*DEAN SMITH	NORTH CAROLINA	55
John Wooden	UCLA	47
*Bobby Knight	Indiana	38
Jerry Tarkanian	Long Bch St, UNLV	37
*Denny Crum	Louisville	35

*still active

• • •

All-Time NCAA Tournament Appearances By A Head Coach

Times In NCAA	COACH	SCHOOL
23	*DEAN SMITH	NORTH CAROLINA
20	Adolph Rupp	Kentucky
18	Lou Carnesecca	St. John's
17	*Denny Crum	Louisville
17	*Bobby Knight	Indiana

*still active

Guthridge And Williams Had Their Own Contest

Bill Guthridge looked at some tapes of Donald Williams shooting the ball late in the season, at a time when Williams was having trouble with his shooting consistency. Guthridge, who has been an assistant on Dean Smith's Carolina staff for 26 years, serves as the team's shooting coach.

Guthridge is the only person who talks to Carolina's players about shooting. Too much information, too much instruction could cause even the best shooter to freeze. If that instruction should come from various sources, each with different ideas about how to shoot a basketball, the athlete could end up a nervous wreck.

Guthridge noticed in looking at the tapes that Williams hit a high percentage of his shots when he was in good position to take them. In other words, when Williams squared up, got a good look at the basket, and stepped into his shot, his shooting percentage was high. But when he took running one-handers, or wasn't fundamentally sound in his shot, his shooting percentage dropped significantly.

Guthridge had a conversation with Williams about this, showed him some tapes. "If you square up and take good shots and are fundamentally sound, then the misses are on me," Guthridge said to Williams. "But if you rush your shots and have poor mechanics, the misses are on you."

Guthridge and Williams played their own little game down the stretch. "That one is on me," Guthridge would tell Williams when a good shot was missed. But when Williams misfired while off balance or otherwise in bad shooting position, Guthridge would say: "That one is on you."

Williams related to this approach and it seemed to relax him. He was a torrid shooter in Carolina's last three games. He hit two 3-pointers in overtime to help beat Cincinnati, and then he was 5-7 in Final Four wins over Kansas and Michigan. He hit 12 of the last 16 shots he took from 3-point range during the NCAA tournament.

Guthridge, a man with a dry sense of humor, would be the last to take any credit for Williams' success. He shuns the spotlight, seldom talks to reporters, is satisfied and fulfilled with his role as

Smith's top assistant. Make no mistake, though, about his competitiveness. He recovers from defeat quickly, even sleeps well after a loss, but losing is not something that he enjoys.

Guthridge is the perfect assistant for Smith. The two men share a basketball philosophy, but their personalities also show a striking contrast. Guthridge does not like to leave the office at night until his desk is clear of all paper. Smith, on the other hand, who gets hundreds of pieces of correspondence each week, often has a desk stacked high with letters, video tapes, basketballs and other tools of his trade. Smith has been known to slip into his assistant's office after Guthridge leaves for the day and pile letters and assorted papers on his desk. When that happens, Guthridge has no trouble targeting the culprit.

Guthridge has had many chances to become a head coach since he's been at Carolina. He could have gone to Penn State and Arkansas to name just two, but he's said that his job at Carolina is better than most head coaching positions. When he believed that his reluctance to leave Carolina was hurting the chances of former assistants Eddie Fogler and Roy Williams to get head coaching jobs at other schools, Guthridge stated publicly that he was going to remain at Carolina and would not consider any head coaching offers. Fogler and Williams went on to head coaching jobs soon thereafter and have done well. It's almost certain that Guthridge would have had similar success had he chosen to leave, but he says he's never regretted his decision to stay at Carolina.

Guthridge takes the front seat on the bus when Carolina's basketball team is on the road. The players laughed at him some this season because he told them after nearly every game that "you are a special team."

Why did Guthridge feel compelled to say this so often during the season? "I just felt that this was a special team," he explained. "It might have been after the Michigan game that we lost in Hawaii. I told the players to hold their heads high, that they were a special team and good things would happen to them. I really did think it was a team that could do some great things. The chemistry and the ingredients were there. I just really felt like this team could win it all."

Carolina teams usually have excellent senior leadership, but even by the program's standards, the leadership provided by the five seniors on the 1992-93 team was exceptional. Guthridge talks about a highly recruited player such as Matt Wenstrom "who was willing to play the (reserve) role he did with enthusiasm. It was a real plus for the team and something that Matt should be proud of."

Guthridge also said Henrik Rodl "didn't miss a beat" when he was replaced in the starting lineup by Donald Williams. George Lynch was the principal leader. Guthridge said Lynch worked hard every day, and although he didn't talk a lot, when he did speak, the players responded. "All of the seniors were excellent," Guthridge said.

Many head coaches don't want their assistants talking to them during the heat of a game. It's distracting. "Coach Smith likes us to give him our ideas during the game and anytime," Guthridge said. "He likes to have things thrown at him, and then he digests it all and figures out what he wants to do."

During Carolina's win over Arkansas, the Tar Heels held a one-point lead and had the ball with less than a minute to play. Smith called timeout, made some substitutions and then told the team it was going to run a backdoor play. Smith doesn't often draw plays on the bench during games. His general philosophy is that if you've prepared properly in practice, you don't need to draw the play. But this time, Guthridge convinced Smith to diagram the play so there would be no chance for a misunderstanding.

"Although that was a play that we had run before, sometimes a picture is worth a thousand words," Guthridge said. "Our goal is to get ideas to Coach Smith and let him decide which ones to keep and which ones to rule out."

Guthridge is always early to the game site. His ritual is to buy a bag of popcorn and a program and go up into the stands and read before the team takes the floor for warmups. He says he didn't see anything unusual on the bus ride to the Superdome to play Michigan, and the atmosphere in Carolina's locker room was much like it had been all year.

"We all knew what we were playing for," he said. "This team was ready to play just about every game this year. We probably weren't ready to play at Wake Forest, but outside of that one game, I can't think of another one when we weren't ready. I thought the team would play well against Michigan. I was sure they'd play hard."

One of Guthridge's roles is to direct the office staff in Smith's absence. After Carolina beat Michigan to win the national championship, the UNC basketball office was overwhelmed with mail and phone calls and visitors dropping by.

It got so bad that Smith and Guthridge just shut the office down for two days to give the secretaries and staff a chance to recover.

A friend called about that time and asked Guthridge how he was doing. "I've been confused ever since Donald Williams made those free throws in New Orleans," Guthridge replied. "But it certainly is nice." ●

> "
> *I've been confused ever since Donald Williams made those free throws in New Orleans. But it certainly is nice.*
> "

Ford Celebrated For Players And Coaches

Even though 16 years have passed since Phil Ford's junior basketball season at Carolina, he thinks of those days often, and the heartbreak of losing to Marquette in the national championship game is still there. The memory will never grow dim and the sadness attached with coming up one game short of his dream won't disappear.

Ford's 1977 team deserved a better fate, that is for sure. It was a powerful team, almost certainly the nation's best, but when it came time to begin play in the NCAA tournament, the Tar Heels were devastated by injuries. Ford, the team's leader and point guard, had a hyper-extended elbow on his shooting arm that made it painful to shoot from beyond close range. Walter Davis, a senior small forward, had a broken finger on his shooting hand. And Tommy LaGarde, 6-10, the starting center, tore up a knee midway through the season and did not play again at Carolina.

Ford's Tar Heels still made it through a brutal NCAA tournament schedule to reach the championship game. Dean Smith, with injuries forcing his regulars to the bench, had to call on reserves to beat a good Purdue team in the opening tournament game. Then the Tar Heels edged Notre Dame on St. Patrick's Day and won the NCAA East by beating Kentucky in College Park. Ford sat out most of the second half against Kentucky with his injury as John Kuester performed brilliantly in the clutch. Many people thought the best two teams in the nation in 1977 were Carolina and Las Vegas, and the Tar Heels beat Vegas 84-83 in Atlanta in the NCAA semifinals, as freshman Mike O'Koren had 31 points.

Marquette coach Al McGuire was coaching his last game when his team went against Carolina in the championship game. UNC came from way behind at halftime to tie the game in the second half, but the Warriors came back to win, 67-59.

Ford, a three-time All-America and the national Player of the Year in 1978, is a fierce competitor. He's also very sentimental, and he's probably the most popular basketball player ever to wear a Carolina uniform. His fifth season as an assistant coach to Dean Smith ended in the Tar Heels winning the 1992-93 NCAA championship. That won't erase the hurt of 1977 from Ford's mind, but it does ease the pain somewhat.

"I've been around Carolina basketball for so long as a player, a fan and now a coach," Ford said. "I grew up in this program where we all run for another person's mistake. When you're part of a program like this, you find that you're happiest when you celebrate for someone else. I was on the 1976 USA team that won the Olympics, and winning the NCAA championship this year made me happier. I was pulling so hard for these players and for Coach Smith."

Phil Ford liked this Carolina team from the early days of pre-season practice. No player in Dean Smith's 32 years of coaching at Carolina ever understood or embraced Smith's philosophy better than Ford. As a point guard, Ford was close to perfect, at least for the way Carolina plays. He had all the offensive skills. He could shoot outside, he had a deadly jump shot off a driving dribble, he took the ball to the basket fearlessly. He was competitive and extremely smart, and when UNC went to the Four Corners with Ford running it, Smith said it was "almost like stealing." Ford thought the game right along with Smith until the two became almost one in their approach to winning.

He was unselfish, not only as a player but in the way he led his life, and he held to the strong belief that if he and his teammates did as Smith instructed them, they would win. Ford still believes those things as an assistant coach, which led him to like this team from the outset.

He knew that Carolina had had teams with more individual talent. But he looked beyond that, and what he saw was a team that had all the pieces to fit the puzzle. This team meshed. Ford saw the 1992-93 Tar Heels as a team that went eight or nine players deep, and they could read each other.

"Team chemistry was great from the start," Ford said. "These players like each other. They believed in themselves and in each other and also in what Coach Smith was teaching. They played hard in practice and in games."

Ford points out another interesting fact about this team, one that wasn't written or talked about much during the season. The players on this team had a habit of winning. George Lynch, Eric Montross and Henrik Rodl all played on state championship teams. Brian Reese and Derrick Phelps played on teams that claimed high school national titles of some sort. Freshman Dante Calabria led his team to the Pennsylvania state championship, and sophomore Donald Williams played on a championship AAU team.

"Winning breeds winning," Ford said, "and many of our players had won championships before. They knew what it was like and that it took hard work."

The thing that Ford liked best about this Carolina team was that all the parts seemed to fit. He can talk on and on about the players, about Montross and Reese and Williams and the others. He admires Montross' competitiveness and toughness, Reese's improvement as a player and his natural skills, the ability of Williams to score.

He's at a loss for words when he tries to describe Lynch, finally saying: "George is different. You don't become the second leading rebounder in the school's history at his size unless you're special. Go back and look at our game down at Clemson. We wouldn't have won that game without George's rebounding."

Ford was a point guard, though, so it is easy for him to describe Derrick Phelps. It's doubtful that Phelps has a bigger fan than Ford. The two of them have a close relationship. Why not? Phelps knows how good Ford was as a player and respects him. And when Ford talks about Phelps, he has a hard time staying in his chair. The urge for him is to stand and pace.

"You have to watch Derrick over a period of time to appreciate everything he does," Ford said. "For sure, there have not been many better defensive players around here than Derrick. He runs the team so well for a couple of reasons. First, he's talented and smart and understands what Coach Smith wants. Second, our players have tremendous confidence in Derrick. They don't think he's going to make the right decision, they know he is. They believe in him."

Several times during the season, Ford sat there on the bench and watched the Tar Heels carve up good opponents. They closed the regular season with three outstanding victories--beating Florida State on the road and winning by wide margins over Wake Forest and Duke at home. During those stretches, Ford would whisper to Smith: "I fear no man when we play like this."

He liked the team's versatility, its confidence, its determination. "To begin with, this team was as good on defense as any we've had here in a long time," Ford said. "The players played hard, they always played hard. They could also play any style. They could play against teams that wanted to slow us down, they could run against teams that wanted to speed up. People questioned our shooting, but go back and look at our December offense. We came out of the box shooting the ball really well."

The Tar Heels stumbled in the ACC tournament championship game when they lost to Georgia Tech by two points. Phelps missed that game due to injury, but many people still thought that the defeat would hurt Carolina's chances in the NCAA tournament.

"Don't get me wrong," Ford said. "Our players wanted to win that Georgia Tech game. But it did not hurt their confidence at all. They looked ahead. This was a team that didn't worry about its opponent. Our players felt deep down that if we played our best, we were going to win."

Ford watched with tears in his eyes as Carolina's players hugged each other and celebrated after beating Michigan for the national championship. It was quite a contrast from that night in Atlanta 16 years earlier, when Ford sat on the bench next to his best friend, Walter Davis, as the clock ticked down to zero and Marquette cut down the nets. Ford and Davis tried to console Mike O'Koren, who wept.

The emotions in college basketball run deep and the memories from some games are indelible. Phil Ford will never forget his 1977 team's bid for basketball history, nor should he. But as he left the Superdome on the night of April 5, 1993, he was happier than he had ever been over the outcome of an athletic event. His heart was full for George Lynch and Eric Montross and Henrik Rodl and all of the players.

Phil Ford is indeed happiest when he celebrates the victories of others. This was another night in his life that he would never forget, and the memories would be much, much sweeter this time. ●

...When you're part of a program like this, you find that you are happiest when you celebrate for someone else.

Wiel Says Championship Was 'Icing On The Cake'

Randy Wiel will never forget his seventh season as an assistant varsity basketball coach and head junior varsity coach at North Carolina. The Tar Heels won the national championship, and just a few days later, Wiel accepted the job as head basketball coach at UNC-Asheville.

Wiel, who played at Carolina from 1975-79, coached the 1992 Dutch Olympic basketball team. He is a tremendous athlete and a linguist of some note. He speaks six languages fluently.

Wiel said winning the national championship in what turned out to be his last year on Carolina's coaching staff is a thrill that will stay with him the rest of his life.

Question: Just how meaningful was it to win the NCAA championship in your last year as a North Carolina coach?

Wiel: "I think we've always had real good teams at North Carolina. We've always been able to win and compete in the ACC and go to the NCAA tournament. We had some very strong teams during my years of coaching at Carolina, such as the 1987 and 1991 teams. It was like icing on the cake that we won the championship this year."

Question: What were the special qualities that you saw in this Carolina team?

Wiel: "This team was very close, not to say our other teams weren't. But defensively, this team was very, very consistent. I think that was the mainstay of the team. Even when we didn't play well offensively, we won a number of games by being consistent on defense. Our defense carried us through the season. Coach Smith stresses defense, and this team was a good example of that."

Question: Why was this such a good defensive team?

Wiel: "Probably because the majority of the team had been together for at least three years. The defensive principles are pretty much reacting to situations, and of course, it started with Derrick Phelps because he put pressure on the ball on top. There was a lot of pressure on the ball, which gave other players time to get into good defensive position, overplay, and Derrick usually didn't give opposing guards any breathing room. It started with him, but I think everybody played exceptional defense. Eric Montross played good post defense. He got good help from Henrik Rodl. I think we improved so much as a team defensively. It was fun to watch."

Question: You were close to the players on this team, and they seemed to gain confidence as the season went along. Why was that?

Wiel: "I approach every game from a positive side. I made them feel that they were as good as any team in the country, each one of them. I talked to George Lynch a lot. The thing I like the most about him is that he has the heart of a lion, and with him, I knew he could guard a bigger guy or a smaller guy. He, along with Eric, were the ones that I tried to make sure were playing tough defensively. They played the most physical positions. George guarded a lot of bigger guys, so he had to compete. I always tried to beef him up. George would always say, 'Coach, you watch me.' He called himself a baby Moses Malone."

Question: You saw some great leaders in your years at Carolina. How does George rank among them?

Wiel: "George pretty much was a leader in the way he played. The players fed off him. We had some great leaders over the years. When I played, we had Phil Ford. We've had some great senior leadership right on down the line. The seniors this year were very close, which I think was a big part of their success this year. They enjoyed being in each other's company. They banned together. Practices were fun. They helped each other in practice. They did some social things together. There was almost no bickering, and that was a strength of our team."

Question: Was this an enjoyable team to coach and be around?

Wiel: "It was. The guys really played together, liked each other. We won, but even when we lost, they gave it their best, and the next day in practice they tried harder. Nobody wanted to miss a practice for any reason, even an injury. Everybody wanted to be in there, and that was fun. You could see how guys like Scott Cherry improved so much, and Coach Smith had no problems playing him in important situations."

Question: What were your emotions as the team cut down the nets in New Orleans?

Wiel: "I remember standing there thinking, my goodness, you start off in November knowing you are one of 30 or 40 teams that has a chance to win the national championship. Only one team can be champions. The other ones lose, and many times even when you lose, it doesn't mean you aren't good enough. There is a luck factor involved. When we won the whole thing, I remembered Coach Smith saying when we recruited that big class (1990) to give them time. They were juniors this year, and their time had come."

Question: This team wanted to win for themselves and for Coach Smith, didn't it?

Wiel: "Yes. It was good in that manner. Coach is so close with the team. The players have such a good personal relationship with him, and they felt the way they could do something for him was to win the championship. 🏀

Hanners Had Bird's-Eye View Of Best Comeback

When it comes to Carolina basketball, Dave Hanners believes that anything is possible. He believes because he was a sophomore on Carolina's team on March 2, 1974 that came from eight points down against Duke with only 17 seconds left, tied the game and won it in overtime.

Hanners recalls being on the bench in that game, listening to coach Dean Smith plot strategy. "Coach Smith actually convinced us that 17 seconds is an eternity and that we could win the game," Hanners said. "He was so calm and sure of what he was saying, that he gave the players confidence."

Hanners remembers that Smith broke that comeback plan down into tiny segments, looking only three or four seconds ahead, and the players were amazed when things kept happening the way their coach said they would.

"Duke had the ball out of bounds in the backcourt," Hanners said, "and Coach told us we had three options. One, we would not let them get the ball in within five seconds. Two, we would steal the inbounds pass. Three, we would foul immediately if they did get the ball in."

All kinds of improbable things happened in those 17 seconds, and when Walter Davis banked in a shot from about 35 feet out at the buzzer, UNC tied the game at 86 and won in overtime, 96-92. It ranks as probably the most miraculous comeback in college basketball history, and in many ways that one game defines Carolina basketball under Dean Smith's teachings. Nothing is out of reach.

Hanners coached high school basketball and served as an assistant coach at UNC-Wilmington, Furman and East Tennessee State before coming back to Carolina in 1989 to replace Dick Harp, who retired and moved back to Kansas. Hanners was caught up in the NCAA's cost-saving economic plan last year and served as an assistant athletic director. But with Randy Wiel leaving at the end of the season to become head basketball coach at UNC-Asheville, Hanners will return next year to his first love, coaching college basketball.

Hanners didn't coach the 1992-93 team. But he saw every game. He liked the team's closeness, its competitiveness, the willingness of the players to put aside individual honors and concerns for the good of the team. The team, as Hanners saw it, was a perfect blend of senior experience and youthful enthusiasm.

It was a team that soaked up Smith's coaching. Really believed in it. Smith tries to get his team to play hard, execute, worry about the quality of its own play, not look at the scoreboard. "This team was sold on Coach Smith's ideas," Hanners said. "The players didn't look at (statistics). They knew that Coach Smith knows what he is talking about. The team did what it was supposed to do and kept on doing it."

Hanners expresses amazement when he talks about George Lynch and the many things he brought to the Tar Heels' championship drive. That campaign didn't begin on Dec. 1 against Old Dominion, or even on Nov. 1, the first day of practice. It began way back in the steamy days of summer when the players worked out on their own. Lynch came early to those sessions and left late. The

other players saw Lynch set the tone and joined him.

"The work ethic of this team was strong," Hanners said. "It also was a team that paid attention to the task at hand. It made no difference to them if the opponent was Old Dominion, Ohio State or Florida State. Anybody who was paying attention could tell early on that this was a special team. Look back to the Diet Pepsi tournament in Charlotte. Those were our second and third games of the season, and we were already pretty doggone good."

Hanners said Carolina's players gained more and more confidence as the season went along. They played their best basketball late in the season and were really rolling when they lost to Georgia Tech in the ACC tournament finals.

"That loss bothered me a little bit," Hanners said. "I still had a good feeling going into the NCAA tournament, though. There is a fine line between being confident and being cocky. This was not a cocky team, but it was a very confident team. The players were truly not afraid to play anybody. I think they knew if they played their best, they could beat anybody."

Hanners was impressed with the team's consistent excellence on defense, the way it handled late-game situations. He felt pretty sure that Lynch and Eric Montross would do the job inside on a game-to-game basis. In games when Derrick Phelps penetrated, and Donald Williams hit his outside shot, and Brian Reese slashed to the basket, Hanners believed the Tar Heels were the best.

His strongest and most lasting memory of this team, however, is the way the players reacted to Smith. "They listened and responded," he said, "and Coach has the ability to get players to perform beyond what they think are their limits."

UNC TEAM AWARDS 1992-93

Dante Calabria
Butch Bennett Award (Given in memory of Bob Bennett, a member of the 1967-68 freshman team who died of leukemia, to the freshman member of the varsity or junior varsity who exemplifies determination, sportsmanship and sacrifice for the good of the team, as determined by a vote of team members.)

George Lynch
Oscar Vatz Award (Given by Dr. Ben Vatz in memory of his brother, Oscar, to the outstanding rebounder, as determined by statistics.)

Eric Montross
Mary Frances Andrews Award (Given by Mrs. James Dempsey in memory of Mary Frances Andrews, to the best field-goal percentage shooter, as determined by statistics.)

Henrik Rodl
Scholar-Athlete Award (Presented annually by the UNC athletic department, to the varsity team member recommended by coaches as one who best exemplifies "student-athlete.")

George Lynch, Henrik Rodl
Team Captains

Derrick Phelps
Carmichael-Cobb Award (Given by Whit Cobb in memory of Cartwright Carmichael and Jack Cobb, Carolina's first basketball All-Americas and stars on UNC's 1924 national championship team, to the outstanding defensive player, according to coaches' game statistics.)

Donald Williams
Martha Jordan Award (Given in memory of Martha Jordan, to the best free-throw percentage shooter, as determined by coaches' statistical sheets from the season.)

Derrick Phelps
Foy Roberson Award (Given in memory of Foy Roberson, a former UNC basketball player who was killed in World War ll, to the most inspirational player, as voted upon by teammates and coaches.)

Eric Montross
Herb and Pauline Wall Memorial Award (Given in memory of Herb and Pauline Wall, to the best screener, according to statistics.)

Scott Cherry, Matt Wenstrom
Rick Sharp Award (Given in memory of Rick Sharp, the Emmy Award-winning producer of CBS sports, and a 1964 UNC graduate, to the player who contributed the most to the team in practice sessions and behind the scenes, as determined by a vote of team members and coaches.)

George Lynch, Brian Reese
Jimmie Dempsey Award (Given to the team's overall statistical leader, as determined by statistics, including most offensive and some defensive statistics.)

COACHES AWARDS (WINNERS DETERMINED BY COACHES' STATISTICS DURING THE SEASON.)

Derrick Phelps
Most Assists

Derrick Phelps
Most Charges Drawn

Kevin Salvadori
Most Blocked Shots

ALL-STAR AWARDS

Eric Montross, George Lynch
First-Team AII-ACC

Brian Reese, Eric Montross
First-Team AII-ACC Tournament

Donald Williams, George Lynch
Second-Team AII-ACC Tournament

Donald Williams, Eric Montross, George Lynch
AII-NCAA East Regional

George Lynch
NCAA East Regional MVP

Donald Williams, George Lynch, Eric Montross
AII-NCAA Final Four

Donald Williams
NCAA Final Four MVP

Eric Montross, George Lynch
District All-America

Eric Montross
John Wooden All-America
Second-Team Sporting News All-America
Second-Team Basketball Weekly All-America
Third-Team UPI All-America
Third-Team Basketball Times All-America

Henrik Rodl
GTE District Academic All-America

George Lynch
Outstanding Senior (Winner determined by a vote of team members.)

George Lynch
Most Valuable Player (Winner is determined by a vote of team members.)

Call 'Em Champs

North Carolina's 1993 basketball team had 14 players on the roster. One came from Germany and the others from different parts of the United States.

There were no barriers on this team, no petty jealousies. The players genuinely cared for one another. They had a common goal to win a national championship. They listened to their coach, believed in his teachings, knew and appreciated the value of teamwork.

They were tough and adversity made them stronger. This was a confident team, supremely confident, but not cocky. The players believed if they performed at their best, they would win. Every player on the team had an important role, from star forward George Lynch to Travis Stephenson, the last man off the bench.

This team knew how to laugh and wasn't ashamed to cry. It took every opponent seriously, but never themselves too seriously. It was a team that stayed the course, never backed down, never asked for favors and certainly didn't give any.

This was a team, all right. A special team. And the following pages are devoted to its heroes.

Season For Dreamers

GEORGE LYNCH LAID IT ON THE LINE

George Lynch doesn't do a lot of talking and never has. He knew, though, before the 1992-93 basketball season ever began that he would have to take a major leadership role if Carolina's team were to reach the heights that he had in mind.

Sure, those who are expert in goal-setting say you take it a step at a time. You shoot for a short-range goal, then for a next step and a next before you finally decide on your long-range target. That's the orderly process, the so-called correct way, the way a business consultant might draw it on a chart. But George Lynch, who had only one season of college basketball left, was impatient. His college career had been just about perfect, with for one major exception, and thus when he set his aim for Carolina's basketball team, he found that his mind jumped over all intermediate goals and focused on only one--the national championship.

That was the missing piece in Lynch's career and it was his dream.

This was Lynch's fourth year at Carolina. His first three seasons at Chapel Hill were hardly a disaster. The record was 73-29 and included two trips to the NCAA Final 16 and one to the Final Four. It wasn't that Lynch wasn't appreciative of that success, it's just that he's such a competitor that he wanted more. And, quite frankly, he was tired of hearing about Duke and he was especially weary of hearing people question Carolina's ability to win "big" games. He knew the allegation was outrageous, but he wanted to bury the talk forever.

To get to where he wanted to be in April, Lynch, the quiet man, knew deep down that he was going to have to be this team's leader, the guy that everyone else on the team looked to for a source of confidence when things got tight. To play this role effectively, Lynch would have to open up, be willing to offer his advice--even his criticism--and he would have to earn the respect of his teammates. The last part would not be hard. Seniors have a special place on Carolina's basketball team. For three years Lynch had earned respect every day. He never missed practice, played through aches and pains and at times when he didn't feel well, and he always competed at the highest and most intense level.

Coach Dean Smith was asked after the season to write a caption under Lynch's picture, and the coach scribbled: "Heart of a lion." That's Lynch, 6-8, senior, a forward from Roanoke, Va., and a man who hates losing. He hates it so much, in fact, that when his team was 20 points behind to Wake Forest in Winston-Salem with just three minutes to play, Lynch crashed through his own bench and into the stands in pursuit of a loose ball. It's the only way he knows how to play and the score of the game didn't matter. That kind of thing made big impressions on his teammates.

"When you decide to come to Carolina," Lynch said, "your goals aren't limited to winning the ACC regular season or the ACC tournament. We wanted to win the national championship. We had the coach and the players to do it. We had to be willing to dream and work hard and put it all on the line. No excuses. Me? I was going to play hard every day, every game, and I was going to let the team know that we all had to do that if we wanted to win it all. I set

the tone and every player on the team took the challenge and competed. The players on our team didn't respect me because I talked a mean game; they respected me because I competed and worked hard."

Lynch had to be careful that the fire flaming in his belly would produce positive results. Some players he prodded, some he praised, others he challenged. "Let's see who gets the most offensive rebounds tonight," he said to one teammate before a big game. "I think I've won the last five times. Don't you think it's time you won once?"

Lynch did not tempt his teammates with selfish goals, such as who would get the most points. Offensive rebounding. Now that was something that would help the team win. "I had to get a feel for what the players wanted," Lynch said, "and I had to be careful not to step on shoes and mess up the shine. I had to say the right thing and then hope that it would inspire them."

> *...The players on our team didn't respect me because I talked a mean game; they respected me because I competed and worked hard.*

He was also not reluctant to look at his own game and come down hard on himself. He did that in Hawaii after Michigan's Jalen Rose batted in a follow shot at the buzzer to give the Wolverines a 79-78 win and hand Carolina its first loss of the season. This was a spectacular college basketball game that was played in the semifinals of the Rainbow Classic. Many basketball observers called it the best college game ever played in Hawaii. Lynch competed fiercely. He got 16 rebounds against Michigan's tall, athletic and talented frontline. But he hit only 5-18 shots from the field and many of them were poor shots.

Lynch agonized over that game and his role in it. He knew that for Carolina to contend for national honors, he couldn't play that way. He didn't need anyone to tell him. After all, he was a veteran player with keen intelligence, and it made sense that the team needed him close to the basket to rebound, not outside launching 3-pointers. That one game had a major impact on Lynch's season. His game would be to rebound, take high percentage shots, play tough defense. He hawked the ball so effectively that he became Carolina's all-time leader in steals. He made very few poor decisions the rest of the season.

That game, even though it ended in defeat, gave Lynch and his teammates confidence. They lost to Michigan, one of the nation's best teams, by one point. The Tar Heels knew they could play better, and Lynch had this feeling in his gut that the two teams would face each other again down the road.

"Team chemistry" might be a hackneyed term, but it was without question one of the strengths of Carolina's team. The players were able to talk to each other, ask questions and tease one another without it causing problems. Lynch caught it himself after that first Michigan game when some of the younger players on the team accused him of having "Senior Syndrome. You thought you had to take every shot."

"They were right," Lynch said, "and I remembered it in every game that we played after that. I wasn't going to let it happen again. We were able to talk and joke with each other, usually without anyone getting upset, but if we took it too far and did upset a player on the team, the person responsible was always man enough to apologize. This was a team that was able to talk things out."

The Tar Heels didn't have many disappointments in a 34-4 season. The Michigan loss in December was the last for UNC until Jan. 30 when Wake Forest won, 88-62. That was followed by a loss at Duke, and Lynch called that part of the season the team's "checkpoint." The Tar Heels used those losses as their new beginning. Lynch says that more than ever, the players knew they had a team that could become great. But they also learned that they could be beaten if they weren't ready to compete at a high level every night.

Carolina went through the second half of its ACC schedule unbeaten to win the regular season championship by two games over Florida State and by four over Wake Forest and Duke. It had relatively easy wins over Maryland and Virginia to reach the championship game of the ACC tournament against Georgia Tech, but in the late stages of the Virginia game, Derrick Phelps was fouled hard from behind and left the court on a stretcher. Phelps had a severely bruised tailbone and would not be able to play against Georgia Tech.

"The players on our team sort of looked at each other," Lynch said. "Each player on this team was very important to the program, and we knew we'd have a major void without Derrick in there. We didn't have one player who kept this team together, because ours was a team effort."

Carolina lost 77-75 to Georgia Tech. Then the team got on a bus and headed back to Chapel Hill to learn it had been seeded first in the NCAA East region. There was not a whole lot of talk about the loss, but the team was deeply disappointed.

"We didn't dwell on the Georgia Tech game," Lynch said. "It was obviously a game that we wanted to win, but it was not a disaster because we were able to play another game and still had a chance for our number one goal--the national championship."

North Carolina beat East Carolina and Rhode Island in Winston-Salem to advance to the East Regionals at the Meadowlands, where Arkansas and Cincinnati both lost close games to a Carolina team that was playing well and with confidence. Lynch says the Tar Heels were thrilled to be going back to the Final Four, but when workers at the Meadowlands brought out a stepladder so the team could cut down the nets and take them back to Chapel Hill, Carolina declined.

"It was no big deal, no major decision," Lynch said. "We were still in pursuit of our goal, and the nets we wanted were those in the Superdome."

Lynch was going back to the Final Four for the second time in his Carolina career. The first time, in 1991, the Tar Heels lost in the

semifinals to Kansas, which, ironically would also be the opponent this year. Michigan and Kentucky were the other Final Four participants.

"We looked at it like we had two games left to play, two games left to win," Lynch said. "Kansas was the first team that was in the way of what we wanted. I could have stopped playing basketball earlier in the year and still would have accomplished everything that I wanted--except winning a national championship. It's not possible for me to describe how badly I wanted to win the championship. I can't put that feeling into words. I spent so many hours working towards this moment. Carolina basketball means so much to so many people, especially to the players. It had been 11 years since Carolina had won the national championship, and you have to be a player in this program, you have to spend four years here, to really know how that feels."

Kansas never led Carolina but once, and that was early. Late in the game, with the Tar Heels protecting a lead, Darrin Hancock of Kansas took a rebound and dribbled the length of the court against Lynch and Eric Montross, who had four fouls at the time. Lynch was on one side, Montross on the other, and when Hancock made it through the defense, Lynch reached in to foul, and he thought Mon-

LYNCH'S LINE:								
FIELD GOAL M-A/Pct	FREE THROW M-A/Pct	3-POINT M-A/Pct	Reb/Avg	A	TO	S	Pts	Avg
235-469/50.1	88-132/66.7	2-11/18.2	365/9.6	72	89	89	560	14.7

tross should have been more aggressive. The two had a brief exchange.

"I want to play on Monday night," Lynch said sharply. He knew that his words could be taken the wrong way. "I think I said it in a nasty voice," he said. "Eric was offended by it. After the timeout, I apologized for the way I raised my voice. Both of us were competing hard. He had four fouls and didn't want to reach, and I understood his situation. But one play can determine a game and that's why I made the point."

Instead of this being an uneasy situation, the two players left the timeout huddle with Lynch's arm wrapped around Montross' huge shoulders. The team chemistry that had been such a strength all year was still there. Carolina went on to finish off Kansas, 78-68.

It was down to two teams--Carolina and Michigan--for the national championship. Lynch's dream was alive. Since the beginning of the NCAA tournament, he had told his teammates, "I don't want this to be my last game." It became the team's battle cry. "Don't let this be the last game we play together."

But now, the college season had one game left. There would be no game on Tuesday.

A rematch from Hawaii.

Lynch slept well the Sunday night before the game and awoke about 8 a.m. Monday. He knew that he had to gear himself down, because he was ready to play upon awakening and game time was 12 hours away. Monday was a slow day and Lynch wondered if the tipoff of the biggest game of his life would ever arrive.

Once the game began, Lynch's emotional tank was on full. Coach Smith took him out of the game early to let him watch a minute and settle down. Lynch sat on the bench next to assistant coach Bill Guthridge. Lynch cheered for his teammates, screamed instructions, used his arms to demonstrate how they should rebound and play defense.

After getting pounded by Lynch, Guthridge said to Smith: "You need to get George back in the game before he kills me over here."

Once in the first half, Lynch was in the right corner with Michigan's Chris Webber guarding him when he fired one from deep. Seeing what was about to happen, Coach Smith said: "Don't, George." But Lynch did, and when Webber didn't block him out, Lynch got his own rebound and scored.

"He was just passing to himself," Guthridge told Smith.

Lynch said he used the play to send a message to Webber. "It was sort of disrespectful for him not to box me out," Lynch said. "In practice, Coach always had two or three players trying to box me out. I said, 'Hey, Chris Webber, you're not going to box me out? Let me show you what happens when you don't.' I got the rebound and scored."

Carolina led 42-36 at halftime, and coming out of the locker room to start the second half, Lynch had a few words to say. "Do you guys remember last year when we were back home watching Duke play for the national championship?" he asked his teammates. "We said we should have been there. Well, we're here now, so let's take full advantage of it. Don't leave anything in here. We don't want to leave that floor tonight wishing that we had boxed out or wishing that we had set a screen. Let's do it. Let's play harder in the second half than we did in the first. We're one half away from our dream."

Lynch was magnificent and scored 12 points and got 10 rebounds. In one of the biggest plays of the game, with Carolina leading 68-67 with 2:28 left and the shot clock down to four seconds, Lynch spun into the lane and shot over the outstretched hands of Juwan Howard, a 6-10 superb defender. The ball seemed to stay in the air for an unusually long time for such a short shot before dropping into the basket. It was almost as if Lynch had willed it in.

After Carolina won a brilliantly played game, Lynch put on his championship hat and shirt, hugged his teammates, helped cut down the nets--the ones the Tar Heels wanted. He and Coach Smith embraced and enjoyed a private moment and a thank you.

"I wanted this for Coach as much as for myself," Lynch said. "You have to understand that Coach Smith is not just about winning the 'big one.' He's much more than that to his players."

One week to the night after Carolina won the national championship, the team had its banquet. George Lynch was named team MVP.

Coach Smith spoke about his five seniors and did just fine until he got to Lynch. Suddenly, the confident and poised Smith was overcome with emotion and stopped in mid-sentence and sat down.

"I understood," Lynch said. "If I had been up there trying to talk about Coach, I would have become emotional, too."

There was a special bond between Smith and Lynch that went far beyond a player-coach relationship. Towards the end of the season, when explaining why Carolina had won a tough game, Smith sometimes just said: "We had George Lynch on our side."

So, George Lynch lived his dream. The 1993 national championship belongs to him and his team and his coach, and his college career is fulfilled, his blessings runneth over.

"How many people," he asked, "can look back at the last four years of their lives and truly say that they don't have one regret?"

Not many. But not many wear championship rings, either.

'I'm All Carolina Blue'

MONTROSS FAMILY HAS MICHIGAN TIES

Eric Montross, 7-0, North Carolina's starting center, was in the locker room in the Superdome 40 minutes after the Tar Heels had beaten Kansas, 78-68, to advance to the NCAA championship game against the winner of Kentucky-Michigan, which was being played a couple of hundred yards away.

Sitting on a bench in front of his locker, Montross was asked by a reporter from Detroit: "Since you have so many ties to Michigan, are you pulling for them to beat Kentucky?"

It was a fair question, because after all, the Montross family of Indianapolis did indeed have a strong affiliation with the University of Michigan. Scott Montross, Eric's father, went to school there and played basketball. One of his grandfathers was an All-America basketball player at Ann Arbor. Eric's mother went to school there. One of his uncles went to Michigan and his sister is enrolled there now. The Montross family ought to get a discount from Michigan's alumni office.

So, Eric Montross, since you have such close ties to Michigan, are you pulling for them to beat Kentucky? Montross looked the reporter in the eye and said: "My family has close ties to Michigan. I'm all Carolina Blue and don't care which team we play."

Montross didn't clutter his mind with trivia when he and the Tar Heels went to New Orleans to compete for the national championship. He had been to the Final Four as a freshman in 1991 when it was played in his hometown of Indianapolis, and that year UNC was beaten in the semifinals by Kansas. This time, he wanted to leave a winner.

North Carolina's team was focused and primed to play when it took the court late on Saturday afternoon, April 3, to play Kansas. This game, too, had many ironies. Kansas was coached by Roy

Williams, a former assistant to Dean Smith at North Carolina. Of course, Smith played at Kansas on the 1952 team that won the national championship. Williams and Smith are close friends, and the playing styles of their teams are strikingly similar.

Montross and his teammates, though, pushed all that aside. They had heard that song and dance in 1991 and it was distracting. As far as they were concerned, Kansas was just another team and it stood in the way of what Carolina wanted. Montross was active and effective from the start against the Jayhawks. He scored 23 points and hit 9-14 from the field, but he also picked up his second personal foul with 11:45 left in the first half and had his fourth personal with 8:11 left in the game.

He had to be careful, and that was on his mind with less than three minutes to play and Carolina leading 68-63, and Kansas' Darrin Hancock came down the court with the ball against Montross and Carolina senior leader George Lynch. Lynch ended up with a foul on the play and Hancock made the two free throws to make it a 68-65 game.

Lynch discussed the play with Montross, questioned why he had not been more active on defense and said: "I want to play another game on Monday night."

Montross recalls the moment well. He might have been able to come up behind Hancock and bat the ball away. It would have been a gamble. Montross had the four fouls and had never tried that ploy before in game situations. Carolina calls that defensive maneuver a "flick."

"George is quite accomplished at it," Montross said. "He has speed and the experience in doing it. I don't know how to do it and had never done it before, and I had four fouls and it was a crucial part of the game. George asked me why I hadn't gone after it and I explained it to him. George is very competitive and so am I. That game was the first time we'd ever been in conflict, and it certainly wasn't a big one. I think it improved us for the next game and got us in a better state of mind."

There is a perception that Montross plays better when he's angry. He is a big man, easily noticed on the court, and his jersey number of 00 makes him stand out even more. There is a vivid memory of him playing at home against Duke as a sophomore, blood dripping from two open cuts on his head, blocking shots and scoring inside in an emotional Carolina victory. Newspapers and television stations across the country ran pictures of him in his blood-stained jersey from that game, and it sort of became his signature performance. "Make the big guy angry," some people have said, "and he becomes a bear on the court."

Not true, Montross says.

"I don't play better mad," he said. "I play better in a competitive situation. I don't get mad. It may appear to people that I'm mad, but in those times I just get in a competitive state of mind. I don't put up with mistakes on my part. I don't yell at my teammates, but maybe I am at my best when something happens to upset me. It's not anger that drives me, though. I just know that I can do better, the team can do better, and that competitive state drives me."

Montross came to Carolina as a highly recruited player and after he had narrowed his college choices to UNC, Michigan and Indiana. There was tremendous pressure for him to stay in his own state and attend Indiana, and because of his family's association with Michigan, many expected him to go there. But he chose Carolina. He was big and strong and determined when he checked into Chapel Hill, but like most big freshmen, his basketball skills needed sharpening. If one would go back and look at tapes of Montross playing as a freshman and compare it to his play as a junior, he would notice a dramatic improvement.

Montross and Carolina's other big men get special work, concentrated work, designed to help them keep the ball up, to aid them in moving their feet on defense, and to learn to shoot with both hands. Montross has developed his left-hand shot and his jump hook, weapons that make him a versatile offensive player.

He has spent many sessions working with Carolina assistant coach Bill Guthridge on pivot moves and post defense.

"He has really made me a better post player," Montross said. "He's developed my post game almost totally. When I came to Carolina, I didn't understand the concept of playing inside at the college level. I wasn't feeble in there, but I wasn't where I wanted to be, either. He's helped me set goals. It's apparent to Coach Guthridge and to me how much I've improved, but we both know there is still improving to do."

Carolina coach Dean Smith had the feeling from early in November practices that this could be one of his best defensive teams. It was an experienced team, and veteran players usually do the best job of running Carolina's intricate defensive schemes. One of the keys on defense would be Montross. How effective would he be playing defense in the post area? Carolina's defense doesn't work unless all five men play it effectively, which is why it's true when people say if you don't play defense at North Carolina, you don't play.

The turning point there came on Dec. 22 when Carolina played Ohio State in Columbus. The Buckeyes, playing before a loud ca-

pacity crowd of 13,276, led 38-35 at halftime, and center Lawrence Funderburke, 6-9, had been the catalyst. He had 13 points at halftime, and several of them were thunder dunks that inspired his teammates and stoked the crowd's enthusiasm.

In the locker room at halftime, Coach Smith was not a happy man. He didn't like his team's shot selection in the first 20 minutes and he certainly didn't like the defense, which had allowed Ohio State to shoot 53.3 percent in the first 20 minutes. Smith told Montross that he had to get in front of Funderburke and make it tough for Ohio State to get him the ball.

Montross fronted Funderburke in the second half, denied him the ball, frustrated him. Funderburke got only three shots in the second half, Ohio State was able to hit only 26 percent of its shots in the second half, as Carolina won, 84-64. "I started out that Ohio State game by not getting in front of Funderburke," Montross said. "It wasn't that I couldn't front him, I just didn't. Coach Smith made me aware at halftime of what I had to do in order for us to win. That's when I realized that playing post defense was not that hard to do. It doesn't take that much more effort, and it really pays off."

Carolina's defense, which had been good up to that point, was on the way to becoming great.

Carolina went to Hawaii after Christmas for the Rainbow Classic, and over there the Tar Heels lost 79-78 to Michigan in a tremendous basketball game. When Michigan's Jalen Rose batted in a follow shot at the buzzer to win it for the Wolverines, Montross just stood on the court, wondering how Carolina had let this one slip away. When he awoke the next morning and reflected on the game, he had a strong feeling that the two teams would meet again in the NCAA tournament.

"It was obvious that both North Carolina and Michigan had good teams," Montross said. "We had confidence that we could reach the Final Four and we expected them to be there, too. We knew then that if we were lucky enough to play them again, we'd be ready. It would be a challenge that our team would welcome."

Montross said he thinks the turning point of Carolina's season came when Brian Reese, 6-5, junior, got over a series of injuries that nagged him for about half of the season. "Brian has so much skill and talent," Montross said, "and when he got well, we could feel the difference immediately. Brian is a scary opponent when he's healthy."

Montross also didn't pay attention to those who alleged that Carolina was too slow and not athletic enough to compete with quicker teams, opponents that would show up in the NCAA tournament. "It isn't fair to our team for people to say that we don't have good athletes," Montross said. "We have good athletes, good quickness. We can stay with those teams. We showed that all year long."

> "
> *I don't play better mad. I play better in a competitive situation...I don't yell at my teammates, but maybe I am at my best when something happens to upset me.*
> "

MONTROSS' LINE:

FIELD GOAL M-A/Pct	FREE THROW M-A/Pct	3-POINT M-A/Pct	Reb/Avg	A	TO	S	Pts	Avg
222-361/61.5	156-228/68.4	0-0/00.0	290/7.6	28	66	22	600	15.8

those plays were being drawn. "He amazes us, even in practice," Montross said of Smith. "We practice last-second situations and he comes up with something that works perfectly. You saw it in the Arkansas and Cincinnati games. In that Cincinnati game, he drew up a play and said: 'This will work.' Then he said, 'No, no, no. This one will work better.'"

Cincinnati coach Bob Huggins called timeout after looking at Carolina's alignment for the inbounds pass, and on Carolina's bench, Smith changed plans. "He just came up with another play, a new one," Montross said. "And it was beautiful to see it unfold."

Finally, after winning the NCAA East and taking care of Kansas, it was time to play the NCAA championship game, and it would be a rematch between Carolina and Michigan. Monday, game day, was tedious for Montross. He played a lot of cards. He didn't want to walk around town so much that he would tire his legs. He had time to think about this Final Four and what it all meant.

"This one was more special than the one in Indianapolis, even though that one was played in my hometown," Montross said. "I was a more integral part of this team than I was in 1991. I was really into every game. I was anxious to play. I wanted the day to pass faster. I couldn't sit in my room all day, because that got old quick. I didn't want to get out of the mood to play the game, but I didn't want to sit around all day thinking about it, either."

Montross knew that he would be going against Michigan's Chris Webber, whom he considers a friend. While a lot of people accused Webber of being a big trash-talker, Montross didn't see that in Webber's game. Instead, he saw Webber as a talented player, a competitor, a man who hates to lose. Nothing wrong with any of that. Webber scored 23 points in the championship game and Montross had 16.

After Carolina won 77-71, Montross took a couple of deep breaths and tried to relax. "It was a great sense of relief to win and have the game over," he said. "So much energy went into this, there was so much anxiety. To know that we had finally achieved the biggest goal that we had worked for all season was just a tremendous feeling of relief. We started enjoying our victory later. It is the pinnacle of a college athlete's career. Very few experience anything like this."

Montross admits that winning the national championship over Michigan carried special meaning for him. After all, Michigan had beaten the Tar Heels in December and had knocked Carolina out of the NCAA tournament in a great game in 1989. It was payback time.

Meanwhile, up in the Superdome stands, a former Michigan basketball player took off his light blue sport coat and waved it over his head. Scott Montross had seen his son and his Tar Heel teammates win the biggest game of their young lives. They were the 1993 national champions, and this Michigan man, at least for this one moment, was just like his son--all Carolina Blue. ❧

After the disappointment of losing the ACC tournament championship game to Georgia Tech, Carolina tried to put that part of the season behind and build some NCAA tournament momentum. The Tar Heels did that with lopsided wins over East Carolina and Rhode Island, but then there were close, competitive games in the NCAA East Regional against Arkansas and Cincinnati, teams that were quick and athletic and loved to press. In the wins over Arkansas and Cincinnati, the Tar Heels got big play calls from the bench. One was a backdoor cut from George Lynch to Donald Williams when UNC was leading Arkansas by only one point with less than 50 seconds to play, and the other was a play that Coach Smith designed for Brian Reese with the score tied against Cincinnati with eight-tenths of a second left in regulation. Reese missed an open shot in the lane at the buzzer, but the play call had freed him for the easy attempt.

Montross remembers being in the huddle on the bench when

He Wanted A Rematch

DERRICK PHELPS LOVES BIG GAMES

You have to watch Derrick Phelps, North Carolina's point guard, play over a period of time before you get a feel for how valuable he is. He's not the kind of player who will convince you after watching him for one game, or even five or 10 games. But if you watched him play an entire season, then you would understand why North Carolina's national championship basketball team couldn't get along without him.

Phelps ranks right up there with Bobby Jones, who was one of the NBA's best defenders for a decade, as the best defensive player at Carolina in the Dean Smith era. In fact, for two years running, Smith has pushed Phelps for college basketball's defensive Player of the Year.

Bob Oliva, who coached Phelps at Christ the King High School in Middle Village, N.Y., says he saw Phelps completely dominate an important playoff game in high school when he scored only five points. "His defense in that game stopped the other team from being able to run an offense," Oliva said.

As good as Phelps is as a defender, don't get the impression that he's a one-dimensional player. He also runs North Carolina's offense. He gets the ball to the right player at the right time, and he himself scored 8.1 points a game and averaged 4.4 rebounds, not bad for a point guard.

Phelps, 6-3, from East Elmhurst, N.Y., was a junior on Carolina's 1992-93 championship team. It was his second year as a starter at point guard, and he gained confidence in his game throughout the season. He plays basketball with a smile on his face and malice in his heart. Go back and check the tapes of Carolina's 38 games during the season, and you would not be able to find even one game when Phelps had extended bad periods of play.

Phelps might sometimes give the impression that basketball doesn't mean as much to him as it does his teammates. For instance, after Carolina lost a stunning 79-78 game to Michigan in the Rainbow Classic in December, UNC's players sat in a silent dressing room, heads bowed. Then Phelps walked in and broke into song. "It was just another game and we lost," Phelps explained. "I didn't want the team to be down about it. It wasn't the last game of the season, we had plenty of games left to play. I said that night in the locker room that you never know, we might play those guys again before it's over."

Phil Ford, now an assistant coach on North Carolina's staff and one of the best point guards ever to play college basketball, recruited Phelps. He, too, upon watching Phelps play a few games, wasn't completely sure how much basketball meant to him. But the more Ford saw, the more impressed he became. "Derrick is a bottom line competitor," Ford says, "he hates to lose."

He is also relentless. He pressures the opponent's point guard every time, challenges him, keeps him from penetrating, forces places he doesn't want to go. Over a period of a game, that has a wearing effect that makes it difficult for opposing teams to get into a set offense. Duke point guard Bobby Hurley, certainly one of the most talented and experienced in the nation, hit only 6-24 field goals against Phelps in two games in 1992-93.

Go back to the first of the season, all the way back to summertime when Carolina's players were involved in pickup games on the Smith Center floor, and Phelps had a good feeling about this team. The pickup games were competitive and often involved some former Carolina players who now play in the NBA. J.R. Reid, now of the San Antonio Spurs, was in one game and playing on a team against Phelps. Reid had watched with a smile on his face as Phelps said to freshman Dante Calabria: "You put the ball on the floor, I'm going to take if from you." Calabria didn't believe it and started dribbling in front of Phelps, who stole it almost immediately. A few minutes later, Reid had the ball and Phelps showed that he played no favorites. He said the same thing to Reid: "Put the ball on the floor and I'm going to take it." As Phelps stole the ball from Reid and headed down the court, he yelled over his shoulder: "I warned you that I'd take it from you." J.R. Reid was not amused.

> "...Some of us went into this season as second-year starters. Suddenly, we were the main producers...This time we had experience and we knew what we were doing on the court."

"I always thought that we had the people capable of winning a national championship," Phelps said. "I knew what I could do and what our other players could do. But it was a matter of doing it when it counted. Some of us went into this season as second-year starters. Suddenly, we were the main producers. We had gone to the Final Four as freshmen, but we weren't really the main factors then. This time, we had experience and we knew what we were doing on the court."

North Carolina's basketball program gives a lot of authority to its point guard, while at the same time putting much responsibility on his shoulders. Coach Dean Smith hopes for a point guard that thinks along with him, and Smith likes it when he stands to call a play, only to have his point guard call the same one before Smith can flash the signal. Phelps does that with regularity, and he is so good at understanding the game, that sometimes when Smith is about to call one thing but Phelps calls something else, Smith defers. That's how much he believes in Phelps.

"I think our relationship is special," Phelps said, speaking of his head coach. "It's different from other players on the team. There is more involved with me knowing the plays, knowing where everyone is on the floor, just running the team, period. That's what he wants me to do. He wants me to know things first."

Said Phil Ford: "I never saw a team where the players had the confidence in their point guard that ours have in Derrick. They

Pat Kennedy told his team to stay aggressive, and "if we score 45 points, they'll have to score 60-something to match us."

It was a lot quieter in North Carolina's locker room. The Tar Heels were getting killed on their homecourt. Phelps spoke up, told the team that it wasn't playing its game. "I said that we were passing the ball once and then shooting," Phelps said. "They left us wide-open, and they wanted us to take the quick shot. We had to do things they didn't want us to do. We moved the ball around in the second half and got good shots. We had to make them play defense."

North Carolina came from 21 points down late in the second half to beat Florida State. But then came two straight ACC losses to Wake Forest and Duke. "Wake Forest just spanked us," Phelps said. "They were better than we were that day. Then we lost to Duke, but we woke up after that."

As the Duke game in Durham was winding down and the students were celebrating a victory over the dreaded Tar Heels and Duke coach Mike Krzyzewski and point guard Bobby Hurley embraced in front of Duke's bench, Derrick Phelps told Phil Ford: "We're not losing again this year."

Phelps looked like a prophet. The Tar Heels started winning and went to Florida State on Feb. 27 to play a big game. Carolina could clinch at least a tie for the regular season championship with a victory. FSU wanted revenge for losing a 21-point second-half lead in Chapel Hill, and it was Senior Day in Tallahassee. Carolina played one of its best games of the season and won, 86-76. "We showed our character in that game," Phelps said. "People were doubting us going down there. Florida State was really hyped up for that game, so we got together and made sure we were ready to pull together. We were No. 1 at that time and we wanted to stay No. 1."

Carolina was on a hot streak, which carried all the way into the semifinals of the ACC tournament against Virginia. UNC had the game well in hand with less than two minutes to play when Phelps, breaking loose for a layup, was fouled hard from behind and took a nasty spill. It was a frightening experience.

"My legs went numb," Phelps said. "At times like that you wonder if you'll ever play basketball again. There were a lot of serious faces standing over me, and then they got a stretcher to carry me out."

Dean Smith tried to relieve a little of the pressure of the moment when he leaned over and asked Phelps: "Do you think (Pat) Sullivan will make them if I let him shoot your foul shots?"

Phelps suffered a severely bruised tailbone and could not play in the ACC championship game against Georgia Tech, which UNC lost, 77-75. He sat on Carolina's bench, saw things that he could have done to help his team win. But when that game ended, it was over and done with. The Tar Heels looked ahead to the NCAA tournament, because their top goal all season long was the national championship.

Georgia Tech broke their winning streak at 11 games. They would have to put together another six-game streak to win the top prize. The loss to Tech did not damage the team's confidence. "We had good chemistry," Phelps said. "We listened to each other and everybody did their job. We were a confident team going into the NCAA tournament."

Phelps, still nursing the tailbone injury, didn't start the first NCAA game against East Carolina. But once in the game, he played

know he is going to make the right decision, the right call. They believe in him."

There are always key points in a basketball season, at least for a good team, when it must measure up to adversity. Carolina's loss to Michigan in December, while deeply disappointing, was also encouraging. UNC took on one of the most talented teams in the nation and lost by a point at the buzzer, in a game that every Carolina player felt they should have won. That game served as a confidence-builder, Phelps recalls. "We all said that night that we might play them again," he said. "We knew we could compete with them. We knew they got lucky on that last shot. We knew it would be a great game if we played them again. It would come down to which team would play better in that game, and all of us hoped that we would play them again."

The team put together a nice winning streak after the Michigan loss, but in an ACC game at home against Florida State, the Tar Heels were down 45-28 at halftime and the Seminoles were strutting. Over in the FSU locker room, guard Sam Cassell was going on about how he was "embarrassed" that North Carolina thought that Donald Williams or Henrik Rodl could guard him, and later coach

PHELPS' LINE:							
FIELD GOAL M-A/Pct	FREE THROW M-A/Pct	3-POINT M-A/Pct	Reb/Avg	A	TO	S	Pts	Avg
111-243/45.7	56-83/67.5	15-48/31.3	157/4.4	196	110	82	293	8.1

for keeps, which included stepping in front of ECU's speeding Lester Lyons and drawing a charge. Phelps hit the floor hard, which brought Dean Smith jumping off the bench, holding his head. He saw in the Georgia Tech game how much Phelps meant to his team, and he knew Carolina had to have him in the NCAAs.

"I took that charge because that's the way I play," Phelps said. "It was instinct. I was playing my game and trying to do a good job."

The Tar Heels kept winning and reached the Final Four. Phelps came up limping badly in the semifinals against Kansas. He had to go to the bench, but he said he knew he was going back in the game. "I wasn't going to be out at that point," he said. "I had to play."

Smith turned to Phelps' close friend and teammate, Brian Reese, who knows Phelps well, and asked Reese if Phelps was ready to go back in. "I didn't know why Coach asked Brian instead of me," Phelps said, "but I guess he knew I'd tell him I was all right, no matter what was wrong. I would have told him that I was fine and gone back into the game."

Carolina beat Kansas and Michigan beat Kentucky to set up a rematch. In the game in Hawaii, Phelps remembers that Michigan's players did a lot of talking on the court. "But after that game they knew we could play and they respected us," he said.

Phelps was anxious on Monday, the day of the championship game. He sat around, got bored, wished that the game would start at 4:20 New Orleans time rather than 8:20.

"But we had to be ready," he said. "We couldn't change the starting time. We tried not to think about the game all day, but you have to think about it. Everywhere we walked outside, we saw people with Michigan hats or Carolina hats. There was no way to block out the game. You turned on the TV and people were comparing the teams, guessing which one would win. It was a hard day."

Finally, game time. Phelps went up against Michigan point guard Jalen Rose, 6-8, talented and talkative. It was some battle, just as the game was. Carolina led 42-36 at halftime. "We knew at halftime that this was it, the final game," Phelps said. "We also knew that we could win, so all of us were intent on doing our best in the second half. We had come this far, so winning was the only acceptable outcome."

Phelps wasn't real comfortable when Michigan's Chris Webber pulled down a missed UNC free throw with 20 seconds left and Carolina leading 73-71. His mind raced back to that night in Hawaii a little more than three months earlier, when Carolina also led the Wolverines with seconds left only to lose on a wild shot at the buzzer. "I was thinking they might do the same thing again," Phelps said. "When Webber called the timeout, I thought they had timeouts left. Once I found out they didn't, I felt pretty good about our chances."

Phelps, the cool one, said he was pretty sure that teammate Donald Williams would make the technical foul shots resulting from Webber's improper timeout. "But if he hadn't," he added, "I would have done something."

Phelps, who always seemed to play his best under pressure, probably would have. His mind had been set on winning this game since last summer. There was no turning back now.

'It's All Over, Donald'

DONALD WILLIAMS TOOK THE CHALLENGE

It was a long basketball season for North Carolina's basketball team--38 games long--but one game stuck in Donald Williams' mind. It was a memory that wouldn't go away.

It was Carolina's game at Duke on Feb. 3. It was a close game, anybody's game, until the last couple of minutes. Carolina couldn't hit its shots and Duke pulled away to an 81-67 win. Williams had good shots in the game, got some real good looks at the basket, but he hit only 3-15 from the field.

"I was real hard on myself after that game," Williams said. "I was so disappointed, because I felt that I had let the team down. Everybody was supportive of me, the players and coaches, but it's still one of the worst feelings I ever had after a game. I usually make the shots that I missed in that game. I felt good going into the game, but as the game went on and I kept missing, maybe I shouldn't have taken as many shots. Maybe I should have helped the team win in other ways."

That was the second straight ACC loss for the Tar Heels and it ended the first half of the league season. "Everybody on our team was determined to stop that losing," Williams said.

North Carolina zipped through the second half of the ACC season and had already clinched the regular season conference championship when Duke came to Chapel Hill to close the regular season on March 7.

"I remembered what happened over there," Williams said. "I remembered the disappointment. This was the last home game for our seniors. The game didn't mean anything in the ACC standings, but it was a game for pride and for our seniors, and I certainly wanted to make up for my game in Durham."

Williams wasted no time making his point. He hit a couple of 3-pointers and had Duke juggling its defensive alignment trying to find somebody to stop him. Before the day was done, he hit 10-15 from the field, 5-8 from 3-point range and scored 27 points, as Carolina won, 83-69.

"It was a great way to end the regular season," Williams said. "I didn't think anybody could stop us if we played our game."

North Carolina carried an 11-game winning streak into the ACC tournament championship game against Georgia Tech. Unfortunately for the Tar Heels, Derrick Phelps was hurt in the tournament semifinals and didn't play against Tech, and the Yellow Jackets won the game, 77-75. Williams had another off shooting day--4-18 and 11 points.

"We felt bad after that game, because we thought we should have won," Williams said. "I know we didn't have Derrick, but that was like using an excuse. We still lost. Georgia Tech played great, but we should have won. Some good came out of it. To see how close we came to winning without our point guard gave us a lot of confidence. We knew all year long that when we had all of our players healthy, we were the best team in the country. That was the attitude this team had all season long, and even after we lost the Georgia Tech game, we knew that when we got Derrick back, we'd be much better."

There was no more room for slipups. The NCAA tournament is single elimination. The finality of it creates great pressure. One loss and you don't play again until next year.

Williams was only 3-9 from the field in Carolina's opening NCAA tournament game, an 85-65 win over East Carolina, but he regained his touch and knocked down 7-11 from the field in scoring 17 points as Carolina smashed Rhode Island 112-67 in round two. Those two wins sent Carolina to the East Regional in the Meadowlands and a game with Arkansas, a team with quickness and de-

32

fensive daring and a whole lot of confidence.

Williams was 7-19 from the field against Arkansas, certainly not a great percentage, but a couple of his baskets were key. One came with Carolina leading 73-71 and about two minutes left in the game and the shot clock about to expire. An Arkansas defender touched the ball in Williams' hands, but Williams regained control, turned and shot a beauty to give Carolina a 75-71 lead. Then, with North Carolina leading 75-74, UNC coach Dean Smith called timeout with 51 seconds to play. He drew a backdoor cut--George Lynch to Williams--that worked perfectly, as Carolina went on to win, 80-74.

The next game against Cincinnati went into overtime, and it was then that Williams got on a streak that would help carry his team to the championship. With the score tied at 68 in overtime, Carolina's Eric Montross got an offensive rebound, fired it outside to Williams, who hit a 3-pointer. Next time down the court, Williams nailed another 3-pointer to give Carolina a 74-68 lead. The Tar Heels went on to win, 75-68.

The men in light blue were on their way to the Final Four for the second time in three years, but for Donald Williams, this was his first trip to the mecca of college basketball. His first "official" trip, that is.

When Williams grew up in Garner, N.C., he would go into his backyard and shoot baskets and pretend that he was playing in the Final Four. He dreamed of one day playing in these games and he wondered how he would feel.

Williams went to New Orleans with a lot of confidence in himself and his team. He made the big shots against Cincinnati in overtime, which helped. But what happened to him during his freshman year at Carolina, a time that seemed so long ago as he prepared to play in New Orleans, not only enhanced his confidence, but also made him a better player.

Williams came to North Carolina with press clippings that detailed his ability to shoot the basketball. But during his freshman college season, he learned the difference between high school and college basketball, and it was a shock to him. Furthermore, Carolina had Hubert Davis, a senior, as the starter at big guard, and since Kenny Harris had transferred to Virginia Commonwealth, UNC did not have a backup to Phelps at point guard.

Dean Smith used Williams as Phelps' backup at point guard. Not only was Williams learning to adjust to college basketball, he also had to learn a new position. He didn't play much as a freshman and he says he was frustrated and sometimes discouraged. Smith was criticized for using Williams in this manner, but the coach was thinking about Williams' future as a basketball player, not just his freshman season. Williams went against Phelps every day in practice. He learned to put the ball on the floor and drive against smaller, quicker players. He learned to pass,

WILLIAMS' LINE:

FIELD GOAL M-A/Pct	FREE THROW M-A/Pct	3-POINT M-A/Pct	Reb/Avg	A	TO	S	Pts	Avg
174-380/45.8	97-117/82.9	83-199/41.7	71/1.9	46	39	38	528	14.3

and most of all, he learned how important it was to play effective defense.

The season at point guard made Donald Williams a much better basketball player. It changed him so that when Carolina trailed Michigan in Hawaii by one point with less than 30 seconds to play this season, Smith called timeout, gave the ball to Williams at the top of the key and told him to take Dugan Fife one-on-one. Williams drove Fife into the lane, got him on his heels and then pulled up for a short jumper that went in and gave Carolina a one-point lead in a game that it eventually lost, 79-78.

"...It was my first trip to the Final Four and I had dreamed about it for so long. The first time I stepped on the Superdome court for practice, my eyes just caught fire...That took time to sink in, but when it did, I wanted to finish it off. I wanted to leave a champion.

"

There was a new side to Donald Williams' game, and he learned it the year he spent playing point guard.

"Everything about my game improved after that year," Williams said. "Hard work was the answer. I got frustrated sometimes, but I had people to motivate me. I created a lot of enthusiasm and motivation myself because I wanted to become a better player. I knew I had things to learn. Coach Smith wanted me to improve my ballhandling, and point guard helped there. It really helped my on-the-ball defense because I guarded smaller, quicker guys, and it helped my decision-making. I learned to make the easy pass, the sure pass."

Williams has a shooter's mentality. His challenge was to be able to tell a good shot from a bad one, the proper time to shoot and when to back it out. He has the confidence and courage to keep shooting even when the shots are not falling. He also has a quick smile and can take teasing. When he went into a mild shooting slump late in the season, teammates Pat Sullivan and Scott Cherry started calling him "Sports Illustrated," because he didn't show up but once a week.

But after nailing those two 3-pointers in overtime against Cincinnati, Williams went to New Orleans on a high. He knew he was ready.

Although Williams had for years dreamed of playing in the Final Four, he still wasn't prepared for the magnitude of the event. In the first place, the Superdome is a huge building. Some shooters have trouble there with depth perception, but Williams said he was never bothered with it, not even in practice.

Carolina's first game in New Orleans was against Kansas, and Williams was especially nervous as he went out to warm up for that game. The Superdome was packed. The building has big screens and the fans who sit in the upper decks for basketball games have to watch on those screens. Williams was amazed by it all.

It wasn't long after the start of the game that he took himself out. He was so nervous, so fired up that he became winded shortly after the opening buzzer. "I'm nervous before every game," he said,

"but this was a different kind of nervousness. The Final Four, the big crowd. I was so nervous that I got tired after a couple of times down the court. I kept taking myself out of the games. After I took myself out of the game and watched for a couple of minutes, it seemed to relax me. Our guys were like that. It was like we said, 'Yo, we're here, we're actually here.' Funny, but all the hype before the games didn't bother me. l didn't become nervous until I stepped on the court to play the game. Then it hit me."

Williams was outstanding against Kansas. He hit 7-11 from the field, and 5-7 from 3-point range in scoring 25 points. When Kansas cut Carolina's lead to 68-65 with 2:47 left, the Jayhawks tried to trap Phelps. But Carolina's point guard lobbed a pass to Williams, who didn't hesitate. He fired a 3-pointer from the right of the key for a 71-65 Carolina lead. It took the Tar Heels exactly four seconds to answer the Kansas threat.

Carolina won 78-68 to set up the championship game with Michigan.

Williams had played with Michigan's starters, known as the "Fab Five," in some high school all-star games. He knew them well, and they tried to play with his mind some during the championship game. He and Michigan star Chris Webber came eye-to-eye in pregame warmups and Webber said: "It's over, Donald, it's all over."

When Williams hit a 3-pointer over Michigan guard Jalen Rose early in the game, the Wolverines put Jimmy King on him. "I'm going to have to stop these 'threes' from happening," King said to Williams. To which Williams replied: "Bring it on."

It was a game fitting for the national championship. Carolina and Michigan were great teams and each played well when the pressure was at its peak. Neither team backed down, each survived what could have been knockout punches to come back.

Williams saved his best for last. Hit hit a baseline jumper with 4:45 left after Michigan had gone ahead 65-61. Then, with the Wolverines ahead 67-63, Williams answered with a 3-pointer.

Back and forth it went like this until Carolina took the lead late and Chris Webber called the timeout and got the technical foul with Carolina leading 73-71 with 11 seconds to play. Dean Smith called Williams over and told him to shoot the two technical foul shots. That didn't surprise Williams. He thought he would be the man. "Coach goes by (shooting) percentages in situations like that," Williams said, "and I had the best percentage. He also did things like that all year to boost my confidence. I was ready."

Carolina freshman Ed Geth tried to say something to Williams before he went to the line, but Williams pulled away. He wanted to be alone with his thoughts for a second. He stood there at the foul line, with 64,151 watching in the Superdome and millions more looking in on TV. He was nervous, real nervous, before the first shot. He put a little higher arc on the ball because he wanted to make sure it got over the front rim. Swish. He made the second one and then two more foul shots with eight seconds left.

Since overtime of the Cincinnati game, Williams hit 12-16 from 3-point range, and Carolina had what it had spent months pursuing- -the national championship.

"I wanted it so bad," Williams said. "It was my first trip to the Final Four and I had dreamed about it for so long. The first time I stepped on the Superdome court for practice, my eyes just caught fire. At first, I couldn't believe I was there. That took time to sink in, but when it did, I wanted to finish it off. I wanted to leave a champion."

Sometimes, dreams and wishes do come true. Donald Williams knows it now for sure, because even when he pinches himself, the 1993 national championship still belongs to him and his Carolina teammates.

Last Team Standing Tall

BRIAN REESE LIVED MAGIC MOMENT

It was not the easiest season for Brian Reese, even though it ended in a national championship for his North Carolina team. After a summer of hard work, Reese, 6-5, a junior from The Bronx, was primed for his best college season. His first few days of preseason practice in early November were, according to UNC coach Dean Smith, the best he had played at Carolina. Reese agreed. He said he was playing defense, rebounding, taking charges, playing an all-around game.

Then he hurt his right leg and missed much preseason work, which hampered his conditioning and slowed his development. Then, as Carolina was routing Texas in the championship game of the Diet Pepsi Tournament of Champions in Charlotte, Reese twisted his right ankle and had to leave the game, a game that saw him hit all four of his field goal attempts and get four rebounds in only 14 minutes of play.

Reese missed the following two games against Virginia Tech and Houston. It was one thing after another, until early in February, when he suffered a freak back injury while warming up for practice.

"I worked harder in the offseason than ever before in my life," Reese said, "but at the beginning of the season, I was wondering if it helped me any. I'm sure it helped early in preseason, because I was in great shape. I was rebounding, taking charges. I was all over the floor and very aggressive. The injuries really set me back. All through the first half of the season, I probably practiced 10 times. All of that work I did during the summer didn't help me except during the first two days of preseason practice. I started out in November like I was in middle-of-the-season shape. I started out slow my first two seasons here and came on strong in the middle of the year. The same thing happened this year because of the injuries."

Reese, who sat out Carolina's win over N.C. State on Feb. 6 because of the back injury, said he first felt injury-free on Feb. 9 at Maryland when he scored 16 points and got six rebounds in 20 minutes, as Carolina won 77-63. "I felt good up there," Reese said. "I didn't have any tape on my ankles. I just felt comfortable rebounding and passing."

Reese's athletic ability, particularily his slashing moves to the basket, were vital to Carolina's offensive plan. He often broke down defenses when he drove to the basket, and his outside shooting gave the Tar Heels another threat from the perimeter. Not only that, but Reese also was an excellent receiver of lob passes that resulted in dunks and easy baskets.

Reese won much acclaim for his 25-point performance in Carolina's 86-76 win at Florida State, a game that Florida State had pointed to ever since it lost a big lead to Carolina in Chapel Hill in January. Although many people point to that game as Reese's best of the year, he disagrees.

"I won't say Florida State was my best game," Reese said, "because even though I scored 25 points, I didn't do well rebounding or in getting assists. I didn't have a complete game. I'm after the complete game. Ten points, six rebounds, six assists, that's the kind of game I like to have."

Reese says he isn't bothered that many fans and media people look first at points to determine how a player performed in a certain game. "That doesn't matter to me," he said. "I know what wins games. I was so happy in the NCAA tournament because I was second to Derrick (Phelps) on our team in assists. I think he had 29 and I had 28 in the NCAA tournament. You don't ever hear about things like that. I thought I helped the team a lot with my passing and rebounding. I know Coach Smith and my teammates like that, and I do, too. They thank me for that. That's all I need. I don't worry about how much I score."

Carolina's 1991-92 team advanced to the NCAA Final 16 before it lost a close game to Ohio State in Lexington, Ky. That game didn't set well with the Tar Heels, not at all, and some think it set the stage for what happened in 1992-93.

> *This team was able to focus on one game at a time and treat each game as important. The only thing that changed at the end of the season was how we talked to each other before and during the game, one-on-one, not with the whole team together.*

"We wanted to prove to ourselves that we could do better than that," Reese said. "All of us thought--we knew--that we could have played better in that game against Ohio State. We went back and looked at the tape and we could see that we didn't put out enough effort throughout the game. It seemed like we were just out there playing. We weren't playing Carolina basketball, because we didn't dive for every loose ball. Our goal was to play Carolina basketball all through this season. Even if we didn't play well, we wanted to give the good effort in every game. Coach Smith told us at the beginning of the season that we might play the worst game of our lives, but we were going to give him that effort and do it in every game. We wanted to give him 100 percent every time we played."

Reese came to Carolina in that recruiting class that also included Eric Montross, Derrick Phelps, Pat Sullivan and Clifford Rozier. Rozier played one year at Carolina and then transferred to Louisville. Reese admits that winning a national championship was on his mind when he signed with the Tar Heels. "I'm glad we did it as juniors," he said, "so that gives us another year to try for another one."

Reese said he started thinking about winning a national cham-

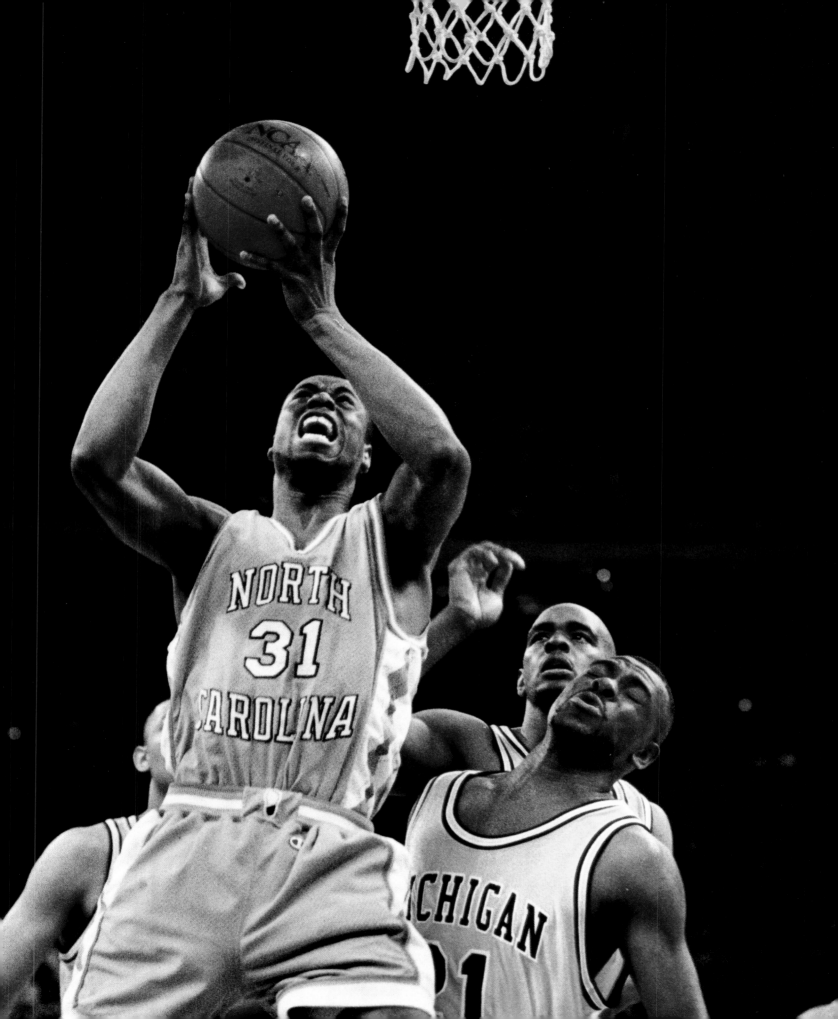

pionship early in the 1992-93 season. Coach Smith gave each player a picture of the Superdome, site of the 1993 Final Four, and printed across the picture were these words: "North Carolina, 1993 NCAA Champions."

Carolina, even though the press and opponents talked all year about the team's size, wasn't real big across its frontline. Montross is huge at 7-0, 250 pounds, but after that you had George Lynch, 6-8, and Reese, 6-5. To be a great team, Carolina had to get rebounding help from Reese. Coach Smith, in a private conversation with Reese at midseason, told him that he wanted to mistake Reese for Lynch when it came to rebounding.

"At the beginning of the year, before I got hurt, I was doing a lot of good rebounding," Reese said. "I played with a lot of confidence until the injuries hit, and then they set me back in the first half of the season. I picked up my game again, including the rebounding, in the second half of the season when I became injury-free. I was comfortable with my role on the team. One of my goals was to hit the offensive backboards hard, and I think I did a good job of that."

Injuries wouldn't be the only adversity that Reese would face during the season. His maternal grandmother, with whom he was extremely close, died during the week of the ACC tournament. Reese went home to The Bronx to be with his mother and family and didn't practice that week, but he did come back for Carolina's opening game against Maryland.

"My grandmother and I were very close," Reese said. "I doubt that she would have wanted me to stop playing basketball, even though it was a difficult time for my family and me. A lot of things were going through my mind. My main concern was my mother and how she was taking this, how she was feeling. She told me to go ahead and play. Even when I had the injuries, I still felt that I needed to be out there to help the team."

With Reese back for the ACC tournament, Derrick Phelps, one

of his closest friends, got hurt in the semifinals against Virginia. Phelps took a hard fall and left the court on a stretcher. "I was worried," Reese said. "I was the first one over there and I asked him what was wrong. He said, 'I can't feel my legs.' Later, he started getting some feeling back in his legs, so I was relieved. I felt then that he would be all right. But when they carried him off the floor on a stretcher, that was scary."

It was a hard week. Reese's grandmother died and Phelps was hurt. The two friends and basketball teammates tried to encourage each other.

"That's what friendship is all about," Reese said. "Derrick, Donald Williams and I are real close friends. We help each other, no matter what. Somebody is always there with a shoulder for you to lean on. No matter what happens, I know Derrick and Donald will always be in my corner. They really helped me out when my grandmother passed and when I went through the injuries. When I was injured, they would say, 'Yo, B. We need you.' That's the way it is supposed to be instead of always trying to baby you. We rise to the occasion, and that's one of the reasons we won the national championship."

There were times during the NCAA tournament, however, when it appeared that Carolina would not make it all the way. In the finals of the NCAA East Regional in the Meadowlands, Cincinnati broke to a 29-14 lead with seven minutes left in the first half. The Bearcats were sassy and confident. Reese said Coach Smith gave the team confidence when things were not going well in that game.

"Coach kept saying, 'Don't worry about it, it's all right. We have plenty of time.' He kept us calm. He doesn't fall into that business of saying: 'We have to score this time down the court because we are so many points behind.' He's not like that. He's more likely to say: 'Don't worry, because we are going to score this time. We're going to run this play and we are going to score.' Lo and behold, we end up scoring and we feel good about it, because our coach told us what would happen. That builds the team's confidence to a higher level and we take it from there."

Carolina knocked Cincinnati out, 75-68, in overtime to move on to the Final Four in New Orleans. The first opponent there was Kansas and the media had already started on the hype, a coaching battle between Carolina's Smith and his former assistant, Roy Williams, now head coach at Kansas.

Carolina's team refused to listen. Instead, the Tar Heels talked all week about having two more games to win, and Kansas was the first one on the list.

"We don't worry about anything but each other," Reese said, explaining how Carolina's players approached the Kansas game. "How are we doing? What should we be concentrating on? That's what concerned us. The two coaches weren't playing against each other. It was our team against theirs."

After beating Kansas, Carolina had one more hurdle to clear to reach its goal. But it was a formidable challenge. Michigan was good, athletic, confident. The Wolverines had been to the championship game the prior year. They had the experience. This time, they wanted the ring.

Reese tried to stay relaxed on the day of the championship game. He spent a lot of time with Derrick Phelps and his family. They tried to approach this like it was a regular season game, just another name on the schedule. It was hard to do. Reese kept think-

REESE'S LINE:

FIELD GOAL M-A/Pct	FREE THROW M-A/Pct	3-POINT M-A/Pct	Reb/Avg	A	TO	S	Pts	Avg
152-300/50.7	72-104/69.2	22-60/36.7	125/3.6	83	82	24	398	11.4

ing that he had to remain cool, because even in championship games, some things were going to go wrong.

"This team was able to focus on one game at a time and treat each game as important," Reese said. "The only thing that changed at the end of the season was how we talked to each other before and during the game, one-on-one, not with the whole team together. I might say to George Lynch, 'Yo, baby, this is it. Let's go.' We knew what we had to do. Derrick and I had this special talk that we gave to each other during the second half of the season. George and I had a little thing going before the games, and Derrick, Donald and I would say things to each other. We all had these little talks and you could look into the other player's eyes and know that we had to get the job done, no matter what it took, no matter who had to score or who had to rebound. We knew we had to get it together."

Before the Michigan game, Phelps said to Reese: "It's on. Once again, it's on." Reese was nervous when he took the court, but that was not unusual. He gets that way before games. "You're always nervous when you go onto the court for warmups under the lights," he said. "But with me, once the ball is tipped and I touch it a few times, run up and down the court a few times, that's it. I don't have time to think about being nervous anymore."

It turns out that Carolina and Michigan were up to the challenge. It was a game worthy of the national championship, both teams playing well and hard. Reese remembers many things that happened in the game, special moments. He recalls setting a screen that led to a Lynch dunk. He recalls Eric Montross being so strong from start to finish. And Donald Williams hitting big shots down the stretch. "After all of those things, we would look at each other," Reese said, "and say, 'Let's go,' and then race back on defense."

After Carolina had secured a dramatic 77-71 victory for the national title, Reese's first thoughts were about his mother. He knew she was watching from their home in The Bronx and he knew how happy this would make her. "I know she is so happy right now," he recalls thinking to himself.

Then he and Phelps hugged and Phelps said to him: "We did it, man, we did it." Reese says that Phelps repeated it, over and over.

Back in the locker room, where this Carolina team would be together for the last time, Reese slumped in front of his locker. He thought of the long season, how hard he and his teammates had worked, of all the injuries, of his grandmother's death and how much this moment meant. It was like magic, almost surreal. "We were the last team standing tall," Reese said.

He went home to The Bronx, where his neighbors and friends were happy to see him. "Everybody was really excited for me at home," Reese said. "But it's always like that when I go home. I'm the only one in my neighborhood who has gone to college. They see me playing basketball on television all the time. I get along with everyone in my area and they don't treat me differently. They gave me congratulations, but it's New York, they're not going to be all over me. They all gave me a hug for winning the national championship."

How could anyone want a better homecoming than that?

Season Of Redemption

PAT SULLIVAN PASSES BIGGEST TEST

Pat Sullivan knew that as far as his college basketball career was concerned, he faced a crossroads year. The previous season, 1991-92, had not been an easy one for him. He lost confidence in himself about midway through his sophomore season, grew so unsure of his abilities that he turned down open shots and became tentative with his passing. In the season-ending loss to Ohio State in the NCAA tournament in Lexington, Sullivan heard the crowd groan and laugh as a pass intended for him bounced off the back of his head and out of bounds.

Many fans turned on him. They wrote critical letters to newspapers and called in their gripes to the radio talk shows and were certainly not hesitant to let Carolina coach Dean Smith know how they felt about Sullivan's play.

Sullivan, from Bogota, N.J., is a sensitive young man. He heard the furor going on around him, and it didn't help as he battled to regain confidence in his ability to play basketball. He came to Carolina in that highly-acclaimed recruiting class that also included Eric Montross, Clifford Rozier, Derrick Phelps and Brian Reese. The recruiting nuts build the high school players up to ridiculous extremes, and their book on Sullivan was that he was a shooter with excellent range and a passer with unlimited potential.

Promises unkept. Suddenly, here he was at the end of his sophomore season not knowing for sure if he was good enough to play college basketball. "I was questioning myself, asking: 'How good am I?' I lacked confidence in myself."

Sullivan didn't make a big deal out of it, but deep down he knew that it was time for him to prove that he could play at this level. And the person that he had to prove it to first was himself. Inner turmoil is a tough opponent to conquer.

Sullivan's way of dealing with this crisis was by the sweat of his brow. Basketball people call players like Sullivan a "gym rat," because he loves the arena, enjoys being there. He checked in at weird hours during the summer before his junior season to fire jump shot after jump shot at the baskets in an otherwise empty Smith Center.

This would be his summer of hard work and redemption.

Basketball never was very far from Sullivan's mind during the summer, most of which was spent in Chapel Hill. At times when he felt like going downtown to enjoy evenings with some of his buddies, he was first pulled back to the Smith Center to work on his game. He found a willing partner in senior teammate Scott Cherry, and the two of them would be in the gym twice a day shooting, dribbling, defending, working to get better. Sullivan loves basketball and the smell of the arena. It is his sanctuary. But make no mistake, this was hard work.

Chuck Lisenbee, a manager on the basketball team, was Sullivan's roommate. He didn't know what he was getting involved in when he drew that assignment. Lisenbee had keys to the gym, and sometimes as he and Sullivan sat around the apartment talking late at night, the urge would hit and Sullivan would talk Lisenbee into opening the gym door.

Sullivan recalls being in the Smith Center some summer mornings at one o'clock. He would shoot and Lisenbee would retrieve the basketball. Hundreds of shots. When you're young and competitive and trying to rebuild lost confidence, the time of day hardly matters.

You do it until you get it right.

This was not a battle, however, that Sullivan could win by himself. During those summer months, he often found himself visiting friends in the basketball office. The door to the corner office would sometimes open and Dean Smith would walk out and invite Sullivan in.

Sullivan recalls hearing the words that inspired him, words that made him believe. "You are a good player," Smith told him, "and you can play the game."

"It helped out tremendously to know that he had confidence in me," Sullivan said, "especially when I lacked it in myself. I told myself that if Coach Smith thinks I'm a good player, then I should think that about myself. It was a big boost."

Smith asked Sullivan to listen to some tapes about positive thinking and goal setting. Smith is not one who thinks that you can gain confidence just by acknowledging that you've lost it. He sees it as a step-by-step process: Hard work plus success equals confidence.

"We both listened to this one tape about a guy whose goal was to make $100,000," Sullivan recalls. "He made a photocopy of a big green bill and wrote $100,000 on it and put it on his ceiling where he could see it all the time. I think that's where Coach Smith got the idea for the picture of the Superdome that we had in our lockers."

Sullivan let his mind imagine success. He pictured himself playing defense against Duke's Grant Hill or Wake Forest's Rodney Rogers and stopping them. He was building himself up, and he was feeling better about his progress.

"To be honest, Coach Smith probably should have given up on me," Sullivan said. "But he didn't. I really had some rough times during my sophomore year and so did some of the other guys. As great as Hubert Davis was, we depended on him too much my sophomore year. I know I did. I wanted him to come take the ball from me. I just didn't feel comfortable. Maybe the turning point came after the loss to Ohio State in the NCAA tournament. I was depressed that we lost that game, but it was also about that time that I thought things could get better for me. I was determined to work harder, gain my confidence back, and see some improvement not only in my game, but also in myself. Not only did this hard work help my game, it also helped my overall attitude about life. I felt like I became a stronger person by going through that adversity, and in the process, I think I also became a better person."

Sullivan, hearing the voices of his critics, was sometimes confused. He knew that he had a hard time pleasing them, and he let what they thought bother him. It was here that he got help from his older brother, Matt Sullivan. The two of them are close.

"A lot of people tell me to shoot the ball more," Sullivan said. "Matt took the opposite approach. He told me to do what I felt comfortable doing, to work hard and do what Coach Smith wants me to do. He made me understand you can't please everybody. My goal should be to please myself, my teammates and my coaches. I wanted to make the guys on our team and the people most important in my life happy. I feel I have done that."

Still, after the hard work in the offseason, Sullivan had to make things happen in the season. There was no dramatic eye-catching change in his game. Rather, the changes were subtle. He moved crisply to do the things that it takes for teams to win--setting screens, playing good defense, making that extra pass, boxing out on rebounds.

And, yes, he had to be willing to take the open shot, which wasn't an easy adjustment for him. "I hurt the team when I didn't take the open shot," Sullivan said. "That was a big change for me this year. I felt confident shooting the ball when the shot was there. But against N.C. State at home this year, Coach Smith took Henrik Rodl and me out of the game because we passed up wide-open shots. He sat us down and told us to shoot the ball when we had open shots."

Great teams need a player like Sullivan. He doesn't hunt his shot, nor does he shoot often, but he hit 51.8 percent from the field in averaging 6.4 points a game last season. He cut down on his turnovers and increased his assists over the previous season. The hard work paid off.

Still, there were low moments. The Tar Heels lost 88-62 at Wake Forest on Jan. 30. It was the kind of loss that could have devastated a team, so thorough and humiliating was the beating.

Carolina's coaches and players were very careful after that game to give full credit to Wake Forest, which played at the top of its game and deserved to win. But away from the public eye, the Tar Heels looked within for answers.

"That wasn't us," Sullivan said, recalling that game. "Even before the game in the locker room, we were just sitting around. It's bad to say, but it's almost like we didn't want to be there. We have

to give Wake Forest a lot of credit. They played well and gave us a beating, but it was like our heads were somewhere else."

As the players looked at tapes of that game, the team's unquestioned leader, senior George Lynch, pointed out many instances when the effort was lacking. Even though the Tar Heels lost the next game at Duke, Sullivan could sense a strong determination building among the team's members.

Sullivan's role was off the bench as a reserve. As the team roared down the stretch, losing only to Georgia Tech by two in the finals of the ACC tournament when point guard Derrick Phelps was out with an injury, Sullivan's confidence in his own game continued to build. The Tar Heels kept winning until they found themselves matched with Michigan in the game to determine the national championship.

On the bus ride from the hotel to the Superdome to play one last game with the stakes at their highest, the team was quiet and reflective. Sullivan said it was a little strange, because win or lose, it was going to be the last game of the season. From the beginning of the NCAA tournament against East Carolina in Winston-Salem, George Lynch had told the team: "I

"
To be honest, Coach Smith probably should have given up on me. But he didn't. I really had some rough times during my sophomore year and so did some of the other guys.
"

don't want this to be my last game."

"But this was Monday night and it was the last game, no matter what," Sullivan said. "Everyone on the bus was quiet. The guys were listening to their music. We pretty much treated it as we did the other games. In the locker room, we did the same things we had done all season. We were loose. Scott Cherry and I were kind of messing around, trying to stay loose. But we all knew what we were about to do. We knew we were getting ready to go out that door and play for the national championship."

Coach Smith knew his team was ready to play. He didn't need to do anything to stoke the fire.

"He treated it exactly the same as other games," Sullivan said. "He told us to keep Michigan off the boards, to use our depth, to create tempo and wear them down. He did not put pressure on us. He wanted us to do the things we had done all year to get to this game."

It was a beautiful game, and when it got down to the last 20 seconds, with Carolina leading 72-71, Sullivan was fouled by Michigan's Rob Pelinka. All the hard work of the last 12 months rushed through his mind as the official handed him the ball on the foul line and Michigan's Jalen Rose sharply reminded him: "This is for the national championship, baby."

"I wasn't scared," Sullivan recalls, "but I was nervous. I was thinking back to all of the things that had gone wrong my sophomore year. Then I looked over at our bench and all the guys were clapping and cheering for me. I felt I couldn't let the guys down. We had been through so much together, I just couldn't let them down. After Rose told me I was shooting for the national championship, I thought to myself that I was going to show him, I would make the shot. I made the first one and Rose kind of hit me on the release. On the second one, I don't know if I was thinking about that or not, but the shot felt good, but it was long. I sprinted back on defense. I saw Chris Webber trapped in the corner and I was trying to read his passing lanes when he called timeout. At first, I didn't know what was going on, but then I saw the official call a technical on Michigan, and I felt that we had it won."

Sullivan said his teammate, Donald Williams, "was like ice. He hit all four of those foul shots and we had our dream. We were national champions."

As the horn sounded to end the game, Sullivan embraced Coach Smith and then ran to midcourt to join his teammates. Many thoughts went through his mind later that night, but he thought not only of this team, but of past Carolina teams that were good, even great, but weren't able to enjoy this moment. He thought of Rick Fox and Pete Chilcutt and King Rice and Hubert Davis, and in his mind, this championship belonged to them the same as it did to this team.

And he also thought back to the previous summer, to those late sessions in the Smith Center when he and Chuck Lisenbee and the sound of a basketball swishing through the nets penetrated the silence and the still of the early morning.

Pat Sullivan thought about those lonely nights as he walked out of the Superdome late on the night of April 5, 1993 as a member of the national champions of college basketball.

The long battle to rebuild his game and his confidence had been won and the reward was sweet and worth all the sweat.

SULLIVAN'S LINE:

FIELD GOAL M-A/Pct	FREE THROW M-A/Pct	3-POINT M-A/Pct	Reb/Avg	A	TO	S	Pts	Avg
88-170/51.8	60-76/78.9	9-30/30.0	92/2.4	51	35	26	245	6.4

The Sweetest Memories

RODL HAS THEM FOR LONG TRIP HOME

Every college basketball team that seeks greatness needs a player that absolutely gives himself up for the good of the team. He is usually someone who would rather pass than shoot, who plays defense, who never worries about personal statistics.

His only goals are team goals and his only concern each game is that the team wins. His play is so unselfish that the coach has to threaten to take him out of the game if he doesn't take his open shots.

Meet Henrik Rodl, Carolina senior, from Heusenstamm, Germany. He did all of the little things--set screens, moved without the ball, passed inside to the big men, played defense--that helped UNC's 1992-93 team go 34-4 and win the NCAA championship. He did it quietly, usually without publicity, and he never complained about his role.

When you talk about team chemistry and its importance to Carolina's season, give Rodl much credit for making it a team strength. "He was one of our best passers," Carolina coach Dean Smith said, "and his contributions to our team often went unappreciated, but not by his teammates and certainly not by his coaches."

Rodl sat alone in front of his locker in Carolina's Superdome dressing room not long after the Tar Heels beat Michigan 77-71 to win the NCAA championship. Reporters and TV camera people were all over the place, surrounding Eric Montross and Derrick Phelps and George Lynch and others. One reporter approached Rodl and asked him if there had been much trash-talking in the game.

"I'm not a player who induces much trash-talking," Rodl said. "I guess I'm not good enough for the other teams to worry about me."

Rodl was being modest. He had some key moments in Carolina's season, including a prominent role in the team's sensational comeback from 21 points down late in the second half to beat Florida State. His first 3-pointer cut Florida State's lead to 71-54 with just over nine minutes to play. He hit another 3-pointer shortly after that to make it a 73-63 game and Carolina's rally was well underway and would not be denied.

North Carolina opened the season shooting the ball well. The Tar Heels hit a shooting slump midway through the season, and it was at this point that Rodl lost some confidence in his shot. He went a couple of games when he turned down wide-open shots and saw Coach Smith giving him the shooting motion from the sidelines. Finally, Smith sat Rodl down and told him that he if didn't take the open shot, he would take him out of the game.

"Coach was right," Rodl said, "because when I didn't take my open shots I hurt the team. Even if I missed, at least we had a chance for an offensive rebound."

Rodl says a key to Carolina's season came after the Tar Heels lost back-to-back ACC games to Wake Forest and Duke. He recalled the year before when the team, facing a brutal stretch of road games late in the season, lost four straight ACC games.

"We lost confidence during that losing streak the year before," Rodl said. "When we lost the two games in a row this season, we came back and played really well against N.C. State. We beat them (104-58), and that seemed to get us going again. We never reached the point where our confidence suffered."

There seems to be no doubt that the comeback over Florida State sapped Carolina emotionally for its next game at Wake Forest. Many of the players say it was obvious in the locker room that the team wasn't ready to play. Why? The players differ on that. Some

think the team might have grown a little cocky after coming back to beat the Seminoles. Some think the team was emotionally drained from the big comeback and hoped that they could play their way into the Wake Forest game.

"That win over Florida State was a hard game and it did take a lot out of us," Rodl said. "Maybe the team just felt like we couldn't lose anymore. After all, we had been 21 points down to a team as good as Florida State and won. Maybe we thought we could come back from any kind of deficit. We weren't as focused for the Wake Forest game as we had been up to that point, and our concentration left something to be desired. It was a devastating loss for us, but I think some good came of it. It taught us that we had to give our best and our all to win in this league. We couldn't afford to be off in any game. It was a big lesson and I think we learned it well."

Rodl says Carolina's team, after it broke that two-game losing streak, gained confidence as it went along. The team had the ability to focus on the game at hand and not look ahead. By the time the regular season came to an end, Rodl thought that the Tar Heels had as good a chance as anybody of winning the NCAA title.

"The Duke game in Chapel Hill was a special time for us," Rodl said, "because it was going to be the last home game for the seniors. We played very well in that game. Even though Duke played without Grant Hill, it was nice to beat them the way we did. We wanted to play them again because some people said the only reason we beat them was because Hill didn't play."

Carolina was a confident team heading into postseason. Rodl found himself in the spotlight in the ACC championship game against Georgia Tech because he started in place of Derrick Phelps at point guard. Phelps was injured in the semifinals of the ACC tournament and didn't dress out for the championship game. As hard as Rodl played, it was clear that Carolina missed Phelps at both ends of the court.

"Derrick is definitely an important part of this team," Rodl said. "During the Georgia Tech game, I think the team did feel less confident with Scott (Cherry) and me running the point. The team had developed so much confidence in Derrick's leadership, it was hard to replace. I think we would have won that game if he had played. We gave it a good effort, but we're a lot better team with Derrick in there. Derrick was always supportive of me. He cheered me on and wanted badly for us to win that Georgia Tech game when he couldn't play."

Rodl says rather than being deflated by the loss to Georgia Tech, Carolina seemed to come out of the game more determined than ever to win the NCAA championship. It would take a six-game

winning streak to make this happen.

Before Carolina went into NCAA play, Coach Smith met with his team. The players were asked what they could do better to help the team advance in the tournament. The players told what they could do and Smith added his remarks.

"I was the only player in the meeting that Coach forgot to ask," Rodl said. "He came back in practice the next day and asked me. He wanted me to hit the open jumper and continue working hard. I knew what he expected from me and the other guys on the team knew what he expected from them. That made it easier for him and for us to do the job."

Rodl, who along with Lynch was elected permanent team captain, said he could sense from the beginning of the season that the team really wanted to win the national championship. "There was never a time," he said, "that I thought this team wouldn't give everything it had to win."

Rodl viewed his leadership responsibilities as different from the way George Lynch led. In the first place, they have contrasting personalities. Rodl is older than Lynch, is married, and is more subdued.

"I had a role on the team to support my teammates," he said. "I tried to give them confidence and help them maintain poise. I wanted to lead by example and make right decisions. I am not the type of person to stand up in a crowd and tell the guys what we need to be doing. Usually, when I saw someone doing something wrong, or I wanted to tell him something that he could do better, I took him aside and suggested it to him. I think maybe I helped a couple of my teammates, but you'd have to ask them."

Rodl says it wasn't an easy season for UNC freshman Dante Calabria. "He kept his confidence up for much of the season," Rodl said, "but there came a point when his confidence left him a little bit. He wasn't as confident in practice anymore, and you could see the disappointment in his face. When we were on one of the bus rides, I talked to him and told him about my experience as a freshman. I told him to keep playing hard. I wanted to help him out, to support him, to be a friend for him. I think we got a lot closer by talking like that. Those little things make a team special. Team closeness did play a very valuable role for us. George (Lynch) obviously led us on the court and off...I think, by and large, the seniors were more important off the court. Next year's seniors will have to do both, because they will play more than we did."

Rodl says once the NCAA tournament began, and the team got over its short-lived disappointment of losing to Georgia Tech in the ACC tournament, the Tar Heels were confident and focused for NCAA tournament play. UNC and Michigan made their way through the 64-team tournament field to set up a championship rematch from the Rainbow Classic in Hawaii. Rodl said losing to Michigan in December by one point "was very disappointing," but he says he didn't dwell on that game. "It was a pretty lucky play for them at the end," he said. "Either team could have won the game."

Monday, April 5, 1993, the day of the championship game in New Orleans. Rodl says he didn't sleep well the night before the game and neither did some of his teammates. The team went to shooting practice Monday morning and then "wasted time," waiting for the game. "It is hard on everyone's nerves to wait all day to play this game," he said.

Rodl said he knew "the magnitude of the game. I knew that it was why we were there. I don't think I was aware of how much it

RODL'S LINE:

FIELD GOAL M-A/Pct	FREE THROW M-A/Pct	3-POINT M-A/Pct	Reb/Avg	A	TO	S	Pts	Avg
58-117/49.6	25-38/65.8	22-62/35.5	57/1.5	136	60	39	163	4.3

meant to society or the people around us. It was one of the most fulfilling athletic moments in my life."

Rodl never said much in the locker room before games and he didn't before the Michigan game. He said Carolina's players were usually intense before games. "We don't feel that we did anything different for this game than we had done all year," he said. "Everyone was calm, focused and we took it seriously."

It was actually a sense of relief, Rodl said, when the team took the court for pregame warmups. The waiting, the anticipation was over. It was time to crown a champion.

Rodl's view of the game's last 20 seconds, when Michigan's Chris Webber rebounded a missed foul shot with Carolina leading 73-71: "I was sitting on the bench," Rodl recalled. "First, he walked and everyone on our bench was upset because there was no call. Then he called a timeout at the other end of the court. I had no idea that they didn't have any timeouts left. It took me a couple of seconds to realize what had happened. I think people have made too much of it. There were so many things in that game that were more important. First of all, he walked and that was pretty obvious. Second, he was surrounded by Derrick (Phelps) and George (Lynch) in the corner. I don't know where he could have gone with the ball. Even after the technical, Don (Williams) had to make the free throws. Nobody gave them to him. Fourth, without Webber, Michigan wouldn't have even been close to being in the game. It was incredible how well he played."

Rodl, who was named the outstanding scholar athlete on Carolina's team after a brilliant classroom career at Chapel Hill, signed a professional basketball contract to play in his homeland of Germany. Shortly after he went through the graduation ceremonies at Carolina on May 8, he and his wife Susan packed up and left for a new life, a fresh start in Germany.

He carried with him the ultimate joy for an athlete--the right for his team to be called the best in the nation. "I will always cherish the relationships that I made," Rodl said. "I am especially happy for our team because we got along so well. For it to turn out the way it did makes it more special. When the guys get together in the future, we'll have something great to remember and talk about." ◉

Finish Was A Blur

SALVADORI THERE AT THE END

Kevin Salvadori thought that Carolina's basketball team had the goods to win the 1992-93 national championship, but there were some interruptions along the way that gave him pause.

First, he remembers the Rainbow Classic in Hawaii, the night that Carolina played Michigan in the tournament semifinals. The two teams had dressing rooms that were located near each other. The players on the two teams came out of their dressing rooms at the same time, and Salvadori recalls Michigan being brash and cocky.

Salvadori, 7-0, a junior, struggled in that first Michigan game. He played 10 minutes, didn't score, got no rebounds and fouled out.

"Michigan talked a lot of trash in that game over in Hawaii," Salvadori recalls. "They did everything they could to take us out of our game. We did not play well in the first half, which was not characteristic of this team. We played them hard in the second half. They won the game (79-78) but they knew they were lucky. They thought they were going to dominate us in that game. They acted like they had it won before they even took the court. But when it was over, we had their respect. They knew we could play."

All of that would become important later in the season, much later.

Carolina put together a nine-game winning streak after the Michigan loss to go 17-1. The most dramatic of those victories was the comeback against Florida State in Chapel Hill, which saw UNC come from 21 down midway in the second half to win. That game came just before the Tar Heels went to Winston-Salem to play Wake Forest, a team they had dominated in recent years. Not this day, though. Wake Forest erupted in the second half to win, 88-62.

That was a thrashing that no one could ignore.

"I remember clearly before that game that everyone was so dead," Salvadori said. "We really didn't want to play for some reason. We were on a real high after coming back against Florida State. I think our heads got a little big and we became a little cocky after that game. We knew that we had a really good team, but Wake Forest was ready for us and we weren't ready for them. Losing like that was a big disappointment, but I had a feeling that it would help us before the season was over. We were embarrassed about the way we played in that game. It made us hungry again. Even though we lost to Duke in the next game, we felt pretty good about the way we played for most of the game. We felt that we were on the way back up."

Kevin Salvadori is what basketball people call a "late bloomer." He got very little recruiting attention as a player at Seton-La Salle High School in Pittsburgh until well into his senior season. Salvadori was tall and gangly and certainly didn't have the strength to go inside and bang with ACC players. Nevertheless, North Carolina assistant coach Bill Guthridge saw things in Salvadori that he liked. Salvadori was developing into a good shot blocker on the high school level, he ran the court fairly well for someone that tall, he had a soft touch on his shot. Guthridge looked at Salvadori as a player with potential. The recruiting battle was not fierce, but North Carolina signed him.

When Salvadori got to Chapel Hill, it was obvious that he needed more strength and more weight. He redshirted his freshman season and spent a lot of time in the weight room building up his body. His improvement has been impressive, so much so that he was an important man off the bench in Carolina's championship drive.

"I thought that I could eventually play at Carolina, or I wouldn't have come here," Salvadori said. "I didn't know, though, that I would improve as quickly as I did. I played okay when I first came here, but I was dominated by a lot of big men around here. Playing against that kind of competition helped me develop. I never dreamed that one day I would be playing for the national championship. When you come to Carolina, you know that it could happen, but it still didn't cross my mind that we would be playing for the national championship and I'd be in the game at the end."

This Carolina team seemed to have all the pieces to the puzzle. It had size and depth and a lot better quickness than many people realized. Every basketball team must find the answer to team chemistry, which isn't easy. Salvadori recalls seeing how that came together for this team, which had 14 players from different parts of the country, players with different interests, different ambitions.

"The closeness is what I will remember most about this team," Salvadori said. "Everybody on this team got along. I ended up spending at least some time with everybody on the team and everybody liked each other."

For Carolina to become a great team, it was going to be necessary for someone to emerge as the true leader, the person all the others would respect. The name of George Lynch pops up constantly in conversations with Carolina's players, and it was no exception in discussing leadership with Salvadori.

"George was our main leader, on and off the court," Salvadori said. "He was vocal off the court. If he needed to get on somebody, he didn't hesitate. He would get on their case and make sure they got back in line and did what they needed to do for the team to be successful. George hustled more than anybody else on the team. I

> *...When you come to Carolina, you know that it could happen, but it still didn't cross my mind that we would be playing for the national championship and I'd be in the game at the end.*

have never seen anyone play as hard as he does. Seeing a senior and your star player work that hard, compete that hard, lifts everybody and motivates everybody to give their best. With George, it didn't matter if we were killing somebody or they were killing us, he never lost his tenacity. He always played as hard as he could."

That kind of leadership is rare. Lynch not only showed it in games, but also in practice. He got some help, Salvadori said, from the other seniors and also from point guard Derrick Phelps, a junior, who had his say in team huddles and who ran the team on the court.

North Carolina, while it had depth, had certain players that it could not lose and still maintain the high quality of its play. Lynch was one. Phelps was another. The Tar Heels, after losing to Wake Forest and Duke, won the regular season ACC championship and took an 11-game winning streak into the ACC tournament championship game against Georgia Tech. But Phelps was injured in the Virginia game in the ACC tournament semifinals and couldn't play against Georgia Tech.

It made a dramatic difference, as Tech point guard Travis Best spent most of the afternoon penetrating Carolina's defense and pitching off to James Forrest, who had 27 points in Tech's 77-75 victory. Carolina's loss in that game prompted all kinds of questions. Was the team's momentum broken going into the NCAA tournament? Remember, some pointed out, that Carolina goes to the Final Four only in years that it wins the ACC tournament.

"It was frustrating losing to Georgia Tech," Salvadori said. "We didn't have Derrick, but it was still a game that we should have won. Our defense in that game wasn't at a level that it had been. After we lost that one, a lot of people said we couldn't win the national championship for this reason or that. That fired us up. People were talking us down again. It seems for a team as good as we were, we didn't get a lot of respect this year. We had to keep proving ourselves over and over again. We got our focus back."

One more loss and the season would be over. You don't get second chances in NCAA tournament play. Carolina was seeded No. 1 in the East, and Salvadori says the team was confident that it could win the national championship, as long as everyone took care of the task at hand. On the other hand, if the team got the NCAA brackets out and started looking ahead to this game or that one, there would be trouble.

Carolina took care of East Carolina and Rhode Island to advance to the NCAA East. The first game in the Meadowlands was against Arkansas, and the Hogs were quick and talented and had the underdog role, which coach Nolan Richardson exploited to near perfection. Carolina led 75-74 with 52 seconds left and had the ball. Coach Dean Smith took timeout and called for a backdoor cut, with Lynch making the pass to Donald Williams. Why Williams? Because Smith knew that Arkansas defender Corey Beck would be guarding Williams, and Beck was aggressive, a defender who liked to gamble and overplay his man.

The play worked just as drawn. Williams got the layup and Carolina the victory to survive and advance.

"That was so typical of Coach Smith," Salvadori said. "He drew the play for Donald because he knew the defender on him was a gambling defender. Coach knew exactly what was going to happen. What he told us would happen in the huddle happened on the court. I will always remember the exactness of Coach Smith's approach to that play. I was in awe as the play developed, because the whole thing unfolded just as he said it would."

Carolina found itself in trouble in the next game against Cincinnati, down 15 points and not playing very well. It is at times such as this that leadership becomes crucial. Salvadori again points to Lynch, saying he would not let Carolina lose. "He fought as hard as he could to get us back in the Cincinnati game," Salvadori said, "and when we got back in it, we put Derrick on (Nick) Van Exel, which shut him down for the rest of the game."

The game went into overtime, but Salvadori says he was confident that Carolina would win because of its defense. "Cincinnati did not get any good looks at the basket against our defense in the second half or in overtime," Salvadori said. "Our defense shut them down, which was the key to the game."

The Tar Heels, champions of the NCAA East, were off to New Orleans to play in the Final Four. Carolina's players, Salvadori recalled, celebrated briefly, but then they reminded themselves that they weren't happy just to be making one more basketball trip. They were going to the Final Four to win it.

Salvadori played an important role in the win over Kansas in the semifinals. He went in for Eric Montross, who encountered early foul trouble, and scored six points, got three rebounds, blocked a shot and had no turnovers. He did it while fighting a nasty cold that made it hard for him to breathe.

The necessary step had been taken. Kansas was out of the way, and now Carolina could focus on just one more game, this one for the national championship, and Michigan would again be the opponent.

Salvadori's family stayed in the same New Orleans hotel as Carolina's team. Salvadori spent a lot of time with them on Monday, the day of the Michigan game. While many Carolina players were anxious for the game to get there, and while his family was uptight, Salvadori was loose and relaxed. It wasn't by accident. He learned a lesson in the loss to Duke at Durham. He was so fired up for that game that it hurt his play. He got no points, two rebounds and four fouls in the loss to Duke. He made a pact with himself after that game that he would prepare better. He would be ready to play, but not so fired up that it would work against him. Salvadori recalls getting excited on the bus ride to the Superdome to play the game.

"We knew this was it," he said. "This is what we had worked for. Pat (Sullivan) and Scott (Cherry) usually carry on in the locker room to keep us loose, but they were quieter than usual on this night. They did what they could to relax us, because we didn't want to go out there tight, but there was no mistaking that this game was different. We reminded each other in the huddles that this is what we had worked for, to give it all we had."

Salvadori said that Carolina freshman Dante Calabria had some friends down for the Final Four. One of them was Sean Miller, who was an outstanding point guard at the University of Pittsburgh and also a Carolina fan. Miller's father coached Calabria in high school. "Sean Miller was amazed at how loose we were before a game this big," Salvadori said. "I don't think many college teams were as relaxed and as easygoing as our team was this year. Pat and Scott can act so goofy sometimes. That's something else that I'll always remember about this team."

Salvadori, who remembered Michigan talking a lot on the court in Hawaii, said there was very little talking in this game. "In fact," he said, "I didn't hear anything said in the pivot area. Everybody was playing hard and competing."

SALVADORI'S LINE:

FIELD GOAL M-A/Pct	FREE THROW M-A/Pct	3-POINT M-A/Pct	Reb/Avg	A	TO	S	Pts	Avg
66-144/45.8	38-54/70.4	0-0/00.0	138/3.6	12	24	7	170	4.5

Salvadori was in the game at the end when Pat Sullivan made one foul shot, missed the second, and Michigan's Chris Webber rebounded with 20 seconds to play and Carolina ahead, 73-71. He hustled back on defense to make sure he had his man, Juwan Howard, covered. He heard the crowd roar when Webber apparently got away with a travel in front of Carolina's bench. But everything was happening so fast that it was a blur in Salvadori's mind. Even when Webber called a timeout that his team didn't have and everybody on Carolina's bench started jumping up and down, Salvadori had no idea what all the excitement was about. He finally tugged on the coat sleeve of assistant coach Bill Guthridge to ask what was going on. It was then that Salvadori learned that Michigan would be charged with a technical foul for taking too many timeouts.

"It was a great feeling," Salvadori said. "We had worked so hard. We were sending Donald (Williams) to the line to shoot the technicals and then we would get the ball back. Everybody on our bench was excited, because we all knew that there was no way we would let Michigan back into the game. It was over, and we were national champions."

Memories Will Last

MATT WENSTROM SENSED A BIG SEASON

Matt Wenstrom had a feeling last summer, the summer before his senior Carolina basketball season, that the Tar Heels were going to accomplish some extraordinary goals. He could tell it the way the players worked on their own in the hot summer months to improve individually. He knew it was a team that would work hard and compete.

But what convinced him even more than all of that was the feeling the players on the team had for one another. Wenstrom watched all of this during the offseason and saw a team that was together and extremely focused. He certainly wasn't predicting a national championship, but he felt sure that this group would reach its potential, whatever it was.

"This team was so close," Wenstrom said. "You could tell by the way we worked last summer that this team had common goals and a good work ethic. We knew, all of us did, that this team would be different. We had a feeling for one another that would get us over the rough spots."

Four of Carolina's five seniors came to Chapel Hill together. Wenstrom was in the recruiting class with George Lynch, Henrik Rodl and Scott Cherry. The other senior on the 1992-93 team, Travis Stephenson, walked on two years later.

"The senior leadership that we had this year really began four years ago," Wenstrom said. "George, Henrik, Scott and I were very close. We did a lot of things together, hung around together quite a bit. That's what made this year's team special--the closeness. When you know people that well, you can better react to their moods and to their intensity."

Carolina coach Dean Smith talked all season about his team's senior leadership, which was exceptional. Smith has an open door policy for his players and has for all of his 32 years as Carolina's head coach. He especially listens to his seniors and to their suggestions, which is not to say that he does everything that they might recommend. Seniors do have a lot to say about team rules, however. They make them and the coaching staff enforces them.

This Carolina team abolished one of the shooting rules that it had used since the 3-point shot was introduced to college basketball. The Tar Heels had given some players the green light to shoot 3-pointers, while others had a yellow light, and some had the red light. There was no such rule this season, but the team had to understand that its goal was to take good shots. Except for a few games in December, the players exercised good shot selection.

With Eric Montross and Kevin Salvadori playing in front of him at center, Wenstrom knew that his role on the 1992-93 team would not be one of playing a lot of minutes. He would get important playing time in some games and it would be up to him to take advantage of it, but his main role would come in practice and in leadership situations. One of his key on-court performances came against Florida State in Chapel Hill. The Tar Heels were being run out of their own building in the first half when Wenstrom entered the game for Montross, who was in foul trouble, and hit 4-5 from the field and scored a quick eight points. His play kept Carolina within shouting distance in the first half, in a game that it came from 21 points down in the second half to win.

"We were so far behind in that Florida State game," Wenstrom said. "Coach looked down the bench when Eric got into foul trouble and put me in. It was an opportunity for me to show the team that we could win this game, no matter how far behind we were at the time. My philosophy is that no matter how far behind we are at halftime, we can beat the opponent by at least that amount in the second half. I wanted to show the players in that game that we were not going to quit, that we were going to play hard and come back and win. I did feel good about my contribution to that comeback. It was a big win for the team, a good game for me, but more importantly, it showed what we could do when we put our minds to it."

Carolina was cruising at that point in the season. The team was unbeaten through six ACC games and the only blemish on the record was a one-point loss to Michigan in the Rainbow Classic in Hawaii. But there were storm clouds on the horizon. Trouble loomed ahead.

After the comeback win over Florida State, the Tar Heels went to Winston-Salem to play Wake Forest on a Saturday afternoon. The Deacons broke open a close game in the second half and won in a rout, 88-62. Carolina also lost its next game to Duke on the road, and suddenly the team was looking at a two-game losing streak and the ACC regular season race was again a contest.

"Losing to Wake Forest by so much made us shape up a little bit," Wenstrom said. "A lot of guys went into that game not focused. Some guys stepped up on the bus ride back to Chapel Hill that day and said we needed to get refocused right away. Even though we lost the next game to Duke, that didn't bring us down like the Wake Forest game did. After the Duke loss we renewed our commitment, the one we had made last summer, to having a good season."

Carolina was impressive in winning seven straight conference games in the second half of the ACC regular season to clinch the regular season title and set up the last home game for the seniors. Duke was the opponent. Wenstrom had stood on the sidelines and watched three senior classes wave good-bye to the home crowd for the last time. He knew that his day would come and he wondered how he would react to it.

"It was such an intense day," Wenstrom said. "We were playing Duke, but the thing that really made the day emotional was that it would be the last home game for the seniors. We joked about it some as we dressed for the game. We wondered if we were going to cry when we were introduced. But when it came time to run onto the court for pregame warmups, all of us had straight faces. We were very eager to get down to business. It's hard knowing that you are getting ready to play for the last time on the court that has brought you so much success. We had grown so much as players on that court. It was a hard day, an emotional day, but we had to eventually put that aside and concentrate on beating Duke."

Carolina won 83-69, and Wenstrom and the other four seniors started the game, another Tar Heel basketball tradition. Beating Duke was a good way to go into NCAA tournament play, but Wen-

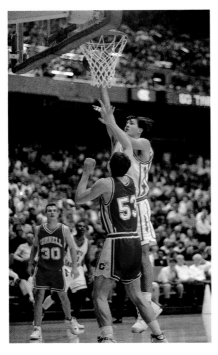

strom saw much more than that to encourage him.

"We had shown all season long that we had what it took to be a serious threat on the national scene," Wenstrom said. "It certainly wasn't just the Duke game. We showed heart in coming back to beat Florida State. Things happened all year to show time and again that our players never quit. We got our tails whipped at Wake Forest, then lost a hard game at Duke, but we never quit. We showed we had the qualities of a winner."

Dean Smith talked several times during the season about how much he admired Wenstrom for the way he kept a positive attitude, even though he wasn't playing much. Wenstrom is a competitor and sitting on the bench, especially when the team was winning and getting national attention, wasn't easy. He wanted to play and be a part of what was happening on the court.

"Everybody's role isn't to score 20 points or get 10 rebounds," Wenstrom said. "Everybody's role is different. A player who knows his role and accepts it is more of an asset to his team than a player who covets another player's role. I knew my role was to go in when I was needed. I did well in those situations, and it showed the team that all of us should be ready for Coach when he called on us. I was ready and that was a big part of what I stood for on this team. My role was to do other things, and the players on the team respected me for that."

Wenstrom recalled that at the team banquet the previous year, Coach Smith had said, "No more Mr. Nice Guy," but the big senior, who had come to Carolina from Katy, Texas, didn't notice much difference in his coach this season. Some subtle changes maybe, but nothing dramatic.

"He was intense this year," Wenstrom said of his coach. "He wanted us to have a goal and a focus. He knew what he wanted from this team and he showed us. He let us know that he wasn't going to accept anything but our best. If your coach demands the best from you every day, you are pushed to work hard and you strive to meet your goals. He certainly demanded intensity and our attention. Words from him are enough for us. We believe him and trust that he means business."

North Carolina went to the NCAA tournament as the No. 1 seed in the East. It had an 11-game winning streak snapped when it lost in the ACC tournament championship game to Georgia Tech. The Tar Heels felt good about themselves and the state of their play, however, as they entered NCAA competition. They promptly put to-

gether another winning streak, this one for five games, to set up a showdown for the national championship against Michigan.

Wenstrom remembers Monday, April 5, 1993, as being one of the longest days of his life. Carolina and Michigan were to play that night in the New Orleans Superdome for the national championship, the prize that some 300 Division 1 NCAA basketball teams had as their dream when they began practice the previous Nov. 1.

Wenstrom spent part of the day with his girlfriend, walking around New Orleans and enjoying the city's beauty. He and his teammates didn't want to sit around all day thinking about the game, talking about it. They wanted to relax and think about other things. That is not easy to do, however, not when the national championship is at hand. Games this big are never very far from a player's mind.

It finally came time for the Tar Heels to board the team bus and take the drive down to the Superdome. It was a quiet ride, a nervous time, the kind of moment that competitors live and work for.

Once in the locker room, Carolina wanted to do its best to treat this game as it had 37 other games during the season. Pat Sullivan and Scott Cherry did their Harlem Globetrotters imitation at one end of the room. They'd done it all season. Wenstrom joked around. Some players wanted to be alone to listen to music or just sit and think.

Nobody needed any extra motivation for this one. After a long season, there was one game left to determine the national champion. The players had extra incentive, one that their coach knew nothing about. "If you watched any television at all, there were all kinds of people criticizing Coach Smith because his teams had won only one NCAA championship," Wenstrom said. "Even though we knew the criticism was ridiculous, we wanted to put it to rest. For all of the things that he does for us and for all of his hard work, we wanted this one for him. That was one of our team goals."

Carolina and Michigan put on quite a performance for college basketball, and the end of the game had more drama than good theatre. Wenstrom felt good with Pat Sullivan on the foul line with 20 seconds left and Carolina holding a one-point lead. Wenstrom knew that Sullivan, Derrick Phelps and Donald Williams were good foul shooters, especially in the clutch. Sullivan made one foul shot, missed the next, and Michigan's Chris Webber rebounded.

"When Webber got the ball, he signaled for a timeout, but the referee didn't acknowledge it," Wenstrom said. "Then Webber dragged his feet and the referee didn't acknowledge that, either. Our whole bench went wild. We were screaming for a travel but the referee waved us off. We knew how good our defense was. Michigan was not going to score. We were active, we trapped Webber and he got nervous and called timeout. I don't blame him at all. It's the coach's responsibility to notify his players of the timeout situation. The people on our bench kept track. We knew instantly that they didn't have a timeout left. When the referee made the signal calling for a timeout, we were thrilled. We knew we had them."

Carolina 77, Michigan 71.

"This was a special season that I was able to share with special people," Wenstrom said. "Great memories like this never fade. The hard work, the tough games, the celebration and the happiness will always be there. This championship season is something that I'll never forget."

WENSTROM'S LINE:

FIELD GOAL M-A/Pct	FREE THROW M-A/Pct	3-POINT M-A/Pct	Reb/Avg	A	TO	S	Pts	Avg
34-61/55.7	16-27/59.3	0-1/00.0	47/1.4	7	13	1	84	2.5

Carolina Was Pumped

SCOTT CHERRY RECALLS COACH'S WORDS

Scott Cherry and his buddy and Carolina teammate Pat Sullivan got together the night before the Tar Heels were to play Michigan for the national championship and talked about what it would mean to be the champions of college basketball. They remembered 1991 when Carolina went to the Final Four and lost to Kansas in the semifinals.

They remembered that feeling, having to say goodbye to family and flying back to Chapel Hill and having people ask what happened. They didn't want that to happen again, no way.

"I thought about how I would feel if we won the championship," Cherry said. "I did not let any negative thoughts enter my mind. I was trying to imagine us winning, using positive thoughts. We were there, we were in the championship game, so why not finish what we had come after?"

Scott Cherry will one day look back at the entire 1992-93 season and see just how spectacular it was for him. He was not a highly recruited basketball player coming out of Ballston Spa, N.Y. In fact, Carolina probably represented his only major college basketball scholarship offer, and when coach Dean Smith signed him, UNC's fans asked: "Who's he?" Carolina's coaches liked Cherry's attitude, his intelligence, his athletic ability.

Cherry was nervous when he checked into Chapel Hill for school and drifted down to the Smith Center to play some pickup games with his future teammates. He had never even seen a sev-en-footer, and the first day he

laced on sneakers at Carolina, he played against one. You can't blame him for wondering then what he had gotten himself into.

He assumed his role on North Carolina's team, improved his play, gained some confidence, and lo and behold, there he was playing in the 1993 Final Four. Not many coaches would have given Cherry a spot on a major college team, but when he went into North Carolina's lineup and played in big games, in championship games, opposing coaches talked about UNC's depth "wearing us down."

This was Scott Cherry's last season of college basketball. He couldn't believe how the time had zipped by, but here he was, a senior leader on a North Carolina basketball team that was on a mission. Cherry didn't spend a lot of time dreaming about personal

goals, but back in the summer when he and his teammates worked on their own to improve their basketball skills, he wanted his last Carolina team to go back to the Final Four. That would be a neat way to end one's college basketball career.

Cherry was one of five seniors on this team, and he and the others knew how important their leadership roles would be. Team chemistry would be as important as defense and rebounding and shooting, if Carolina hoped to contend for national honors.

"I don't think any of us worked at being leaders," Cherry said of his senior teammates. "George Lynch always goes 110 percent. He goes all out and others feed off that. When you see George run the length of the floor, rip down a rebound, score, and then go back to the other end and make a steal, you feel that you have to work hard and play hard, too. Matt Wenstrom and I contributed off the court. We kept people loose in the locker room before games. We wanted people to enjoy practice, but at the same time, we wanted them to be committed and focused on our goals. Henrik Rodl did his part coming off the bench behind Derrick (Phelps). We didn't sit down and figure all of this out. We were just ourselves. Fortunately, our personalities came through and we became pretty good leaders."

The seniors helped change a few team rules. For instance, Dean Smith has never understood why a basketball player would mess around in warmups, take crazy shots that he wouldn't attempt in a game and even try to miss them. It would be, Smith thought, like Jack Nicklaus trying to mess up on the practice tee before the U.S. Open. You know, go out and shank a few to get ready to play. Carolina's managers watch the players shoot layups in warmups, and those who missed did some extra running in practice. The seniors convinced the coach to change that rule this year, as long as it didn't result in sloppy warmups. A small item? Yes, but little things mean a lot in putting together a championship team.

Cherry was serious about his leadership responsibilities. "It would have been easy for Matt (Wenstrom) and me to blow off the season because we weren't playing a lot," Cherry said. "But we knew we could be a good team, maybe even a great team. I wanted us to be the best that we could be. I wanted to be a leader for

guys with tremendous talent, like Eric (Montross), Derrick (Phelps), and Brian (Reese), all of them. It was something that was very special to me. I'm thankful for the opportunity to lead this group."

Cherry developed special friendships with senior Henrik Rodl and freshman Dante Calabria, because the three of them played some at point guard behind Phelps. Cherry wanted Rodl and Calabria to do well, and when they had problems, he tried to help. Calabria was sometimes discouraged because he wasn't playing a lot, but Cherry reminded him that he had three years of Carolina basketball left and his time would come. "You're playing a lot more than I did my first year," Cherry reminded him. Rodl, on the other hand, sometimes lost confidence in his shooting ability. Cherry told him that he was a good shooter and the two of them would engage in shooting contests, most of which Rodl won. It seemed to help.

Basketball teams, even real good ones, have their ups and downs, and Carolina did. But Cherry liked this team from the first day of practice, and then there were points during the season when he was convinced that this team was unique.

"After the Florida State game, when we were down 21 points late in the second half and came back to win, we knew we had a team that would never quit," Cherry said. "That gave us a hint that we were a great team. Even though we lost to Michigan by one point in Hawaii on a fluke shot, that told us that we could play with the best teams in the nation. We knew that we were a talented team."

It took a couple of jolts, though, to really get the team going, as Cherry sees it. Carolina lost back-to-back games to Wake Forest and Duke. "The guys realized at that point in the season that we had to come ready to play in every game, no exceptions," Cherry said. "If we weren't ready, a good team like Wake Forest could beat up on us. We just looked at each other after that game, as if to ask: 'Why weren't we ready to play?' We knew that we weren't going to let that happen again. We were not going anywhere and let somebody beat us like that."

Even though Carolina lost the next game at Duke, there was a ray of encouragement. "We went over and lost to Duke after the Wake Forest game, and that taught us that we had to play for 40 minutes," Cherry said. "We played well for 36 minutes against Duke, but in the last four minutes we let them get some fastbreaks and some easy layups and they won. Derrick (Phelps) told some of our coaches that we wouldn't lose another game this year."

Carolina went on an 11-game winning streak until Georgia Tech stopped the Tar Heels in the ACC tournament championship game, a game in which Phelps did not play because of injury. "Losing that game to Georgia Tech sort of fueled our fire going into the NCAA tournament," Cherry said. "We knew we were playing great basketball and that it would be tough for any team to beat us. If we could get Derrick healthy, then we knew we could win the whole thing. It would be hard, but we could do it. Everybody on the team seemed to step up his game."

Cherry, once he found out that Carolina was seeded No. 1 in the East for the NCAA tournament, didn't want the Tar Heels looking too far into the future. "We looked only at our first two games in Winston-Salem," Cherry said. "After we won those, we looked to the tournament in the Meadowlands. We knew that we had to beat some quality teams before we could go anywhere."

The Tar Heels beat Arkansas and Cincinnati in the East Regionals to earn a trip to the Final Four. This had been Cherry's dream, dating all the way back to the previous summer. He and his teammates had talked about it many times. But going back to the Final Four would not be enough. This time, they would not be denied.

"George Lynch pumped us up all season," Cherry said. "George has that ability. He can motivate people. When he is on the court and his emotions are flowing, he can definitely get guys going. He is a great player and a great person, and one of his attributes is that he can get people ready to play."

Cherry, the little-known kid from Ballston Spa, not only made the trip to New Orleans, he heard Dean Smith call his number in both games of the Final Four.

"It is something you dream about as a kid," Cherry said. "My only concern had been for our team to make it to the Final Four. I certainly wasn't thinking about playing time. I was kind of surprised when I went in the Kansas and Michigan games. I had so much adrenaline flowing in the Kansas game that I think I went up a couple of inches higher for those rebounds. I was so pumped up just to be in there playing. I never expected to be in the Michigan game with six minutes left. It shows that Coach has a lot of confidence in his players and he isn't afraid to go out on a limb and use his bench, even in a situation like that. People would have criticized him for that if we had lost."

Cherry says his most lasting memory of the Final Four was the mood in Carolina's locker room before the championship game against Michigan. The team seemed a little uptight, and Smith noticed this and told them that it was just another basketball game and something else would be news the next day.

"I will always remember some of the things Coach Smith said that night, as well as the looks on some of the faces of the players," Cherry said. "You could see the intensity in the eyes of the players, the concentration to what Coach Smith was saying, and how much all of them wanted to win this game. We fooled around some in there to keep our minds off things, but once we sat down and Coach came in and talked about matchups, it was all business from that point on. There was so much space in our locker room that each guy had his own spot, like his own locker."

Then it was time to go out the locker room door, run the 150 yards from the locker room to the Superdome court. Carolina's players huddled just outside their dressing room and, with Scott Cherry leading the way, a basketball under his arm, they took the court for the biggest game of their lives. Carolina beat Michigan for the grandest prize in college basketball, and afterwards, Cherry remembers looking into the stands and seeing his family and the families of his teammates celebrating. After the celebrating had been done on the court by the players, after the Superdome nets had been cut down, the Carolina team went back to its locker room and shut the door.

The intensity that was there before the game and at halftime had been replaced by smiles and some tears and a lot of hugging. The national championship plaque was in the corner of the room. Cherry and close friend Pat Sullivan talked for a minute in an adjoining room.

Then Scott Cherry took his Carolina basketball uniform off for the last time. He came to Carolina four years earlier scared and not knowing what to expect. He left a national champion.

Folks in Ballston Spa, N.Y., welcomed him home a hero, and when Carolina fans talk about Scott Cherry in the future, nobody will ask, "Who's he?"

CHERRY'S LINE:

FIELD GOAL M-A/Pct	FREE THROW M-A/Pct	3-POINT M-A/Pct	Reb/Avg	A	TO	S	Pts	Avg
20-33/60.6	25-35/71.4	4-8/50.0	23/0.7	30	21	9	69	2.1

Bigger Than A Dream

FINAL FOUR GAVE DANTE CALABRIA CHILLS

Dante Calabria was a freshman on North Carolina's 1992-93 national championship basketball team, but he wasn't your ordinary freshman. He's cool and poised and pretty much unflappable.

Calabria, 6-4, came to Chapel Hill from Beaver Falls, Pa., and as soon as he got to school in August he joined in pickup games with his new teammates. He more than held his own. In fact, he had moments of brilliance. He was brash and confident. The Carolina style of playing shouldn't be a shock to Calabria, because his coach at Blackhawk High School, John Miller, ran a lot of Carolina's stuff.

The veteran players warned him, though, that it would be different once practice began on Nov. 1. A lot would be thrown at the freshmen at once, and it would be a miracle if they weren't at least a little bit confused.

"I was in shock," Calabria said of that first practice. "I had thought that it would be hard, but I was still surprised at how intense practice was. The players didn't say a word. Everyone listened to Coach Smith and concentrated the whole time. The other freshmen and I were confused. We didn't know what to do."

Calabria learned a lot as he went along. He's a versatile player who has the talent to play both guard spots. He can handle the ball against pressure, he reads defenses well, he can shoot from the outside and he's a fine passer. He played a good bit during the month of December, but his playing time diminished as Carolina got into its ACC schedule and settled on an eight-man rotation.

At practice, Calabria learned to listen to the coaches, even when they weren't talking to him. He found out that he could pick up bits and pieces of information that would help him. He also leaned on the older players for advice and encouragement. "You learn by observing the other guys and by listening to Coach Smith," he said.

There was more than just basketball stuff to learn, however. Calabria had to learn to balance basketball and the travel with his schoolwork and social life. He found out that Carolina's players are expected to be in class the morning after returning home late from a road game. "You learn responsibility," he said. "I learned to get my studying done early. Time is precious and important. You have to set aside time to get things done."

There were five seniors on Carolina's team, and Calabria learned different things from each of them. He found George Lynch to be the "big leader on the team. He wasn't real vocal as far as saying something to you in front of everybody. If he had something to say to you, or if he wanted to help you out, he would take you aside and tell you in private."

Calabria found Matt Wenstrom to be the most vocal of the seniors. He spent a lot of time observing senior Henrik Rodl. Calabria found Rodl to be quiet but effective, a leader by example. Rodl wasn't spectacular, Calabria thought, but he would come out of a game with an assist-error ratio of 6-1. "He would do everything quietly," Calabria said, "but his statistics were there. He was a quiet leader, but he was steady and dependable."

Lynch took the time to communicate with the freshman players. He told Calabria and the three other freshmen on the team to stick with it, learn, don't get discouraged. Lynch recalled that he had gone through some times when things didn't go his way, but he never gave up. "To look at George now, you know the effort he gave through his career was totally worth it to him," Calabria said. "He talked to us before the games and he just wanted everyone to do it for the team. It doesn't matter who scores on our team as long as you play hard and give the effort. George always reminded us of that."

Calabria saw the Tar Heels go through the season with a lot of peaks and very few valleys. He says he knew on March 7, after Carolina beat Duke handily on Senior Day at the Smith Center, that this team might extend its season into April.

"Everyone was so pumped up after that game," Calabria said. "That's when I thought that we had a great chance to win it all. We lost to them earlier, and then to beat them the way we did, I thought that was big for our team."

The loss to Georgia Tech in the ACC tournament championship game, though a disappointment, seemed to make the team even more focused, Calabria thought. "Because Derrick (Phelps) was out of the Georgia Tech game, it seemed like all of our players felt like they had to do something extra to make up for his absence," he said. "We knew he'd be back for the NCAA tournament, which put us back into the right frame of mind. We knew what we had to do. I had the feeling then that our real season had just begun."

The Tar Heels, seeded No. 1 in the East, made it through four games, including two close ones in the NCAA East Regionals in the Meadowlands, to win an invitation to the Superdome in New Orleans to participate in the Final Four. Kansas would be the team's first opponent there, with Michigan and Kentucky playing in the other game.

Calabria had dreamed of playing in the Final Four. Growing up in Beaver Falls and practicing his game, he often wondered what it would be like to play college basketball in a setting like that. He's a Pittsburgh Steelers football fan, so he had seen football games televised from the Superdome. He had watched Final Fours on television. Many of them.

Still, he wasn't prepared for what he would find in New Orleans. His mind had not even come close to capturing the enormity of the event. Calabria saw newspaper and TV reporters all over the city. Basketball fans wore their school's colors in the hotels and in restaurants and just out walking around. The Final Four leaves the sports page and becomes Page One news. It's not unusual to walk into the hotel lobby and hear a pep band strike up the school's fight song, and impromptu pep rallies break out like a measles epidemic. Calabria observed all of this and just shook his head in wonderment.

"The Final Four was bigger and better than I had dreamed about as a child," Calabria said. "It's hard to imagine all the hype that goes along with being there. Actually, being there is much different than watching on television. Everybody was going crazy on

Bourbon Street. The whole town was involved."

It takes a lot to shake Calabria. He had taken everything in stride, until he and his teammates took the Superdome court for pregame warmups to play Kansas. Then the whole thing hit him as if he were standing under a mountain waterfall.

"We ran out there and the crowd was cheering and going nuts," he said, "and I got chills. I was so pumped up during layups that I had a hard time concentrating. I had never played in front of that many people. We went back into the locker room and everyone had his say. We were all ready to play after that. The initial shock was gone, the butterflies were over, we were ready to play the game. Everybody was anxious to play. It had been written and talked about for a week, so everybody was ready to get their first sweat."

Carolina beat Kansas 78-68, but Calabria says the Tar Heels didn't celebrate long. He could tell, he said, that the "older guys were focused on winning it all. Beating Kansas was a necessary step. There was one left. It wasn't time to celebrate yet."

Michigan and Carolina practiced on Sunday. There were big press conferences for UNC coach Dean Smith and Michigan coach Steve Fisher. Many of the players from each team also sat for interviews and heard questions that they had been asked since the first of the season.

Once Monday arrived--championship day--it was time. The players killed time in their own way. Calabria went shopping on Bourbon Street. He played some video games down there and then just sat around, waiting for game time. He talked to some relatives. Sean Miller, the son of Calabria's high school coach, who played at Pittsburgh, also visited with Calabria. "We all kept talking about this

being the big game, the big dance," Calabria said. "There is a lot of pressure in a game like this, but once it starts, you have to consider it just another game."

Calabria said it was very quiet on the bus from Carolina's hotel to the Superdome. But the locker room was loose. "Scott Cherry and Pat Sullivan kept people loose," Calabria said. "It wasn't very tense. Nothing special went on in there. Nobody said anything about the game being for the national championship until we got in the huddle, and then we said this is it, this is for the big one. We thought if we played hard and did what we always do, we could win."

Calabria got in the game briefly. It made an indelible impression. "It was the highlight of my year, as far as basketball is concerned," he said. "To be in the game with the championship on the line is something that I will never forget. It's something I will tell my kids about. It's so great to have this happen after you've thought about it so much as a kid. Funny, but I wasn't as nervous in the Michigan game as I had been playing against Kansas."

Calabria was on the bench when teammate and close friend Pat Sullivan went to the foul line to shoot one-and-one with 20 seconds left and Carolina leading by one point. Six months seemed to flash through Calabria's mind in that one moment.

"I remembered all the free throws that we had shot before the season began," Calabria said. "I thought of all the times he and I had gone to the gym and just shot free throws. I just knew he wouldn't miss it. Pat and I had put so many free throws up together. I was thinking it had to go in, it had to. I was scared to death because it was for the game, for the championship. That's the kind of situation I always dreamed of being in as a kid. Pat had always dreamed about the same thing. He found himself in that situation and he delivered. Everyone on our bench was going crazy. Pat and I have shot around and hung out together a lot. What he did was huge."

Sullivan made his first foul shot to give Carolina a two-point lead, but his second one missed and Michigan's Chris Webber rebounded and appeared to try to call timeout, which the official ignored. Then it appeared that he traveled, but that wasn't called.

"Everyone on our bench jumped up and down when Webber walked," Calabria said. "We all called for a travel. Then he dribbled down the court and all of us stood up, not knowing what to do. We were all watching Webber when he called timeout. When I saw him do that, I jumped up and down and started hollering. We were going nuts, because we knew that was the game. I even saw Coach 'G' (Guthridge) jump up and down. I definitely knew Donald (Williams) would hit the free throws. He's ice."

Calabria knew exactly how long his first college season had lasted--five months and four days. He has enough memories to fill a museum. The most special part of it all?

"The feeling of winning and being together as a team," Calabria said. "The season was pretty long, but everyone stuck together. We had the most wins in the history of Carolina basketball. It was just the greatest feeling to win that last game and accomplish everything we had worked for all year. We had a few times when things didn't go right, but we kept working hard and believed in ourselves and each other. Then, in the end, we reached our ultimate goal. We are the national champions of college basketball."

Not bad stuff for a freshman. Not bad at all.

CALABRIA'S LINE:

FIELD GOAL M-A/Pct	FREE THROW M-A/Pct	3-POINT M-A/Pct	Reb/Avg	A	TO	S	Pts	Avg
24-52/46.2	7-9/77.8	9-23/39.1	27/0.8	29	21	9	64	1.8

'You Are A Special Team'

LARRY DAVIS KNOWS NOW WHAT IT MEANS

Larry Davis, a freshman on Carolina's 1993 national championship basketball team, was anxious and a little nervous on the day of April 5, 1993. His Tar Heels had extended the season to the very last day, and that night in the New Orleans Superdome, they would play Michigan for the right to be called college basketball's best team.

Time seemed to stand still as the players awaited the time when they would board the bus and take the 10-minute ride from their hotel to a back entrance at the Superdome. Davis sat around the hotel that day and talked, killed time, even wrestled some with freshman teammate Ed Geth and senior Matt Wenstrom, as the rest of the players urged them on.

Cabin fever struck for many of Carolina's players, however, and they went their separate ways. Some just took a walk in the cloudy and brisk and breezy New Orleans weather. Others went shopping, some spent time with family members who were down for the game. Just hanging out.

Davis decided to go with upperclassmen George Lynch, Brian Reese and Donald Williams to visit some college campuses in New Orleans, to see how they compared to Carolina. They dropped by Tulane, then visited Xavier and then Dillard. Davis was surprised that many of the people they talked to on the three campuses were pulling for Michigan.

"That hyped us some," Davis said, "and I pushed it even more by saying, 'Hey, George. They don't have any confidence in you and Brian and Donald.' It made those three guys mad. George was really confident. He had been that way all year and he went into every game we played thinking for sure that we were going to win. After we visited those three campuses and heard the people talk, George said he had something to prove and that (Chris) Webber and (Juwan) Howard would have their hands full. He said he was going to try to get every rebound that came off the rim."

Larry Davis heard Lynch talk that way, and as the four of them headed back to the hotel, he grew more confident that this would be Carolina's moment. The team got together about 4:15 p.m. New Orleans time for the pregame meal. Davis observed that the players were confident and relaxed, maybe more relaxed than they had been all season.

"I think it was because we all knew that we had done everything to that point that we could do," Davis said. "We had won the games that we had to win to advance to the championship game. It was just Michigan and us. We were wired to play our best."

Davis was quiet in the locker room before the team went out to warm up. He was sitting and thinking as a couple of veteran players, Pat Sullivan and Scott Cherry, went around the room and tried to keep everybody loose. Brian Reese, a junior forward and starter, thought that maybe Davis was a little apprehensive. The two of them talked.

"Brian told me that I was lucky and should appreciate this time," Davis said. "He said that when he was a freshman, his team made it to the Final Four but lost the first game there. Here I was a freshman and we were getting ready to go out and play for the championship. I appreciated him saying that. I'm in a little world of my own before every game. I try to get my mind ready for the game and for anything that could happen. Then George Lynch came over to me and patted me on the back and reminded me that this was the last game of the season. He told me that he knew I had a bright future, and then he said: 'Anytime you need help, you know you can call on me.' It was a different atmosphere in the locker room because this was the last game of the season, win or lose. It was almost like some of the guys were saying goodbye before the game. George and Matt (Wenstrom) and Scott (Cherry) all talked about it being their last game in a Carolina uniform."

You must understand that the entire Final Four experience was a highlight tape for Davis. After all, his hometown is Denmark, S.C., population 3,762, and when he went into the Carolina-Kansas game in the semifinals, there were 64,151 fans in the Superdome.

When he was a youth growing up in Denmark and shooting baskets in his backyard and dribbling the ball in the street in front of his house, his imagination often soared. Sure, he dreamed of one day playing college basketball, but his mind never came up with anything as wild as this. The Final Four. The many fans and bands and all the media, always asking questions. This, Larry Davis thought, is wild.

"Let me tell you," he said, "that five years ago, I never would have thought that in my freshman year of college that I would be playing for the national championship. I just had never been able to think that big. It was such a great honor to be playing on this team with these guys. It's the thing that kids dream about when they're shooting baskets all alone. I dreamed of one day winning a national championship, but not as a freshman, not in a place with all those people."

Davis wasn't sure of his feelings when the team was warming up, getting set to take on Michigan in the biggest game of the season. He remembered the game between the two teams in Hawaii, what a good game it was, how hard both teams had played. On one hand, he was confident that his team would win, because he knew the players were ready to give it their best effort. There was no doubt in his mind about that. He also thought that it should be pay-back time for the Tar Heels. After all, many people felt that Michigan was lucky to win the game in Hawaii, and this was UNC's chance to more than even that score. But he also knew that Michigan was a talented team, one that deserved to be in the championship game. "My feeling before the game started," Davis said, "was that the game would be close, would go down to the wire just like the one in Hawaii, but this time, we would be the winner."

It turns out that Davis was a pretty good prognosticator. He was on the bench, his heart pounding, when Pat Sullivan went to the foul line to shoot one-and-one with 20 seconds left and Carolina leading 72-71. Carolina's players on the bench yelled encouragement to Sullivan, and then they clasped hands and hoped for the best.

"I was confident with Pat on the line," Davis said. "I always feel that our guys are going to make them when we have to have them. When Pat made the first one, all of us on the bench gave a big sigh of relief. A lot of the pressure was gone. When Pat missed the second free throw and Webber got the rebound, I couldn't believe that he walked and got away with it. It looked to me like Chris was really nervous. Then he dribbled it down the court himself and got into trouble near their bench and took the timeout that they didn't have. We had them then, we knew it was our game."

After the celebrating had been done on the court and after the media had finally left the Carolina locker room to file their stories, Larry Davis and his teammates got on the bus that would take them back to their hotel. Assistant coach Bill Guthridge always takes the front seat on the bus, usually to the right of the aisle.

"I remember after every game this year," Davis said, "Coach Guthridge would say that we were a special team. I wondered why he kept saying that. He would say it, win or lose. He would get on the bus and say 'Great game,' or 'You guys played hard.' He said closeness, hard work and discipline bring championships, and he

said we had all of those qualities. We sort of laughed sometimes because he said it so much."

Larry Davis went home to Denmark, S.C., on April 9, 1993. He returned a hero. Mayor Orlando H. White proclaimed it "Larry Davis Day," and many of the townspeople turned out to greet him and congratulate him for being a champion. There was a reception and Davis was asked to make a short speech. Some of his youth coaches and other leaders of the community said a few words about him.

"I was real happy, because this was a big honor for me," Davis said. "I never thought they would be having a Larry Davis Day in Denmark. Little kids came up to me and said they saw me on TV. They made me feel good and I think all of that will make me work even harder. I'm looking forward to the next three years, and maybe one day some of these kids will say they want to be just like Larry."

It was a season with many twists and turns for Larry Davis. The first day of practice on Nov. 1 was an experience that will stay with him a long time. He knew college basketball--Carolina basketball-- would be a different world from what he had ever seen before. He found that everything was organized to the second.

"I was really excited when I walked into practice that first day," Davis said. "I was kind of out of it, my mind was drifting a little bit. It started out with a couple of laps and some stretching and I thought it was going to be a breeze. But then Coach Smith got into the drills and the freshmen were kind of mixed up. The headaches began. Any freshman that comes through here needs time to adjust."

Davis didn't play much his rookie season. But he learned. He learned defense from Derrick Phelps. He learned from Donald Williams about patience. He learned leadership from George Lynch.

"After we lost to Wake Forest by 26 points in the regular season," said Davis, "George pulled us all together and said, 'That's not going to happen again, and this one game is not going to set us back.' He said we were going to take that loss and build on it, use it to make us better. The coaches thought we had played hard against Wake, but George didn't. He said if anybody on the team didn't want to play hard or play our game, then he should go see the coaches right now because he had a problem. He was straight up with us."

Larry Davis knows that very few freshman basketball players ever get a chance to match his experience. It was a storybook season and seemingly it was a million miles from Denmark to New Orleans.

"I was really nervous in the first half of the Kansas game," Davis said. "I think the guys sitting on our bench had faster heart-beats than the ones playing. We set goals at the beginning of the season and we had met them. When we got to the Final Four, it was like it was a completely new season. It was the last part and it was do-or-die for every team there. You know deep down that you have to play your best to win. Sometimes even your best is not good enough."

This time, the best was good enough for North Carolina, and as the days pass and Larry Davis lets it all sink in, he can be alone and shut his eyes and almost hear Coach Guthridge say it again: "You are a special team."

Larry Davis doesn't laugh now. He doesn't laugh because he knows it's true. ◉

DAVIS' LINE:

FIELD GOAL M-A/Pct	FREE THROW M-A/Pct	3-POINT M-A/Pct	Reb/Avg	A	TO	S	Pts	Avg
14-40/35.0	14-23/60.9	2-9/22.2	16/0.8	4	5	6	44	2.1

The Rookie's Shock

ED GETH WOULD LEARN THE TRUTH

Ed Geth admits that when he enrolled as a college freshman in August 1992, he had no clue how tough basketball is at North Carolina.

Geth, 6-8, from Norfolk, Va., unlike some of his new teammates at Carolina, did not make any All-America teams as a player at Granby High School. He was second-team All-City in Norfolk his senior year. While Carolina was not the only school to offer him a scholarship, he was not the subject of a major recruiting battle involving many of the nation's basketball powers. Some recruiters called Geth a "sleeper," meaning he had potential but would not be ready to play major college basketball right from the start. He would need time to develop and a lot of work.

Geth is not one of those young men who grew up bouncing a basketball on the way to the grocery store. He had other goals, and he didn't really pick up the sport until he reached high school. But once he started playing and got some encouragement, he took the game seriously. He and his high school coach, Jim Harvey, would spend hours working on something as elementary as catching the ball. Harvey would fire passes that were tough to handle and ask Geth to field them. The drill helped Geth improve his hands, his ability to hang on to passes and rebounds.

Geth worked to increase his speed, and the main thing that attracted North Carolina's coaches to him in the first place was his ability to move his feet. He has quick feet, and big men with quick feet and good hands excite college basketball coaches. Carolina's coaches also like Geth's tenacity as a rebounder. He isn't a great leaper, but he likes to mix it up and has an uncanny knack of being where the ball is.

Geth had long been a Carolina basketball fan. He recalls being depressed when Kansas knocked the Tar Heels out of the Final Four in 1991. So, when UNC coach Dean Smith offered Geth a scholarship to Carolina, Geth didn't waste a lot of time making a decision. He knew he wanted to play at Carolina. Some questioned whether Geth had the ability to play at such a high level, but Geth was not discouraged by that talk. In fact, it fired him up.

The summer before his freshman year was spent getting ready for the challenge of major college basketball. At least, Geth thought he was getting ready. "I didn't sit around on my butt," he said.

But looking back, he knows that he didn't do nearly enough. He worked out with his high school football team, ran some sprints with them, lifted a few weights, counted the days before it would be time to leave for Chapel Hill. Geth had been told that college basketball was played at a different level, with much higher intensity, but he thought a game could only be so tough. He thought the Norfolk workouts would serve him just fine upon his arrival at Carolina.

When Geth got to Chapel Hill, enrolled in his classes and then went over to the Smith Center to take part in some pickup games, the truth slapped him in the face. He was not ready for this level of competition, not nearly ready. He was overweight, which slowed him down and made him tire easily. What he saw on the court were athletes who had little body fat, who were strong and ran great distances without dropping out.

Ed Geth was a freshman who was intimidated by early impressions. And for good reason.

"I was not prepared for Carolina basketball," he says. "I definitely underestimated the physical part. I didn't work as hard as I should have. I didn't watch my diet, didn't control what I ate. I never particularily cared about what my fat intake was. I never ran much for distance, and sometimes in practice, maybe I goofed off too much. I learned when I got here what it takes to be a champion. It was a hard lesson, but I'm glad I went through it, because now I know."

Ed Geth, who less than a year earlier played at Granby High, was in pickup games at the Smith Center with former Carolina players who now play in the NBA. He was also going against veteran teammates such as George Lynch and Eric Montross and Brian Reese. This was a rude awakening. Geth was depressed and didn't know if he'd ever reach the point that he could compete in this setting. He was having trouble with the running, making a decent time, even finishing the race. College players, as competitive as they are, get out the needle when they see one of their own not making the grade.

Geth called home and told his mother that he was depressed. His father told him to stick with it, that good things would eventually happen. Geth got a big boost from senior George Lynch, who took him aside and told him to work harder and forget about giving up. "He encouraged me in a lot of ways," Geth said. "He told me how good he thought I was. He told me that I was an excellent rebounder, and coming from him, one of the best rebounders in the country, really picked me up."

Geth still had his problems, though. He had trouble finishing the 12-minute run. He found all of his teammates were in shape and he wasn't. He was learning the hard way, but he was learning. He watched his diet, worked out in the weight room, pushed himself harder. Every now and then he would do something in practice that would give him confidence, that would make him believe that he could play with these guys. He lost weight, did better in the running.

But practice at North Carolina, especially in the early going, is not easy on freshmen. There's a lot to learn and much is thrown at them.

"Practice was mind-boggling," Geth said. "I tried to think too much during the first couple of weeks. Should I be here or there? Was this the right way or that the right way? I was doing all of this thinking and not playing. Coach Smith pulled me to the side a couple of times and told me I had quick feet. He told me things that I had done that he liked. He told me to quit thinking so much and just play. I eventually got into the groove of practice, not right at that moment, but eventually."

Carolina assistant coach Bill Guthridge spoke with Geth after the freshman missed a workout. "He was a little upset that I missed the workout, but he knew it was an honest mix-up," Geth recalled. "He told me why they were working me so hard, and it wasn't because they didn't like me, but because they thought I had the potential to be a good player. He told me that I could score inside and rebound, but that I could only do it for a short period of time. If I could build up my endurance, he told me I could be a big-time player. That stuck in my mind so much that I always tried to be early for my workouts and did as much work as I could."

Geth didn't play much his freshman season, but he improved rapidly in practice. He got in better shape each day, and as that happened, his play improved, which enhanced his confidence. He felt he belonged.

"This coaching staff is very intelligent," Geth said. "They really know the game, but they know more than that. They know people. They know how to motivate people. I think they go about coaching different people in different ways. They don't use the same technique on everyone. They recognize that everyone is different."

Geth says he wasn't surprised by Carolina's success in 1992-93. At first he was in awe of the talent he encountered when he first got to Chapel Hill. Later, he knew them as his teammates and learned from them. "I knew from the first day that this team could be special," Geth said. "Funny, but after we lost those two games in a row (to Wake Forest and Duke), I really began to feel that we could be champions, that we could take it all the way. There was a different attitude in practice after those two games, a different feeling about how to go about winning. We did not like losing. We didn't like being embarrassed by Wake Forest and we didn't like becoming rattled late in the Duke game. It made us more determined."

Carolina put together an 11-game winning streak after those two losses, a streak that carried it to the ACC tournament championship game against Georgia Tech. During that game, when Geth was seated on the bench, he says he saw a Tech player hit Eric Montross with an elbow. Geth jumped to protest when no call was made, as did several other Tar Heels. Official Dick Paparo, who worked the game, called a technical foul on Carolina's bench, and when he made the call, he looked at Geth.

Coach Dean Smith, without bringing attention to what he was doing, walked in front of the Carolina bench. "He didn't tell me who the technical was on," Smith said, speaking to the group. Geth said he had jumped up to protest the no-call, and the technical was probably on him.

"Coach asked me if I had sworn at the official," Geth said, "and I told him I hadn't sworn or said anything at all. I just jumped up. Coach told me he had jumped up, too, and so had some of the other coaches. That was the end of it, as far as Coach was concerned, but I was depressed by the call. I thought that I had hurt our team and was a factor in us losing that game."

Carolina didn't dwell on that loss. It looked ahead to the NCAA tournament and its No. 1 seed in the East. Geth said he and the other reserves felt the same pressure and the same nervousness as the players who were getting the most playing time.

Carolina won four games in a row in the NCAA to advance to the Final Four. Geth was especially nervous now. He thought he was prepared for everything, but when he went into the Superdome to practice, he couldn't believe that a building that big would be host to the Final Four. He was anxious before the semifinal game with Kansas, because he thought back to 1991 when the Jayhawks beat Carolina in this game in Indianapolis. "I didn't want that negative picture in my mind," Geth said, "but it kept flashing back."

Carolina won, then Michigan beat Kentucky, to set up a Carolina-Michigan match for the national championship. Geth remembers Carolina's locker room before the Michigan game as relaxed and calm. He recalls that Pat Sullivan and Scott Cherry put on a ballhandling exhibition, and he and Larry Davis and Matt Wenstrom had a wrestling match.

"It was like we were just hanging out before practice," Geth said. "It was very loose. Nobody was uptight. Nobody added to the pressure of the moment. It was like the entire team was trying to think about something besides the game."

Geth says his spirits during the game went up and down, depending on how the game was going. He recalls holding hands with his teammates and uttering a silent prayer when teammate Pat Sullivan went to the foul line with 20 seconds left to play and Carolina ahead 72-71.

Then there was the confusion when Michigan's Chris Webber took a timeout that his team didn't have with 11 seconds to play. Geth didn't understand why everyone was going wild until assistant coach Phil Ford told him that Michigan was out of timeouts and would be hit with a technical foul.

After Donald Williams made four foul shots down the stretch and Carolina won 77-71, Ed Geth joined his teammates on court to celebrate and later in the locker room. He sat at his locker until most of the reporters were gone, then he said: "I'm no longer a freshman. No more chasing loose balls, no more carrying the projector and somebody else's bags."

Then, before he slipped into the shower, Ed Geth smiled and tried to describe his feelings, which, he said, were overwhelming.

"I like this feeling so much," he said, "that I must do it again. We will win another one before I leave Carolina, and the next time I will have more to say about the outcome of the games than I did this year."

For Ed Geth, it had been a long time between the start of practice on Nov. 1, 1992 and April 5, 1993. He couldn't remember a six-month period of his life when he had learned as much.

He learned what it took to become a champion.

GETH'S LINE:

	FIELD GOAL	FREE THROW	3-POINT						
	M-A/Pct	M-A/Pct	M-A/Pct	Reb/Avg	A	TO	S	Pts	Avg
	16-25/64.0	12-17/70.6	0-0/00.0	28/1.3	0	7	4	44	2.1

The Good Luck Charm

STEPHENSON'S HEAD WAS 'THE ROCK'

North Carolina's basketball team came out of its locker room in a corner of the Leon County Civic Center in Tallahassee on the afternoon of Feb. 27 and lined up to take the court to play Florida State in an ACC game with many ramifications.

As the players lined up single file, Travis Stephenson, a senior reserve, became the center of attention. First, Eric Montross walked up to Stephenson and rubbed his head. Then Scott Cherry followed, and then the serious and studious Henrik Rodl was standing there rubbing Stephenson's head.

It must have worked, because Carolina won, 86-76. But what's going on here?

"The players always joked about my hat size, about how big it was," Stephenson said. "They always wanted to know how big my helmet was when I played football. Scott Cherry started calling me 'helmet head.' When we went down to play Clemson this year, the players saw the rock on the hill leading into the football stadium that Clemson's players rub for good luck. They call it Frank Howard's rock at Clemson, but after that game, Scott (Cherry) referred to my head as 'the rock,' and then the guys started rubbing my head before the games. Sometimes they'd rub it a little bit, other times they'd rub it a lot, depending on how much luck they figured they needed for that particular game."

Travis Stephenson played very little basketball for the 1992-93 national champions. He was the last man off the bench and played only when the games were decided. That isn't to say that he didn't make contributions to the team, because he did. He was a spirited practice player. He was also a popular player with his teammates, one who understood his role and liked it, and he contributed to team chemistry and leadership.

Stephenson, from Angier, N.C., turned down an appointment to the Air Force Academy to attend UNC. First, he walked on at Chapel Hill as a football player, and he also spent two years playing jayvee basketball for the Tar Heels. Coach Dean Smith promoted him to the varsity for his last two seasons, prompting Stephenson to call himself "one of the luckiest people in the world."

Stephenson was there for every game as the Tar Heels went 34-4 en route to winning the NCAA championship. He got a view of Carolina basketball that thousands of young boys dream about as they shoot baskets on backyard goals across the state of North Carolina.

"The wonderful thing about the guys on this team is that they never treated me differently just because I came to the team as a walk-on," Stephenson said. "I knew I wasn't going to play as much as they would, and they knew it, too, but they still treated me as a regular team member."

Stephenson roomed during the school year with Eric Montross, one of the team's starters, who comes from Indianapolis. The two first struck up a friendship because they each like country music. And all you have to do to get Stephenson to go hunting or fishing is to mention it, which also appealed to Montross.

Stephenson recalls how ready Montross was to play against Duke on Senior Day in the Smith Center and also against Florida State on the road, a game that FSU was primed to win on its Senior Day.

"Eric and I hadn't roomed together on the road for a long time," Stephenson said, "but they put us together for the Final Four. We talked all week about going to New Orleans and winning the national championship. The night before the championship game, we went to bed and Eric said, 'We've got to win this one.' The team had accomplished a lot up to that point, but none of it seemed remotely important the night before the championship game. We had one more game we had to win to finish our dream. We felt like we deserved it, like we'd done everything we could to prepare for this moment."

Stephenson says the team got exceptional leadership from its seniors, though he saw his role as different, somewhat more subdued than that of the four seniors who had been in the program for four years. He especially respected the work ethic of George Lynch, who emerged as the team's most effective leader.

"You could always find George in the offseason working," Stephenson said. "He'd be in the weight room, or out in the gym shooting jumpshots or playing pickup. When we saw that kind of work from a guy who had been in the program for four years, it made us want to work that much harder. George is a great player, and if he was going to work that hard to make us a better team, that's real leadership, leading by example. George didn't have to be a vocal leader all the time, but he was always the first to say something when it needed saying. He wasn't afraid to get in someone's face and tell him to get going--in a positive way. The thing that I'll remember most about George is how hard he worked."

Stephenson also remembers Lynch from the championship game against Michigan, how serious he was on the court. Lynch was intense, Stephenson said, ready to play, and when he was taken out of the game for brief intervals, he didn't want to be sitting there. "I remember looking at him on the court in that game," Stephenson said, "and noticing how ready to play he was. I also saw him get in the face of a couple of our players and tell them to get going."

Stephenson says North Carolina's players didn't look too far ahead once NCAA tournament play began. After beating East Carolina and Rhode Island in the first two rounds, he says his teammates merely said: "Four more games to win."

> *The wonderful thing about the guys on this team is that they never treated me differently just because I came to the team as a walk-on.*

It was an excited Carolina team that won the NCAA East Regional with wins over Arkansas and Cincinnati to go to the Final Four, but there was always this reminder, all the way back on the plane ride from New Jersey to Chapel Hill: "We are going to New Orleans to win."

Carolina got by Kansas in the semifinals on Saturday, practiced Sunday, and then had to wait for game time to roll around on Monday. "We were so ready to play," Stephenson said. "We were ready to play that game before it was even time to eat lunch."

Carolina and Michigan had a real battle in the first half. Back and forth it went. Michigan, down early, got hot from 3-point range to lead 23-13, only to see Carolina tie the game at 25. The Tar Heels had a surge late in the half to lead 42-36 at the break.

Stephenson says Carolina's locker room at halftime was calm but determined. Coach Smith talked about how the team was playing on offense and defense, went over the foul situation.

"We felt we were where we needed to be," Stephenson said. "We were in the game with 20 minutes to play. It got a little more tense as we prepared to leave the room for the second half, because all of us knew we were that much closer to winning. Derrick Phelps said if we played North Carolina defense, we could stop them. Then right before we went back out, George (Lynch) and Matt (Wenstrom) said we'd played for this all year, and now it was down to a last half of basketball. They told us if we didn't leave everything we had on the court, we'd regret it for the rest of our lives."

North Carolina, down late in the game by as many as four points on two occasions, got big baskets to stay close, and then the Tar Heels pushed ahead and won, 77-71. Travis Stephenson, a walk-on, is part of a national championship story.

By the way, Travis, what was "the rock's" record? "I'm not sure, but I did well," Stephenson said. "In fact, Eric has asked me to come back for games next year, just so they can rub my head before they take the court."

STEPHENSON'S LINE:

FIELD GOAL M-A/Pct	FREE THROW M-A/Pct	3-POINT M-A/Pct	Reb/Avg	A	TO	S	Pts	Avg
5-11/45.5	0-0/00.0	0-1/00.0	6/0.3	3	4	0	10	0.5

Smith Has Always Liked Tough Non-ACC Schedule

Dean Smith was impressed with the basketball team that reported to practice at North Carolina on Nov. 1, 1992. It was a team with five seniors, and it looked from the beginning of practice that the seniors were going to be good leaders, which is crucial in building team chemistry.

The so-called experts sat in judgment in the preseason and questioned Carolina's quickness and athletic ability and its outside shooting.

The only senior from the 1991-92 team was Hubert Davis, but Davis, a No. 1 draft pick of the New York Knicks, was also the team's best outside shooter.

"I'm not worried about our outside shooting," Smith said. "I think we'll be an adequate outside shooting team. We won't hesitate to shoot the outside shot when we're expected to shoot it. All of our players worked hard on their outside shooting, as well as other skills, throughout the summer, and that should pay off."

Probably the thing that impressed Smith most in the preseason was the way his team went about playing defense. This was a veteran team, and teams with experience usually are Carolina's best on defense. The previous year's team had not been one of Carolina's best on defense, and Smith was determined to make defense a top priority in 1992-93. His players not only accepted that challenge, they enjoyed it.

Smith knew that in point guard Derrick Phelps he had one of the nation's best defenders. Phelps could be counted on to set the defensive tempo. George Lynch, the senior forward, was quick, strong and determined, but sometimes he free lanced on defense, and other players would have to cover for Lynch when he went out on his own. Veteran players should be able to do that. The defensive strength of the team might well be determined by how well Eric Montross, 7-0, a junior, played pivot defense, and how much improvement Donald Williams, a sophomore at big guard, had made on defense since his freshman season.

The team's November progress was set back when Brian Reese, junior, a starting forward, slipped on the second day of practice and sustained a groin injury that kept him out of a lot of the preseason work. Reese was being counted on, and his absence from practice was of great concern to Smith.

The team picked things up quickly in preseason. It was obvious from the outset that team chemistry was strong. The five seniors had done a good job in the summer. Also, Lynch emerged early on as the team's inspirational leader. Lynch worked overtime and he worked hard, and any player who didn't put out the same effort got his attention.

Carolina's December schedule was a tough one. Smith has believed in tough and competitive schedules since his first year as Carolina's coach in 1961-62. When he inherited a program that was on institutional probation, he was allowed to play only two non-conference games that season. Smith dropped the easiest games off the schedule and kept Indiana and Notre Dame.

Smith's philosophy about non-conference scheduling pretty much mirrors his personality. A highly competitive man, Smith does not enjoy those rare games when Carolina is a prohibitive favorite. He wants a contest. His belief is that teams get better by being exposed to strong teams that play every style of basketball. He is more concerned about learning about his own team in December than he is the about winning and losing. If there is a team weakness, he wants to be able to work on it before the start of the ACC season.

His teams have always played more road games than just about any top-ranked program. Smith knew his team would get a good road test on Dec. 22 against defending Big Ten champion Ohio State. He knew the Tar Heels would face pressure defense and fast offenses against Old Dominion and Houston, two teams that made the NCAA tournament the previous season. And in the Rainbow Classic in Hawaii, the Tar Heels would be joined by such powerhouses as Michigan and Kansas. UNC would also get a stern test on Jan. 24 when it went to the Meadowlands to play at Seton Hall, the favorite in the Big East. Carolina routed Seton Hall on the road the previous year and the Pirates would have this game underlined on the schedule, you could be sure.

Carolina in December would play teams that like to run, teams that like to play a half-court game. The Tar Heels would see man-to-man pressure and zones. They were going to play teams with great athletes.

UNC would be tested in December, no question. Smith should learn about his team's outside shooting, its defense, its ability to play against quick teams with good athletes. If Carolina made it through this December schedule in good shape, it should be a contender in the ACC, and maybe even for national honors.

Old Dominion was first on the schedule. The Monarchs liked to run and press, and they had quick athletes. Smith, after a month of practice, was anxious to see how his team would perform. ⬢

Donald Williams goes strong to the basket against the cougar defense.

Hot Shooting Carolina Destroys Old Dominion

North Carolina coach Dean Smith liked what he saw as his Tar Heels opened the 1992-93 season at home by routing Old Dominion, the defending champions of the Colonial Athletic Association, by the unlikely score of 119-82.

119-82

Old Dominion was a team of excellent athletes, players with good quickness and jumping ability, and the Monarchs would test Carolina's ability to handle defensive pressure. After all, the book on the Tar Heels from the previous season was that they were a slow, prodding team, not quick or fast enough to beat athletic teams.

To exacerbate matters for Carolina, it was without point guard Derrick Phelps, who bruised a knee in the Blue-White scrimmage on Nov. 20 and sat out this game. Could Carolina handle pressure?

The answer was a resounding, yes. Carolina's plan going into the game was to punish Old Dominion every time it tried to press. The Tar Heels were not content to beat the press and then set up a half-court offense; they wanted to shoot layups against it. So effective were the Tar Heels that Old Dominion had to abandon the press in the second half and try some zone. That didn't work, either.

Carolina showed in this game that it was a team that had a lot of different ways to beat you. The scoring was balanced, as five players hit for double figures. Donald Williams led Carolina with 21 points, but it was also encouraging to see Pat Sullivan come off the bench for 18 points. Forward Brian Reese and center Eric Montross took 16 shots from the field between them and hit them all, as Reese scored 19 points and Montross 20.

Henrik Rodl started in place of Phelps at the point and had 11 assists and only one turnover. In fact, when Old Dominion switched to a zone in the second half, Rodl read the defense immediately and threw an alley-oop pass to Reese for a spectacular dunk.

Carolina took control of the game from the outset when it jumped to a 10-2 lead. Old Dominion stayed in the game in the first half, however, by hitting 16-16 foul shots and 5-16 from 3-point range, and the Monarchs trailed 54-41 at halftime.

Carolina's second-half offense was a clinic. It ran through Old Dominion's press for easy shots, and when the Monarchs went zone, Carolina used its size advantage and some excellent screening, cutting and passing to go inside for shots. The Tar Heels shot 85.7 percent in the second half by hitting 24-28 from the field. That's a pretty good percentage for a layup line in warmups.

While the offense carved up Old Dominion's defense, Carolina's defense caused all kinds of problems for the visitors, who hit only 32.5 percent for the game.

The only disappointment for Carolina in this game was the 29 offensive rebounds taken down by Old Dominion. Though ODU missed 54 shots and therefore had many chances for offensive rebounds, the Tar Heels knew they would have to improve their defensive rebounding.

Carolina sophomore Donald Williams, after spending his freshman year backing up Phelps at point guard, made the move back to big guard. "The game was played at such a fast pace that I rushed things early on," Williams said. "I did a better job in the second half."

Montross was 8-8 from the field in getting his 20 points. "My goal is to help the team win," he said. "If that means that one night I score four points and play excellent defense and have eight rebounds, then that will be a successful night. The next night, if I need to score 24 points and get 12 rebounds, then I'm fine with that."

Rodl, though effective, said that Carolina wasn't the same team without Phelps. There would come a time later in the season when the Tar Heels would find that out for sure. "Derrick is our main ballhandler," Rodl said. "You see tonight that some of the pressure they applied on us gave us some trouble. We looked messy at some points. We'll have a lot more confidence when Derrick comes back to run the show. He also sets the pace for us on defense."

The crowd at the Smith Center on the night of Dec.1 was 18,807. It was a quiet audience, one that didn't know what to expect from the Carolina team. But what they saw, whether or not they recognized it, was a team hungry for success, a team that was very much together.

As far as opening nights go, the critics couldn't find much to complain about.

Carolina	FG	FT	R	A	TP
Brian Reese	8-8	2-5	3	4	19
George Lynch	5-8	2-4	8	6	12
Eric Montross	8-8	4-4	5	1	20
Donald Williams	5-8	9-10	2	3	21
Henrik Rodl	2-3	0-0	2	11	5
Pat Sullivan	6-9	5-6	4	1	18
Dante Calabria	0-2	0-0	0	0	0
Matt Wenstrom	1-1	1-2	4	0	3
Kevin Salvadori	3-4	1-2	5	0	7
Scott Cherry	1-1	0-0	1	2	2
Larry Davis	1-1	4-4	1	2	6
T. Stephenson	0-1	0-0	0	1	0
Ed Geth	3-3	0-0	1	0	6
Totals	43-57	28-37	36	31	119
Old Dominion	**FG**	**FT**	**R**	**A**	**TP**
Petey Sessoms	4-14	10-10	8	0	20
Mario Mullen	5-8	2-3	4	1	12
Odell Hodge	2-4	0-2	1	0	4
Kevin Swann	4-12	4-4	2	3	14
Keith Jackson	4-17	2-2	7	2	13
D. Anderson	3-8	3-4	0	2	9
David Harvey	1-6	0-4	4	1	2
Allon Wright	0-1	0-2	1	1	0
Mike Jones	1-5	1-2	1	0	3
Kevin Larkin	1-4	0-0	1	0	2
Walter Wright	1-1	0-0	2	0	3
Team			7		
Totals	26-80	22-33	38	10	82

Three-point goals: Carolina 5-11 (Brian Reese 1-1, Donald Williams 2-4, Henrik Rodl 1-2, Pat Sullivan 1-2, Dante Calabria 0-2); Old Dominion 8-32 (Petey Sessoms 2-7, Mario Mullen 0-1, Kevin Swann 2-4, Keith Jackson 3-11, Donald Anderson 0-2, Mike Jones 0-3, Kevin Larkin 0-3, Walter Wright 1-1).

Turnovers: Carolina 22, Old Dominion 23

KEYS TO THE GAME: After leading 56-45 early in the second half, the Tar Heels went on a 20-4 run to lead 76-49 and never be threatened...UNC's balanced scoring had five players in double figures...Old Dominion could not solve Carolina's trapping, pressing defense, while UNC shot 75.4 percent from the field.

DEAN SMITH COMMENT: "We were fortunate in some ways to win the way we did. We can't put them on the foul line like we did in the first half, because they made all of their foul shots (16-16). But other than that, we played great defense."

GEORGE LYNCH COMMENT: "We couldn't get our traps working like we wanted to in the first half, mainly because they are good ballhandlers. I think we applied more pressure in the second half and did a much better job."

UNC's Eric Montross didn't miss a shot from the field in the opening win over Old Dominion.

UNC Repays Gamecocks For 1990 Tourney Loss

108-67

Carolina's basketball team has a long memory. As it went to Charlotte to play South Carolina in the opening round of the Diet Pepsi Tournament of Champions on Dec. 4, the Tar Heels thought back to this same tournament in 1990, when the Gamecocks upset them, 76-74.

It was payback time. UNC broke fast and routed South Carolina 108-67 in front of 17,480 fans in the Charlotte Coliseum.

It was never a game. North Carolina led 29-12 when Henrik Rodl hit a 3-pointer with 7:54 left in the first half and by 36-16 when Donald Williams hit from 3-point range a few minutes later.

South Carolina had to be discouraged at halftime. After all, the Gamecocks of coach Steve Newton shot 53.8 percent from the field in the first half and still trailed, 49-34. North Carolina had a size advantage inside and took the ball inside to Eric Montross, 7-0, who had 12 points in the first half, as the Tar Heels shot 59.4 percent from the field and hit 4-8 from 3-point land. Carolina had 18 first-half rebounds to nine for South Carolina.

North Carolina played with unexpected smoothness and efficiency for the second game of the season. The second half was never close. South Carolina closed to within 56-43 with 16:53 left, but North Carolina led by 68-47 on a Montross layup five minutes later.

Donald Williams had a hot night shooting for the Tar Heels. He hit 8-12 from the field, 5-8 from 3-point range and scored 23 points. George Lynch had 18 points and 11 rebounds

"

I learned a lot last year. I feel more comfortable and relaxed out there this year. I feel a lot more comfortable playing the wing, though playing the point improved my overall game.

"

Donald Williams

for the winning Heels, while Eric Montross scored 16 points and got nine rebounds, and Brian Reese had 11 points.

Point guard Derrick Phelps, who missed the opening win over Old Dominion, returned and had eight assists.

Carolina's defense held South Carolina to 33 percent shooting in the second half. UNC, meanwhile, shot 57.7 percent from the field for the game and outrebounded the Gamecocks, 44-28. Another key to the game was Carolina's outside shooting, which produced 9-18 from 3-point territory.

Another encouraging thing for the Tar Heels is that they scored many easy baskets off South Carolina's 21 turnovers. Phelps, who missed the opener with a bruised knee, keyed UNC's defense. He sent a message early when he caused a five-second violation less than a minute into the game.

Though the game was seldom in doubt, South Carolina twice cut UNC's lead to 13 in the second half, prompting UNC coach Dean Smith to say: "I know I was worried about the outcome at that point."

Carolina's trapping defense completely took the Gamecocks out of their game. USC's coach Newton said after the game that "they run their traps very well and they take you out of your offense. North Carolina is going to do this to a lot of people this year. They're certainly one of the best teams that I've faced."

Carolina had stressed defense since the start of practice on Nov. 1. The entire package--offense, defense, rebounding and depth--was impressive for this early in the season. When Smith cleared his UNC bench with 5:37 left in the game, the Tar Heel reserves had some outstanding play. The regulars cheered from the bench, a sign that the togetherness on this team could be a strength.

Senior Scott Cherry provided the exclamation point when he stole the ball at midcourt, carefully took it to the basket, measuring his steps along the way, and got his first dunk as a Tar Heel. That brought the Carolina bench and coaching staff up to cheer.

"Any coach should be pleased if his team plays hard," Coach Smith said after the game. "And ours certainly did that. We also played together. The final score is not indicative of the game. Our (reserves) didn't miss a shot, including the 'threes.'"

Carolina	FG	FT	R	A	TP
Brian Reese	4-8	2-2	2	3	11
George Lynch	7-14	4-5	11	0	18
Eric Montross	7-11	2-2	9	0	16
Henrik Rodl	1-3	0-0	2	3	3
Derrick Phelps	0-3	2-2	4	8	2
Pat Sullivan	2-4	1-1	1	2	5
Larry Davis	1-1	0-0	1	0	3
Scott Cherry	2-2	0-0	0	4	4
Donald Williams	8-12	2-2	2	0	23
Dante Calabria	2-2	0-0	3	2	5
Kevin Salavadori	3-4	2-2	0	0	8
T. Stephenson	1-1	0-0	0	0	2
Ed Geth	1-2	2-2	1	0	4
Matt Wenstrom	2-4	0-0	2	1	4
Team			6		
Totals	41-71	17-18	44	23	108
USC	**FG**	**FT**	**R**	**A**	**TP**
Emmett Hall	7-11	2-5	3	2	16
Jamie Watson	5-14	2-3	2	1	12
Obrad Ignjatovic	2-5	0-0	3	0	5
Carey Rich	1-2	0-0	2	8	2
Terry Bynum	0-6	0-0	2	2	0
Waide Franklin	5-11	0-0	1	1	13
Troy McKoy	2-4	0-0	5	0	4
Shannon Hoskins	4-7	0-0	2	0	9
Edmond Wilson	1-4	4-6	4	0	6
Chris Leso	0-1	0-0	1	1	0
Team			3		
Totals	27-65	8-14	28	15	67

Three-point goals: Carolina 9-18 (Brian Reese 1-2, Henrik Rodl 1-3, Derrick Phelps 0-1, Pat Sullivan 0-1, Donald Williams 5-8, Dante Calabria 1-1, George Lynch 0-1, Larry Davis 1-1); USC 5-15 (Jamie Watson 0-1, Obrad Ignjatovic 1-2, Terry Bynum 0-3, Waide Franklin 3-6, Shannon Hoskins 1-3)
Turnovers: Carolina 18, USC 21.

KEYS TO THE GAME: Carolina had a size advantage inside, and when South Carolina sagged in to try to take away the inside attack of the Tar Heels, it left the outside open. This game was another clear indication that Carolina could beat you in a lot of different ways.

DEAN SMITH COMMENT: "We tried very hard and we played very hard, but I think we were fortunate to get the offensive rebounds we did in the first half. George (Lynch) and Eric (Montross) were very active on the boards throughout the game, and it is nice to have Derrick (Phelps) back."

COACH STEVE NEWTON COMMENT: "We learned how good the seventh-ranked team in the nation is. They play awfully hard and they play so well together. Again, that is a credit to what Coach Smith has done with that program."

72

Quick-Shooting Texas No Match For Carolina

104-68

Texas, a team that played in the NCAA tournament in 1992, was at full strength when it met Carolina in the championship game of the Diet Pepsi Tournament of Champions in the Charlotte Coliseum on Dec. 5. Texas beat Princeton the previous night to advance to the final game.

After Texas, coached by Tom Penders, jumped to a 9-1 lead, Carolina put on an absolutely awesome display of basketball. The defense shut the door on the Longhorns, so much so that after the game Texas star B.J. Tyler said: "I've never seen a defense like that. They even guarded us on our bad shots."

Carolina showed the entire package in breaking the game open in the first half. There was a beautiful basket by Donald Williams after a George Lynch rebound. Derrick Phelps stole the ball and fed Henrik Rodl for a dunk. Freshman Dante Calabria came off the bench to hit from outside.

After falling behind 9-1, Carolina led by the shocking score of 61-31 at halftime. Texas shot only 30 percent in the first half while Carolina, getting just about any shot it wanted, nailed 61.5 percent of its attempts in the first half. Lynch and Brian Reese, operating in the open court against Texas' defensive pressure, had 15 and eight points in the first half, respectively.

It did not get better for the Longhorns in the second half. Carolina led by as many as 44, as coach Dean Smith played everybody who was dressed for the game.

One bleak note for Carolina, however. Forward Brian Reese, who had played extremely well in the first half, turned his right ankle early in the second half and had to leave the game. Trainer Marc Davis iced down the ankle and Reese did not return, not that he was needed.

Texas was considered one of the favorites for the Southwest Conference championship. The Longhorns, who later in the season suffered injuries and ran into trouble, were at full strength and ready for North Carolina. This was a quick and athletic team, the type that some critics said that Carolina would have a hard time playing against. Texas trapped and pressed from the start, and Carolina chewed that defense apart with accurate passing and a fastbreak that had the 16,931 fans standing in appreciation.

Carolina, in going 3-0 on the season, scored more than 100 points for the third straight game. While Carolina was shooting 54.9 percent from the field, its defense hounded Texas into a shooting percentage of 28.6.

Donald Williams' drive through the lane gave Carolina its first lead of the night at 19-17, and then the Tar Heels scored eight more unanswered points to start the rout.

Carolina coach Smith took out his regulars with 10:10 left in the game and the Tar Heels winning 83-51. Carolina, after Reese hurt his ankle, had some other scares when Lynch dived after a loose ball, Derrick Phelps aggravated his injured knee, and Donald Williams went down after a hard collision with a Texas player, suffering some bruised ribs.

Reese's injury was a bad omen. It started a frustrating stretch of injuries for him, and he wouldn't get back to true form until the second half of the ACC regular season.

Coach Smith said he wasn't happy with his team's sloppy play in the second half, but was "thrilled with our defense and how hard our team is playing. I am very happy with our effort."

Williams led Carolina in scoring with 19 points. Eric Montross had 14 points and 10 rebounds, Lynch 17 points and seven rebounds.

Texas, a team that likes to shoot the ball quickly, shot 33 3-pointers and only made seven. Carolina outrebounded the Longhorns, 62-55.

UNC's Dean Smith was asked if he was worried when the Longhorns spurted to a 9-1 lead.

"We shouldn't have done anything differently," he said. "We had missed four layups and they had hit two long jump shots with a hand in their face. I'm happy with that. I'm upset that we missed the layups but I'm happy that we got them. Lynch missed two layups, Montross missed one or two. That's a perfect example of why a coach shouldn't take a time-out in that situation. I should be the happy one. Tom should be the unhappy one because we were getting layups."

Lynch was named the tournament's Most Valuable Player, and he was joined on the All-Tournament team by Montross and Williams.

Carolina	FG	FT	R	A	TP
Brian Reese	4-4	0-0	4	1	8
George Lynch	7-14	3-5	7	3	17
Eric Montross	5-11	4-4	10	2	14
Henrik Rodl	3-3	0-0	1	3	7
Derrick Phelps	1-2	2-2	4	3	5
Pat Sullivan	3-9	2-3	6	1	9
Larry Davis	1-4	0-2	1	0	2
Scott Cherry	2-3	0-4	2	2	4
Donald Williams	6-7	4-5	1	3	19
Dante Calabria	3-3	0-0	0	2	7
Kevin Salvadori	2-4	0-1	4	0	4
T. Stephenson	0-1	0-0	3	0	0
Ed Geth	0-1	3-4	2	0	3
Matt Wenstrom	2-5	1-2	6	1	5
Team			11		
Totals	39-71	19-32	62	21	104
Texas	FG	FT	R	A	TP
M. Richardson	8-27	2-2	10	2	20
Gerrald Houston	2-9	0-2	10	1	4
Albert Burditt	6-13	0-5	19	1	12
B.J. Tyler	5-15	1-3	3	4	13
T. Rencher	3-21	2-5	2	0	9
Sheldon Quarles	0-1	0-0	1	1	0
Lamont Hill	1-2	0-1	1	0	2
Tony Watson	3-10	0-0	5	1	8
Michael Chaplin	0-0	0-0	0	0	0
Team			4		
Totals	28-98	5-18	55	10	68

Three-point goals: Carolina 7-8 (Henrik Rodl 1-1, Derrick Phelps 1-1, Pat Sullivan 1-1, Larry Davis 0-1, Donald Williams 3-3, Dante Calabria 1-1); Texas 7-13 (Michael Richardson 2-5, B.J. Tyler 2-11, Terrence Rencher 1-9, Lamont Hill 0-1, Tony Watson 2-7).
Turnovers: Carolina 21, Texas 13

KEYS TO THE GAME: Carolina's defense smothered the Texas attack. Texas likes to shoot quickly, but when Carolina put a hand in the face of its jump shooters, the Longhorns were in trouble...The Tar Heels played well in transition and got some easy baskets after Texas missed shots...The Longhorns had only 13 turnovers, but that was because they took quick shots and didn't handle the ball much.

DEAN SMITH COMMENT: "I'm sorry the second half wasn't pretty by either team. I wish we'd had better concentration in the second half. I thought this game would go down to the wire. That shows how much I know. I know Texas was ranked preseason 18th by the coaches, and I really didn't expect anything like this."

COACH TOM PENDERS COMMENT: "North Carolina has an outstanding basketball team. They don't appear to have very many holes out there. We had to play a great game to be able to hang in there with them, and we didn't have one of our better shooting nights."

Kevin Salvadori and Eric Montross battle Albert Burditt of Texas for a rebound.

Tar Heels Beat VPI On 'George Lynch Day'

Carolina traveled to George Lynch's hometown of Roanoke, Va., on Dec. 9, and on "George Lynch Day" in that city, beat a fired up Virginia Tech team, 78-62. Lynch, a senior, scored 18 points and got 11 rebounds in Carolina's victory. His "homecoming" made it an emotional time for him.

78-62

Virginia Tech, of the Metro Conference, is coached by former UNC Charlotte and Clemson coach Bill Foster. The Hokies fell to 1-1 with the loss.

Carolina roared to a 14-0 lead before VPI got its rhythm. The Tar Heels led 41-26 at the half, and then held off the Hokies in the second half. Carolina won this road game without two of its stars. Brian Reese, a junior, missed the game with an ankle sprain sustained in the win over Texas, and guard Donald Williams, a sophomore, suffered bruised ribs in the Texas game and sat this one out.

The fifth-ranked Tar Heels used their pressure defense to make it hard for Virginia Tech to run an offense. Carolina got several easy baskets in building a 20-4 lead before Virginia Tech staged a mild second-half rally. Carolina held VPI to 39.1 percent shooting for the game, 31.4 in the first half, and outrebounded the Hokies, 49-28. VPI had trouble with Carolina's traps and presses, and couldn't stop the Tar Heels inside.

UNC's Eric Montross had 19 points and 10 rebounds to complement Lynch's brilliant play inside. Henrik Rodl and Scott Cherry had nine points each. Rodl, the starter, and Cherry played the two-guard spot in Williams' absence. Carolina shot 45.8 percent from the

"

All in all, I think it was a great showing for my family members and the people in Roanoke to get a chance to see me play. I wasn't really nervous tonight.

"

George Lynch

floor, but no doubt missed the shooting of Williams and Reese.

"Probably a highlight of the game would be Scott Cherry's play," said Carolina coach Dean Smith. "Scott Cherry, with Donald Williams out, subbed for Henrik Rodl and played like the veteran he is. He just hasn't had much playing time, but he played very well."

Smith also saluted Lynch, whom Smith said continued his "All-America-type play."

"I'm happy with the win for George Lynch, number one, and for North Carolina, number two," said Smith, who schedules a hometown game for each of his players during their careers. "George would have had trouble if we hadn't won this game."

These hometown games are not easy to win a lot of times. The honoree sometimes gets too motivated, puts too much pressure on himself, and Smith was worried about that going into the Virginia Tech game. Lynch attended ceremonies at a noon luncheon that honored him on the day of the game. When it came time to play the game, Lynch was ready.

Carolina improved its record to 4-0 with the win. 🏀

Eric Montross

Carolina	FG	FT	R	A	TP
George Lynch	8-13	2-2	11	3	18
Eric Montross	7-14	5-6	10	1	19
Derrick Phelps	0-7	2-2	8	2	2
Henrik Rodl	3-6	3-3	3	4	9
Pat Sullivan	3-7	1-2	5	5	8
Dante Calabria	2-2	0-0	2	1	5
Kevin Salvadori	2-5	2-3	3	1	6
Matt Wenstrom	0-0	1-2	1	0	1
Scott Cherry	2-3	4-4	0	1	9
Larry Davis	0-1	0-0	0	0	0
Ed Geth	0-1	1-2	2	0	1
T. Stephenson	0-0	0-0	0	0	0
Team			4		
Totals	27-59	21-26	49	18	78
Virginia Tech	**FG**	**FT**	**R**	**A**	**TP**
Corey Jackson	9-17	0-0	6	2	21
Thomas Elliott	4-10	1-3	5	0	9
Jimmy Carruth	3-8	0-1	2	2	6
Jay Purcell	2-7	1-1	2	5	5
Shawn Good	1-4	0-2	2	0	2
Donald Corker	0-1	0-0	2	1	0
D. Watlington	1-8	0-0	4	2	3
Travis Jackson	0-1	2-2	0	1	2
Steve Hall	2-2	0-2	1	0	6
Shawn Smith	3-6	2-2	2	1	8
Team			2		
Totals	25-64	6-13	28	14	62

Three-point goals: Carolina 3-9 (Derrick Phelps 0-3, Henrik Rodl 0-1, Pat Sullivan 1-3, Dante Calabria 1-1, Scott Cherry 1-1); Virginia Tech 6-15 (Corey Jackson 3-6, Thomas Elliott 0-2, Jay Purcell 0-2, Damon Watlington 1-3, Steve Hall 2-2).

Turnovers: Carolina 18, Virginia Tech 14.

KEYS TO THE GAME: Carolina charged out of the gate, with its pressure defense clicking, to a 14-0 lead. That defense held Virginia Tech to just 39.1 percent shooting from the floor. Lynch and Montross, 19 points and 10 rebounds, dominated inside. UNC outrebounded the Hokies, 49-28.

DEAN SMITH COMMENT: "I was a little disappointed offensively. We haven't been sharp this year when our defense doesn't give us the easy baskets. We have some work to do in that area. The game wasn't won until the last five minutes. (Lynch) was the last starter to leave the game. It was a very special night for George."

COACH BILL FOSTER COMMENT: "Our players were nervous, but who wouldn't be? This is a young club that not a lot is expected from. We're playing a team that is averaging more than 100 points a game and is really the talk of the country right now. Sure, they're going to be a little bit nervous, but after that 14-0 lead, I think we settled down a little."

George Lynch prepares to sink a free throw.

Houston's Press Gives Carolina Much Trouble

84-76

When the Houston Cougars came to the Smith Center on Dec. 13, it gave Carolina yet another chance to match up with a quick, athletic team that likes to press. Carolina coach Dean Smith scheduled games like this so his Tar Heels could get used to playing against pressure.

Houston played one of its best games of the season before falling to the unbeaten Tar Heels, 84-76. Carolina improved its record to 5-0 and Houston lost for the first time in the season.

The game was close for all of the first half. Carolina led 42-36 at halftime, but the Tar Heels couldn't feel real comfortable about it. They shot 64.3 percent in the first 20 minutes and had only a six-point lead.

Houston guard Anthony Goldwire had a hot hand in the first half and scored 11 points on some difficult shots. Donald Williams had 13 points and Eric Montross 11 in the first half for UNC.

Carolina got the first six points of the second half and continued its fine play to extend its lead to 66-43 on a Montross dunk on a pass from Kevin Salvadori with 11:51 left to play.

Carolina, which was once again without Brian Reese, led 70-49 when Houston went on a 10-0 run, all on foul shots, and then got a 3-pointer to cut UNC's lead to 70-62. Carolina had trouble with Houston's trapping defense in the second half and ended up with a discouraging 25 turnovers.

Houston played a lot of zone in its half-court defense much of the time. Houston

> *We work on the press every day in practice. But in the games, it's a different story. In the first half, we played pretty well against it, but in the second half, we had a rough time. We just weren't hitting our shots. That's something we need to improve on.*
>
> *Derrick Phelps*

played the previous day in Houston against Illinois-Chicago, and Cougar coach Pat Foster didn't want to wear his team down by playing man-to-man the entire game. Also, he said he didn't think he matched up well enough with Carolina on the inside to play a full game of man-to-man defense.

"Houston will win a lot of games," UNC coach Dean Smith said, "and I hope we will. But we won't if we play like we did the last eight minutes of the game."

Houston coach Foster didn't make any excuses.

"I said I wasn't going to use (playing the day before) as an excuse and I won't," he said. "North Carolina is real good and was better than we were today."

Donald Williams led the Tar Heels with 21 points. Eric Montross scored 15 points and George Lynch and Pat Sullivan added 13 each. Derrick Phelps had a great game at the point for Carolina, finishing with nine points, seven rebounds, 12 assists, seven steals and only two turnovers. 🏀

Carolina	FG	FT	R	A	TP
Pat Sullivan	6-7	0-0	1	1	13
George Lynch	6-12	1-2	8	3	13
Eric Montross	6-6	3-9	7	0	15
Henrik Rodl	2-4	0-0	4	8	5
Derrick Phelps	3-5	3-4	7	12	9
Dante Calabria	1-2	0-0	0	0	2
Donald Williams	7-12	3-4	0	0	21
Matt Wenstrom	1-1	0-0	0	0	2
Kevin Salvadori	2-6	0-0	4	1	4
Team			3		
Totals	34-55	10-19	34	25	84
Houston	**FG**	**FT**	**R**	**A**	**TP**
Derrick Smith	4-9	1-2	2	0	10
Jessie Drain	2-7	0-0	1	2	6
Charles Outlaw	3-3	3-6	8	1	9
David Diaz	4-12	8-9	5	0	17
A. Goldwire	9-14	3-5	0	5	22
Rafael Carrasco	0-2	0-0	5	0	0
Tyrone Evans	4-8	0-0	1	2	12
Lloyd Wiles	0-1	0-0	0	0	0
Team			1		
Totals	26-56	15-22	23	10	76

Three-point goals: Carolina 6-13 (Pat Sullivan 1-1, Henrik Rodl 1-2, Derrick Phelps 0-1, Dante Calabria 0-1, Donald Williams 4-8); Houston 9-23 (Derrick Smith 1-2, Jessie Drain 2-5, David Diaz 1-7, Anthony Goldwire 1-2, Tyrone Evans 4-7).
Turnovers: Carolina 25, Houston 23

KEYS TO THE GAME: Carolina shot 64 percent in the first half to lead 42-36...UNC got a good streak early in the second half to build a 23-point lead, only to see Houston get back in the game when the Tar Heels did a poor job of handling the Cougars' pressure defense. Carolina outrebounded Houston 34-23, shot 61.8 percent from the field, and limited the Cougars to 46.4 percent shooting.

DEAN SMITH COMMENT: "Houston is a good team and I prefer to give credit to them for playing well and bringing the fight to us. You should be happy anytime you beat a team as good as Houston."

COACH PAT FOSTER COMMENT: "If we played them again tomorrow, I still wouldn't play them man-to-man. I think their size was a big factor in the game. They kept getting easy shots around the basket, and we had to work hard for every shot we got...The big difference in the game was early in the second half when we wilted under their pressure."

Kevin Salvadori looks for room under the basket.

Donald Williams aces 3-pointer in scoring 21 points in UNC's win over Houston.

UNC Routs Butler In Montross' Homecoming

103-56

Eric Montross chose Butler, located in his hometown of Indianapolis, as his homecoming game, and he and the Tar Heels thrashed the Bulldogs 103-56 on Dec. 20 in historic Hinkle Fieldhouse.

Hinkle has been the site of many Indiana high school state championship games through the years, including some that Montross played in, and the hit movie "Hoosiers" was filmed there.

Carolina, which was playing well when it went to Indianapolis, added to Hinkle's rich history. The Tar Heels had just finished final examinations from their first semester's work when they traveled to play Butler. UNC's coaches were afraid of a letdown, but it didn't happen. Instead, Carolina played one of its best games of the young season and took the home team out of the game from the very beginning.

Eric Montross tries to find an open teammate.

Carolina, which improved its record to 6-0, forced 16 Butler turnovers in the first half with its defensive pressure. The game was really over at halftime, as Carolina led, 50-26. The Tar Heels missed some easy shots early in the game, but still shot 56.3 percent from the floor for the game and held the Bulldogs to 33.3 percent shooting.

Montross celebrated his homecoming with 13 points and seven rebounds, in a game that saw Carolina's substitutes play almost as much as the regulars. Montross had three straight dunks early in the game. Carolina coach Dean Smith substituted a new lineup with nine minutes to play, and with four minutes to go, every Tar Heel in uniform had played.

George Lynch led Carolina in scoring with 18 points, followed by Montross with 13, Donald Williams and Matt Wenstrom with 12 each, and Henrik Rodl and Brian Reese with 10 each. Reese was playing in his first game since spraining an ankle against Texas on Dec. 5 in Charlotte.

Carolina's defensive pressure bothered Butler the entire game. Butler fell to 1-4 on the season.

"I honestly felt coming into the game that Butler was a good team," Dean Smith said after the game. "I didn't expect to win like this. I was concerned whether we could come away with a win. I've seen that happen on the road before, but I think we'll be a pretty good road team."

This was Carolina's second "homecoming" game in December. The Tar Heels played in George Lynch's hometown of Roanoke, Va., on Dec. 9.

"I was surprised by the number of Carolina fans in the crowd," Coach Smith said. "I didn't know Eric Montross had that many people here."

Smith, who passes coaching milestones with regularity, tied the legendary Phog Allen on the all-time college basketball victory list with No. 746 with the victory over Butler.

"I don't deal with that," Smith said of tying Allen, his college coach. "With this team, I'm just fortunate to have as many good athletes as we do. I'm really not interested in coaches' numbers. I'm interested in this team's sixth win of the season. That means we're six wins closer to the NCAA tournament." 🏀

Carolina	FG	FT	R	A	TP
Pat Sullivan	2-3	0-0	2	1	4
George Lynch	8-16	2-3	8	2	18
Eric Montross	6-13	1-3	7	1	13
Henrik Rodl	3-5	2-4	0	3	10
Derrick Phelps	2-2	0-0	3	9	4
Larry Davis	0-3	0-0	1	1	0
Scott Cherry	0-0	2-2	1	3	2
Donald Williams	4-6	2-2	2	1	12
Dante Calabria	3-3	0-0	1	3	8
Brian Reese	3-6	3-3	6	2	10
Kevin Salavadori	3-4	0-0	3	0	6
Ed Geth	1-1	0-2	3	0	2
T. Stephenson	1-1	0-0	1	0	2
Matt Wenstrom	4-8	4-7	3	1	12
Team			2		
Totals	40-71	16-26	43	27	103
Butler	**FG**	**FT**	**R**	**A**	**TP**
Katara Reliford	2-5	2-4	2	1	6
Brian Beauford	5-15	2-3	7	1	14
J.P. Brens	2-3	0-0	5	0	4
Tim Bowen	0-5	0-0	1	4	0
Jermaine Guice	6-18	0-1	4	0	13
Quincy Bowens	2-4	0-0	0	2	4
John Taylor	3-9	0-0	8	2	6
Jason McKenzie	1-6	1-2	3	0	3
Danny Allen	1-2	0-0	1	0	2
Chris Miskel	2-5	0-2	4	0	4
Burdette Phillips	0-0	0-0	0	0	0
Team			4		
Totals	24-72	5-12	39	10	56

Three-point goals: Carolina 7-13 (Pat Sullivan 0-1, George Lynch 0-2, Henrik Rodl 2-4, Dante Calabria 2-2, Donald Williams 2-3, Brian Reese 1-1); Butler 3-23 (Brian Beauford 2-4, Tim Bowen 0-3, Jermaine Guice 1-9, Quincy Bowen 0-1, Jason McKenzie 0-4, Danny Allen 0-1, Chris Miskel 0-1)
Turnovers: Carolina 16, Butler 26

KEYS TO THE GAME: Carolina, on the road in the first game after final exams, overcame some early-game rustiness and blew the Bulldogs away. The Tar Heels took advantage of their size inside, and finished the game shooting 56.3 percent from the floor, and used their stifling pressure defense to force 26 Butler turnovers and hold the Bulldogs to 33.3 shooting for the game.

DEAN SMITH COMMENT: "I was so worried about Butler that I wanted to show some game films of Butler to the team. We usually don't do that, and in the end, the coaches had to talk me out of it. I just wanted the team to understand that Butler wasn't a team to take lightly."

ERIC MONTROSS COMMENT: "I did have some jitters before this game, but I wasn't as nervous as I thought I would be. If you've ever been in Hinkle Fieldhouse, you'd know that it has a distinct smell. And I think that sort of calms me down. But I couldn't think of a better place to play."

Historic Hinkle Fieldhouse was the stage for Eric Montross' homecoming win over Butler.

Carolina's Second Half Knocks Out Ohio State

Ohio State knocked North Carolina out of the NCAA tournament in March 1992, so when the Tar Heels went to Columbus on Dec. 22, 1992, they wanted to give the Buckeyes a message.

84-64

Playing before a loud capacity crowd of 13,276 at old St. John Arena on the Ohio State campus, Carolina had a great second half to win the game decisively, 84-64.

It was a big win, a major road victory, and it came after Carolina played a first half that left coach Dean Smith most unhappy. The first half was a wonderful game for the spectators. It was back and forth, and it so encouraged the home crowd that the noise level seemed greater than at N.C. State's Reynolds Coliseum when Carolina plays there. Ohio State's biggest lead of the half was 25-19. The Tar Heels would fight back, lead by three, but Ohio State center Lawrence Funderburke, 6-9, was having a huge first half and enjoying it. He hit 5-6 from the field in the first half in scoring 13 points.

"The old man was not happy at halftime," Smith said of himself. Ohio State led at half, 38-35. That's not what concerned Smith. He went to Columbus expecting a tough game. He didn't like the way Carolina was playing. The team was impatient on offense--one pass and a shot. And on defense, Funderburke was getting the ball inside almost at will.

A reporter asked Smith what he said to the team at halftime, and Smith quipped: "I asked them to identify themselves. That wasn't North Carolina basketball we were seeing. It wasn't the team that I had coached for the first six games of the season. We were trying to go one-on-one and force things. We showed no patience, and that's not the way we play at Carolina."

Carolina was a different team in the second half. First, UNC center Eric Montross, after a good lecture from his coach, fronted Funder-

"
There was a time in the second half when they cut the lead to five that it was as loud as I've ever heard it.

"
George Lynch

burke in the post and gave the Ohio State leader only three shot attempts in the second half. Meanwhile, Carolina hit nine of its first 10 shots in the second half and won by 20, which was Ohio State's worse home loss in three years.

Carolina outscored the Buckeyes 16-4 to break open a 45-45 tie and lead 61-49, but the home team had one more punch. With the capacity crowd going crazy, Ohio State scored seven straight points to make the score 61-56. It was crunch time for the Tar Heels.

Eric Montross, who hit all eight of his field goal attempts, answered first by hitting one of two foul shots. Carolina rebounded Montross' missed free throw and Montross got an offensive rebound and laid it in. Brian Reese then scored on a reverse layup and was fouled. Reese missed the foul shot, but UNC rebounded again, and Reese drove through the lane and scored to make it 68-56. Kevin Salvadori scored on a follow shot, Montross made two free throws and Carolina led 72-56 with less than five minutes to play.

"There was a lot of talking going on out there between the players," said Ohio State's star center Lawrence Funderburke, who scored 17 points, but only four in the second half. "But you have to give them credit. They backed it up with a win. They beat us bad on our homecourt and something like that shouldn't happen."

Montross led the Tar Heels with 20 points and nine rebounds, and his work on Funderburke in the second half was key. Dean Smith called it Montross' best game yet. Reese and Derrick Phelps added 14 points and George Lynch had nine points and a career-high 16 rebounds. Phelps, one of the nation's best point guards, controlled the second half the way a conductor leads his orchestra.

The Tar Heels were brilliant in the second half, hitting 18 of 29 field goals, for 62.1 percent, and holding the Buckeyes to 34.5 percent shooting in that half.

Carolina left St. John Arena with a 7-0 record. Coach Randy Ayers' Buckeyes dropped to 4-2. The win gave Dean Smith a 25-12 record against Big 10 teams, and it was win No. 747 for Smith, which moved him past his college coach, Phog Allen, into fourth place on the all-time college basketball victory list. 🏀

Carolina	FG	FT	R	A	TP
George Lynch	5-12	1-2	16	3	11
Eric Montross	8-8	4-8	9	0	20
Derrick Phelps	4-12	6-9	2	4	14
Henrik Rodl	2-2	0-0	2	4	4
Brian Reese	7-11	0-1	2	1	14
Pat Sullivan	3-5	0-0	2	2	6
Donald Williams	4-8	0-0	1	1	9
Dante Calabria	0-0	0-0	2	1	0
Kevin Salvadori	1-1	2-2	4	0	4
Matt Wenstrom	0-0	0-0	0	1	0
Scott Cherry	1-1	0-0	0	0	2
Team			2		
Totals	35-60	13-22	42	17	84
Ohio State	FG	FT	R	A	TP
Greg Simpson	4-11	0-0	0	1	9
Doug Etzler	3-6	0-0	0	2	7
Jamie Skelton	5-11	2-2	1	2	15
Alex Davis	2-6	0-0	4	8	5
Tom Brandewie	1-4	0-0	2	2	2
Charles Macon	2-4	0-1	0	0	4
L. Funderburke	7-9	3-5	6	2	17
Rickey Dudley	1-3	0-0	4	1	2
Antonio Watson	0-0	0-0	0	0	0
Jimmy Ratliff	1-5	1-2	4	0	3
Nate Wilbourne	0-0	0-0	0	0	0
Team			3		
Totals	26-59	6-10	24	18	64

Three-point goals: Carolina 1-5 (George Lynch 0-1, Derrick Phelps 0-1, Pat Sullivan 0-1, Donald Williams 1-2); Ohio State 6-21 (Greg Simpson 1-4, Doug Etzler 1-3, Jamie Skelton 3-7, Alex Davis 1-4, Charles Macon 0-1, Jimmy Ratliff 0-2).
Turnovers: Carolina 17, Ohio State 18

KEYS TO THE GAME: Carolina found patience on offense in the second half, hit nine of its first 10 shots from the field in that period, and Montross shut down Funderburke in the middle.

DEAN SMITH COMMENT: "Our defense was good tonight, but we gave up too many layups in the first half. In fact, we looked like an inexperienced team in the first half, but I am impressed with the way we played the second half. We just didn't have the patience that we needed to break down their defense in the first half. We did in the second half, and it was beautiful basketball to watch."

COACH RANDY AYERS COMMENT: "We competed for 40 minutes, but we didn't execute for 40 minutes against a team as good as Carolina."

Pat Sullivan helps UNC rally in the second half for 20-point win at Ohio State.

UNC Gets It Inside To Beat Scrappy Cajuns

Carolina opened the 1992 Rainbow Classic, which as it turned out had three of the 1993 Final Four teams, by playing a tough Southwestern Louisiana team on Dec. 28, and the Tar Heels came away with an 80-59 victory at Blaisdell Arena in Honolulu.

80-59

For the second game in a row, Carolina started out slowly. The Tar Heels shot 34 percent from the floor in the first half and led only 31-30 at the break. But just as it had done at Ohio State the week before, UNC stormed out of the gates in the second half, shot 58.8 percent in the final 20 minutes and won going away to improve to 8-0 on the season.

Southwestern Louisiana, a favorite to win the Sun Belt Conference, dropped to 5-2. USL knocked Oklahoma out of the NCAA tournament the previous season, and the Tar Heel coaching staff thought that the Cajuns might be the best team UNC had faced up to that point of the season.

The Tar Heels did their damage inside in this game. Eric Montross and George Lynch both scored 17 points. Montross finished with 7-10 from the floor. Lynch was 4-5 from the floor and topped the Tar Heels in rebounding with nine. Carolina outrebounded the Cajuns 44-34. Derrick Phelps and Pat Sullivan scored 10 each for Carolina.

Defense won this game for Carolina, however, and leading the way was point guard Derrick Phelps. Phelps took USL's leading scorer, point guard Michael Allen, out of the game. Allen finished only 7-22 from the field and only 2-11 from 3-point range. The Tar Heels held the Cajuns to just 40.3 percent shooting in the game, 39.4 in the second half.

"Their power and strength eventually wore us down," said USL coach Marty Fletcher.

UNC coach Dean Smith, who was not happy with his team's performance in the first

> "
> *Derrick Phelps was sensational against Allen, and you don't know how hard Allen is to guard.*
> "
>
> *North Carolina Coach Dean Smith*

half, was pleased with what he saw in the second half.

"I am impressed with our defense in the second half," Smith said. "Derrick Phelps was sensational against Allen, and you don't know how hard Allen is to guard."

USL's defense made it difficult for the Tar Heels in the first half. The Cajuns blocked some of UNC's inside shots in the early-going, and the Tar Heels overpassed a bit, which led to some turnovers. Carolina led for most of the first half, but it was close throughout. The Tar Heels' biggest lead was five points and USL led by four at one time.

As is the case many times when the Tar Heels travel on the road, the supposedly neutral crowd at the University of Hawaii's arena fell in behind the Cajuns in the close first half, sensing the underdog was indeed capable of knocking off Carolina. Dunks by USL's Todd Hill and Bryan Collins ignited the crowd in the Cajuns' favor, and fired up the Southwestern team.

It was a different story in the second half, however. The score was tied once at 33, but Carolina started to take control after that. Montross hit two straight baskets and then Lynch got two straight to give the Tar Heels a 46-39 lead. The Cajuns got to within four, 54-50, with just more than seven minutes left, but UNC's Pat Sullivan scored on a follow shot to make it 56-50.

Then, Phelps, still limping from a shin injury suffered earlier in the game, knocked in a 3-pointer to give the Tar Heels a 59-50 lead. Phelps had to leave the game shortly after that and his status for the next game was questionable. With Phelps out, Dean Smith called upon freshman guard Dante Calabria, and Calabria responded by playing very well. He handled the USL pressure defense and got the ball inside to Carolina's big men.

Before he went out, Phelps also had six assists and three steals. Lynch had five steals to lead the Tar Heels in that category. UNC forced 20 USL turnovers.

Make no mistake, though. This was a closer game, much closer, than the final score indicated. Carolina's victory set up a match in the semifinals of the Rainbow Classic between two of the best teams in the nation--UNC and Michigan. It was a game that all of Hawaii hoped for when this tournament field was announced the previous summer. ●

Carolina	FG	FT	R	A	TP
Eric Montross	7-10	3-5	6	1	17
Pat Sullivan	4-6	2-2	5	2	10
Henrik Rodl	4-6	0-3	3	3	9
Scott Cherry	0-0	2-2	0	0	2
Derrick Phelps	4-6	0-0	5	6	10
Donald Williams	2-11	3-3	2	2	7
Dante Calabria	1-2	0-0	2	0	2
Brian Reese	2-8	0-2	3	2	4
Kevin Salvadori	1-6	0-0	5	0	2
George Lynch	8-17	1-2	9	0	17
T. Stephenson	0-0	0-0	0	0	0
Ed Geth	0-0	0-0	0	0	0
Matt Wenstrom	0-0	0-0	1	1	0
Team			3		
Totals	33-72	11-19	44	17	80
USL	**FG**	**FT**	**R**	**A**	**TP**
Michael Allen	7-22	1-2	1	4	17
Byron Starks	7-14	1-2	8	3	15
Tony Moore	0-5	0-0	0	0	0
Todd Hill	5-13	0-0	9	0	11
Shawn Griggs	1-1	0-0	1	0	2
Cedric Mackyeon	3-4	0-1	7	1	6
Bryan Collins	2-4	0-2	6	0	4
C. Boudreaux	2-4	0-0	1	1	4
Team			1		
Totals	27-67	2-7	34	9	59

Three-point goals: Carolina 3-15 (Pat Sullivan 0-1, Henrik Rodl 1-2, Derrick Phelps 0-3, Donald Williams 0-6, Brian Reese 0-2, George Lynch 0-1); Southwestern Louisiana 3-14 (Michael Allen 2-11, Tony Moore 0-1, Todd Hill 1-2.)
Turnovers: Carolina 15, Southwestern Louisiana 20.

KEYS TO THE GAME: Playing on the road right after Christmas, UNC could have panicked after being in a dogfight in the first half and not shooting very well in the first 20 minutes. But the Tar Heels came out in the second half, picked up their defense and got the ball inside to Eric Montross and George Lynch, who finished with 17 points each. UNC outrebounded the quick Cajuns, 44-34, held USL to just 40.3 percent shooting, and forced the Cajuns' leading scorer Michael Allen to just 7-22 from the floor.

DEAN SMITH COMMENT: "Southwestern Louisiana is not an easy team to play against. They bothered some of our inside shots in the first half, and then we hurt ourselves, too. We didn't do well offensively, not by this team's standards. But I am impressed with with our second-half defense."

COACH MARTY FLETCHER COMMENT: "Carolina's power and quickness wore us down. It affected us for six or seven minutes. We turned it over some and they got easy baskets out of it. When you stand around like we did on offense in the second half, you don't get to the foul line. North Carolina is good at running you out of your offense."

George Lynch nails a jumper over Todd Hill as UNC routs Southwestern Louisiana in Rainbow Classic.

UNC-Michigan Put On Great Show In Hawaii

78-79

There was an NCAA-tournament atmosphere in Blaisdell Arena in Hawaii when North Carolina and Michigan got ready to do battle on Dec. 29. A capacity crowd of 7,500 was on hand to see the game, which Michigan won 79-78 on a slap follow shot by Jalen Rose at the buzzer.

The game was so exciting, so competitive that the crowd gave both teams a standing ovation as they left the court. Southwestern Louisiana coach Marty Fletcher, who was in the audience, said: "There might not be a better college basketball game played all season than this one. It was played at such a high level."

The players on both teams, as well as many people in the audience, had the feeling that Carolina and Michigan would meet again in March or April.

After the two teams sparred in the early going, Michigan got a basket and foul shot from Eric Riley to open a 30-21 lead. Donald Williams hit a 3-pointer just before halftime to narrow Michigan's lead to 40-36 at the break.

The second half was simply great basketball, quite a show. Michigan led 44-38 when Carolina went on a 9-0 run to lead 47-44. That spurt featured a 3-point basket by Derrick Phelps and a Henrik Rodl basket after a steal.

It was obvious that neither team would be able to put the other one away. Brian Reese made a strong move off the baseline to put Carolina ahead 62-59 with 7:28 left in the

> *I Think we played well enough to win. Michigan played much better than they had in the tapes that I watched in preparing for this game. As disappointing as this is, it's also proof that we are not far away.*
>
> *North Carolina Coach Dean Smith*

game. But then Michigan went on a tear behind the excellent play of Rose and scored eight points in a row to lead 67-62.

Back and forth it went like this. The game was tied at 71, at 73. Phelps hit two free throws to put Carolina ahead 76-75 with 1:15 left. Then, with the shot clock running down, Rose picked up a loose ball at the top of the key and lobbed it towards the basket, where Chris Webber fielded it four feet short of the rim and flipped the ball over his head into the basket.

With Carolina in possession, down one and 25 seconds left to play, Dean Smith took timeout and gave the ball to Williams in a spread offense. Williams drove his defender into the lane, where he stopped and shot a 10-footer to give the Tar Heels the lead at 78-77 with 13 seconds left.

Michigan, and this would be important later in the season, much later, was out of timeouts. Guard Jimmy King had the ball in the right corner, took a couple of dribbles along the baseline and fired a shot from almost behind the backboard that wasn't even close. In the fight for the rebound, Michigan's Rose, 6-8, slapped the ball from about five feet away from the basket. The ball spun wildly and somehow hit the backboard, then the front rim, and into the nets.

It was a miracle finish that left the fans at Hawaii's Blaisdell Arena stunned. UNC assistant coach Phil Ford fell out of his chair and rolled onto the court. Tar Heel coach Dean Smith held his palms skyward, as if to say, "What else could we have done?" The victorious Wolverines piled on top of each other on the court.

Both of these great teams were 8-1 after this game.

"We're disappointed with the loss," Coach Smith said. "I think we played well enough to win. Michigan played much better than they had in the tapes that I watched in preparing for this game. As disappointing as this is, it's also proof that we're not far away. I think if you talked to the Michigan people right now, they would have to feel very fortunate to win with those tough shots. It wasn't like they got open shots down the stretch."

The two teams left the court to a standing ovation. Would they meet again somewhere down the road? It seemed quite possible.

Carolina	FG	FT	R	A	TP
Eric Montross	5-8	4-6	10	2	14
Pat Sullivan	1-4	2-4	3	0	4
Henrik Rodl	3-3	0-0	1	3	7
Derrick Phelps	4-11	5-7	0	3	15
Donald Williams	4-8	4-4	1	1	13
Dante Calabria	1-2	0-0	1	1	3
Brian Reese	4-4	2-2	3	1	10
Kevin Salvadori	0-0	0-0	0	2	0
George Lynch	5-18	2-4	16	0	12
Team			2		
Totals	27-58	19-27	37	13	78
Michigan	**FG**	**FT**	**R**	**A**	**TP**
Rob Pelinka	2-6	0-0	3	0	5
Chris Webber	10-17	5-6	8	4	27
Jalen Rose	7-14	7-9	5	2	22
Dugan Fife	0-0	1-2	1	1	1
Michael Talley	0-0	0-0	0	1	0
Ray Jackson	0-1	0-0	0	0	0
Jimmy King	3-7	0-2	3	6	6
Juwan Howard	4-7	1-2	7	0	9
James Voskuil	1-5	0-0	1	0	2
Eric Riley	3-3	1-1	4	0	7
Team			1		
Totals	30-60	15-22	34	14	79

Three-point goals: Carolina 5-13 (Pat Sullivan 0-1, Henrik Rodl 1-1, Derrick Phelps 2-6, Donald Williams 1-4, Dante Calabria 1-1); Michigan 4-16 (Rob Pelinka 1-5, Chris Webber 2-3, Jalen Rose 1-3, Jimmy King 0-2, James Voskuil 0-3)
Turnovers: Carolina 19, Michigan 17

KEYS TO THE GAME: Michigan scored on three possessions late in the game, even though Carolina shut down its offense. It showed that Michigan was talented enough to free lance and win. Chris Webber scored 27 points for the Wolverines, including 2-3 from 3-point range.

DEAN SMITH COMMENT: "I think we played extremely well in the second half. I'm a little disappointed with our first-half play. George Lynch was sensational with his 16 rebounds. He usually shoots better (5-18 for the game) and he can improve his shot selection. Our second-half play was extraordinary."

COACH STEVE FISHER COMMENT: "I'm proud of how hard we played. Our priority was to win this tournament. We want a tournament championship. We wanted to play harder and smarter than they did. That was probably a wash."

Michigan's Chris Webber battles Eric Montross for re-bound, as Wolverines win thriller in Hawaii.

Tar Heels Bounce Back To Beat Host Rainbows

101-84

It wasn't easy for Carolina to line up and play in the consolation game of the Rainbow Classic on the night of Dec. 30. The Tar Heels were still thinking about the devastating loss to Michigan the night before. Furthermore, Carolina was playing the host team, Hawaii, and the fans in Blaisdell Arena were thinking upset.

Carolina had a hard time shaking the Rainbow Warriors in the first half. In fact, Hawaii led for much of the first half until UNC went ahead to stay 25-23 with just over eight minutes left in the first. Carolina led 51-34 at halftime en route to a 101-84 victory.

Michigan beat Kansas for the Rainbow Classic championship. Remember the Rainbow Classic field: Carolina, Michigan and Kansas were in the tournament's semifinals, and those three teams would gather in another city for more basketball later in the season.

The victory over Hawaii left Carolina with a 9-1 record and one non-conference game remaining before the start of the ACC season.

"I'm proud of our team for not being flat after last night's disappointment," Carolina coach Dean Smith said. "In many ways, we played better than we did (against Michigan). We moved extremely well without the ball tonight, and we're delighted to have this win."

Carolina shot 57.4 percent from the floor and outrebounded the Rainbows, 36-25. The

"
We still hold some disappointment from the Michigan loss, but overall, we're pleased to come back and get a big win like we did. This puts us back in the right direction for that time in March (in the NCAA tournament). We talked last night about how bad it felt (to lose to Michigan). But in the meantime, we knew that we had to prepare ourselves for Hawaii.
"

Eric Montross

game was rough because the officials let a lot go in this one. UNC center Eric Montross hit the floor four or five times. The Tar Heels went to the foul line 37 times.

"Tonight, (the officials) let us bang and knock, and we're more effective in that style of play," said Hawaii coach Riley Wallace.

George Lynch led the Tar Heels in the first half with 12 points, many of those coming off hustle points inside or on the break.

UNC was never threatened in the second half, but the Rainbows' hot shooting--62.1 percent in the last 20 minutes--kept them from getting blown out. Carolina's biggest lead of the game was 71-48, when Montross scored on a good pass from Lynch and was fouled. Coach Smith cleared his bench with 4:52 left in the game and every Tar Heel in uniform played.

Montross overcame the rough play in the pivot and led UNC with a career-high 28 points on 9-15 shooting. He also had seven rebounds. Lynch finished with 19 points and nine rebounds and Donald Williams added 17 points on 5-7 shooting, 3-3 from 3-point range.

Smith said he was pleased that his team made only 10 turnovers against the aggressive Rainbows. 🏀

George Lynch and Derrick Phelps apply their trademark defense.

Carolina	FG	FT	R	A	TP
Eric Montross	9-15	10-14	7	1	28
Pat Sullivan	2-3	4-4	2	3	8
Henrik Rodl	1-2	1-1	2	4	3
Scott Cherry	1-1	0-0	1	0	2
Derrick Phelps	1-6	1-2	2	6	3
Donald Williams	5-7	4-6	1	1	17
Dante Calabria	1-3	0-0	1	1	2
Brian Reese	2-5	4-4	5	2	8
Kevin Salvadori	3-4	0-0	1	1	6
George Lynch	8-12	3-4	9	1	19
T. Stephenson	0-0	0-0	0	0	0
Ed Geth	0-0	0-0	0	0	0
Matt Wenstrom	2-3	1-2	2	0	5
Team			3		
Totals	35-61	28-37	36	20	101
Hawaii	**FG**	**FT**	**R**	**A**	**TP**
R. Washington	0-1	0-0	0	0	0
Fabio Ribeiro	5-9	5-6	1	1	17
Jarinn Akana	8-11	0-0	3	5	18
Marty Winter	1-1	0-0	0	0	2
Kurt Taylor	0-1	0-0	0	0	0
Kalia McGee	3-4	0-1	2	7	6
Trevor Ruffin	3-8	2-2	0	2	8
Terrance Phillip	3-4	6-9	6	1	12
Gerry Holmes	0-0	0-0	0	0	0
Tim Shepherd	4-8	1-2	4	1	9
Chris Walz	5-13	0-0	7	3	12
Team			2		
Totals	32-60	14-20	25	20	84

Three-point goals: Carolina 3-5 (Henrik Rodl 0-1, Derrick Phelps 0-1, Donald Williams 3-3); Hawaii 6-14 (Fabio Ribeiro 2-3, Jarinn Akana 2-5, Trevor Ruffin 0-2, Chris Walz 2-4)
Turnovers: Carolina 10, Hawaii 14

KEYS TO THE GAME: Carolina was able to focus on this game after the disappointing loss to Michigan...The Tar Heels were patient on offense, and even though Hawaii tried to clog up the inside, UNC still went there for 28 points from Montross and 19 from Lynch.

DEAN SMITH COMMENT: "George Lynch got better looks at the basket tonight than he did last night. I also think that Derrick Phelps (six assists) did a good job passing the ball tonight. Poor Eric Montross, he takes such a beating in there. It was a rough, rough game."

COACH RILEY WALLACE COMMENT: "Dean Smith is a legendary coach, a classy guy, and it was a pleasure for me to compete against him. That might sound crazy after the beating that we took, but it was a good experience for our team. We competed hard tonight. When North Carolina took things away from us, we adjusted. Carolina was probably a little tired from their loss to Michigan, but I never thought for a minute that a Dean Smith team would let it affect them for long. I knew they would be ready to play."

Eric Montross gets two of his 28 points on this hook shot over Hawaii's Tim Shepherd.

UNC Blasts Cornell In Last Tune-Up For ACC

Carolina returned to the Smith Center after its holiday trips to Butler, Ohio State and the Rainbow Classic, and soundly beat Cornell 98-60 on Jan. 4 at the Smith Center.

98-60 This was a game that the Tar Heels figured they should win, but Cornell's upset win over 25th-ranked California by 20 points a few days earlier certainly got their attention.

Carolina's team was still fighting jet lag in this game, played before a crowd of 18,458. The victory, UNC's last non-conference game before the start of ACC play, improved the Tar Heels' record to 10-1. Cornell dropped to 4-4.

Cornell, coached by Jan van Breda Kolff, who after the season accepted the Vanderbilt head coaching job, led 19-18 with just more than 11 minutes left in the first half, but the Tar Heels spurted to a 47-28 halftime lead. Derrick Phelps scored 10 points in the last 10 minutes of the first half to spark that Tar Heel surge.

Carolina shot 54.2 percent from the floor for the game, 58.3 percent in the first half, and held the Big Red to just 41 percent shooting. The Tar Heels, who had a size advantage, clobbered the visitors from the Ivy League on the boards with a 46-30 advantage, and Carolina's pressure defense forced 25 Cornell turnovers. UNC made 5-8 from 3-point range.

"I was a little concerned about whether we'd be too tired," UNC coach Dean Smith said of the jet lag from the Hawaii trip. "But our defensive effort was there, led by Derrick Phelps. We really got a lot of practice on de-

> *I think we're getting over the Hawaii trip. With the big time difference (five hours), I think a lot of us are still trying to catch up on our rest. We looked a little sluggish at times tonight. I think we did some good things, but we still looked kind of rusty.*
>
> *Donald Williams*

fense and fastbreaks, but we must work on our half-court offense."

Carolina missed some easy layups in the second half, but held the Big Red scoreless for the first three minutes of the second half. The Tar Heels went on an 11-2 run early in the second half to end any thoughts of a Cornell comeback. The closest Cornell came after that was 53-34 with 15:38 left in the game, but Carolina soared back out to a 79-42 lead with seven minutes left.

"I thought we played much better than we did (against UNC) last year," said Coach van Breda Kolff, whose team lost to UNC 109-66 during the 1991-92 season. "I think we're a much better basketball team, but I think North Carolina is much better than they were last year, too."

Donald Williams, 6-10 from the floor, and Derrick Phelps, 8-14, led UNC with 16 points each. Brian Reese had 14 points and George Lynch finished with 13 points and nine rebounds. 🏀

Derrick Phelps speeds away from Cornell's Frank Ableson in an easy win at Smith Center.

Carolina	FG	FT	R	A	TP
Brian Reese	5-7	2-2	2	1	14
Kevin Salvadori	3-7	1-2	8	0	7
Eric Montross	2-6	3-5	6	0	7
Henrik Rodl	0-2	0-0	3	3	0
Derrick Phelps	8-14	0-1	6	6	16
Pat Sullivan	3-5	3-5	4	0	9
Donald Williams	6-10	1-2	3	2	16
George Lynch	6-11	1-3	9	3	13
Dante Calabria	2-3	0-0	0	1	4
Matt Wenstrom	3-3	0-0	1	0	6
Scott Cherry	0-2	2-2	1	3	2
T. Stephenson	0-1	0-0	0	0	0
Ed Geth	1-1	2-2	2	0	4
Team			1		
Totals	39-72	15-24	46	19	98
Cornell	**FG**	**FT**	**R**	**A**	**TP**
Zeke Marshall	5-12	2-5	7	0	12
Brian Kopf	1-4	0-0	3	0	2
Justin Treadwell	4-6	0-0	5	0	8
Jeff Gaca	4-14	0-0	1	3	11
Mike Parker	3-6	0-0	1	5	6
Frank Ableson	0-4	2-2	1	3	2
Pax Whitehead	5-12	2-2	5	2	12
Joe Maurer	0-0	0-0	1	0	0
James Escarzega	0-0	0-0	1	0	0
Dave Beck	1-1	0-0	0	0	2
B. Schuckman	1-1	0-0	0	0	3
Reggie Tolliver	1-1	0-0	0	0	2
Howard Hayes	0-0	0-0	0	0	0
Chip Meakem	0-0	0-0	0	0	0
Tim Nash	0-0	0-0	0	0	0
Team			5		
Totals	25-61	6-9	30	13	60

Three-point goals: Carolina 5-8 (Brian Reese 2-2, Donald Williams 3-5, Scott Cherry 0-1); Cornell 4-11 (Jeff Gaca 3-8, Frank Ableson 0-1, Pax Whitehead 0-1, Brandt Schuckman 1-1).
Turnovers: Carolina 14, Cornell 25.

KEYS TO THE GAME: This was another example of this team's ability to concentrate on the opponent at hand. Carolina was tired from the long holiday trip to Hawaii, but it paid attention to Cornell, gave the underdogs proper respect, and won in impressive fashion. Carolina's defense continued to create turnovers, as it forced 25 in this game, many of which set up UNC baskets.

DEAN SMITH COMMENT: "I don't remember us missing that many dead layups at the beginning of the second half and throughout the game. We sure have to do better Thursday night (against N.C. State). But I was pleased with our effort. In all fairness, Cornell was tired, too. That can't be the same team that beat California by 20 at the Meadowlands. They're well-coached, they were trying to be patient."

COACH JAN VAN BREDA KOLFF COMMENT: "This was our fourth game in seven days, and I thought our players were physically tired. On top of that, North Carolina is one of the best-conditioned teams you'll ever see and they just keep running and running. Our whole frontline got very, very tired and every one of them had four fouls in the second half."

Which Team Was Second To Duke In The ACC Lineup?

North Carolina's basketball team did just about everything expected of it during the December non-conference schedule. The Tar Heels came out of that stretch with a mark of 10-1, and the only blemish on the record was the 79-78 loss to Michigan in the Rainbow Classic.

Coach Dean Smith said at the conclusion of those 11 games that he thought his team "was prepared to meet any style of play that we might see in the ACC."

Carolina answered some questions in its December run. In the first place, it showed that it could adapt to any style. The Tar Heels could play fast or slow. Could this Carolina team shoot? Well, it came out of the non-conference schedule hitting right at 55 percent from the field and 45 percent from 3-point range.

But defense keyed this team, there's no question about that. Non-conference opponents shot about 39 percent from the field against the Tar Heels. Carolina's traps were again striking fear in opponents. This team attacked on defense, in the true tradition of Carolina basketball. Opponents had trouble running their offense against UNC's gambling and daring defensive scheme. The defense was also creating turnovers and keying the offense, something that had been missing from the 1991-92 team.

Dean Smith had not settled on his eight-man rotation by the start of the ACC season. George Lynch and Brian Reese were the starters at forward, Eric Montross at center, Derrick Phelps at the point. Henrik Rodl usually started at big guard, but Donald Williams was getting more and more playing time. Kevin Salvadori backed up Montross and Lynch. Pat Sullivan came in for Lynch and Reese. And freshman Dante Calabria was seeing some time as Phelps' backup at point guard.

Team chemistry was good, but Smith was still defining roles.

So, Carolina felt good about itself as it prepared to head into the ACC season. Television commentators love to compare conferences, and in automatically placing the Big Ten at the top of the college basketball world, they had underestimated the strength and balance in the ACC.

Duke was the overwhelming choice to win the ACC regular season. The Blue Devils did nothing to discourage their proponents as they came out of their December schedule at 9-0. But other ACC teams were grabbing some national attention. Virginia, for instance, was 9-0 and playing well. Georgia Tech lost only at Kentucky in December. Florida State, waiting for Charlie Ward to get through football and return to basketball as the team's point guard, was impressive in the preseason NIT. Wake Forest's only loss out of the league in December was at California. Maryland, still in a rebuilding stage under coach Gary Williams, knocked off Louisville.

Area sportswriters voted in the preseason on the ACC's order of finish, and here's the way they saw it: Duke, UNC, Florida State, Georgia Tech, Wake Forest, Virginia, Maryland, N.C. State and Clemson .

As North Carolina prepared to open its ACC season at N.C. State on Jan. 7, the Tar Heels wanted very much to get off to a good start. It had been a season of adversity for coach Les Robinson and his N.C. State team, but a win over Carolina in Reynolds Coliseum to open its conference season would heal a lot of wounds. Carolina was well aware of that. Also, N.C. State beat the Tar Heels twice in the regular season the year before, so UNC was focused to begin the conference season.

While Duke looked solid as the No. 1 team in the ACC, things got a little confusing when you looked beyond the Blue Devils. Carolina had an experienced team, but there were those questions about quickness and outside shooting. Florida State, playing without Ward, lost tough games early to Indiana and UCLA, but with Douglas Edwards and Sam Cassell and Rodney Dobard and Bob Sura, this had to be a team that could contend for league and national honors. Wake Forest had one of the nation's best players in Rodney Rogers, 6-7, and guard Randolph Childress was back after missing a year with injury. Also, Wake Forest had guard Charlie Harrison, a highly recruited transfer from Georgetown, joining the team. Georgia Tech had excellent talent and size in James Forrest and Malcolm Mackey, and one of the league's most talented point guards in Travis Best.

When you looked beyond Duke, it was hard to choose. It would be easy to make a case for Carolina, Florida State, Wake Forest, Georgia Tech or even Virginia to finish second behind the Blue Devils.

Clemson, meanwhile, was a hard team to figure. The Tigers were 9-0, but the schedule was outrageously easy. Clemson had to open the league season at Duke, where it was totally unprepared for this kind of competition and it showed, as Duke won, 110-67. Nevertheless, Clemson had quickness, as well as two of the conference's best players in guard Chris Whitney and center Sharone Wright. The Tigers were dangerous.

One of the reasons that UNC coach Dean Smith likes to take his team on the road to play tough non-conference games is because he knows what awaits the Tar Heels in the ACC. Smith's teams have been so dominant for so long that they find conference road crowds loud and hostile. Beating the Tar Heels is cause to celebrate.

With this backdrop, it was time to get on with the real season, the ACC schedule. Carolina's team had worked hard and been successful in December against good opponents. It was a confident team that made the trip to Reynolds Coliseum on Jan. 7. A crowd of 12,400 awaited the Tar Heels.

Dean Smith knew that if his team had weaknesses, and it did, they would now be exploited by the people who know the Tar Heels best--the teams in the tough ACC.

It was time to get it on.

Carolina Begins ACC Play By Winning At N.C. State

100-67

When North Carolina went to Raleigh to open its ACC season against N.C. State on Jan. 7, some news hit just before the game that was disturbing to UNC's coaching staff. It was announced that three N.C. State players--Jamie Knox, Chuck Kornegay and Donnie Seale--had been ruled academically ineligible.

State had struggled up to that point, and sometimes when adversity strikes just before gametime, a team gets together and plays a fired up game. Carolina coach Dean Smith warned his players of that in their dressing room in the basement of Reynolds Coliseum. He also dropped the reminder that N.C. State beat Carolina twice the previous season.

Carolina, wanting badly to get off to a good start in the conference, was focused. Its pressing, stalking defense hounded N.C. State all over the court, seldom allowing Wolfpack shooters to get an uncontested shot at the basket. State hurt Carolina the year before with the 3-point shot, but in this game the Wolfpack hit only 7-27 from long distance, as Carolina's defenders covered the perimeter as a point of emphasis.

Carolina raced to a 6-0 lead before the capacity crowd of 12,400, which had come to Reynolds hoping for another upset. N.C. State never led in the game, which turned into a lopsided affair early. Donald Williams, from nearby Garner, hit a 3-pointer with four min-

> "
>
> *This is a totally different year for me. I'm playing more on the wing, where I'm more comfortable playing, and I have a new role on this team. I missed my first shot tonight, but Coach Smith told me to settle down and shoot normally. From then on, I felt comfortable.*
>
> "
>
> *Donald Williams*

utes left in the half to boost Carolina's lead to 40-22 and that mounted to 51-30 at halftime.

Carolina's defense held N.C. State to 33.3 percent shooting from the field in the first half, as the Tar Heels got good shots and connected for 59 percent. Carolina also dominated the backboards in this game, getting 49 rebounds to State's 29. And 21 of UNC's rebounds were on the offensive glass.

Carolina improved its record to 11-1, while N.C. State dropped to 3-5, 0-1 in the ACC.

The Wolfpack's offensive plan was to spread the floor, milk the shot clock and hope for some open shots against Carolina's defense. None of it worked. Carolina got the lead early, which made it more difficult for State to hold the ball. Also, Carolina's gambling defense enticed State into a faster offense than it wanted.

UNC also bottled up State's talented center Kevin Thompson, 6-11, and allowed him only 11 points and four rebounds.

"They got the early lead," said N.C. State coach Les Robinson, "and we tried to get it back by hitting the home runs (3-pointers). That's not the kind of team we are. We have to get it back by grinding it out."

N.C. State tried to pack its defense on the inside, as a lot of teams tried to do against Carolina this season, and then dared the Tar Heels to take the outside shot. UNC answered with patience. It still got the ball inside for 21 points from George Lynch, while Williams hit 5-8 from 3-point range in scoring 23 points.

"Donald (Williams) used to come over here to shoot," UNC coach Dean Smith said. "He must like these rims, but I'm glad he's not over here playing now. He's improved every part of his game since last year. He's a much better passer than last season."

UNC's Eric Montross and Brian Reese had 11 points each. Both Lynch and Montross had nine rebounds.

Derrick Phelps went down with another injury, his third of the season. This time, Phelps was blindsided by a pick with about 14 minutes to go in the game and suffered a mild concussion. He was questionable for the next game against Maryland in the Smith Center on Jan. 9. Phelps was having another outstanding game--eight points, five assists and seven rebounds in only 22 minutes. ◉

Carolina	FG	FT	R	A	TP
Brian Reese	4-6	2-2	3	4	11
George Lynch	8-16	5-7	9	2	21
Eric Montross	4-7	3-5	9	1	11
Henrik Rodl	1-4	0-0	3	3	3
Derrick Phelps	4-10	0-0	7	5	8
Donald Williams	7-11	4-5	4	2	23
Pat Sullivan	4-5	0-0	2	1	8
Kevin Salvadori	0-3	3-4	2	1	3
Dante Calabria	0-1	2-2	2	2	2
Scott Cherry	1-2	2-2	2	1	4
Matt Wenstrom	0-0	0-0	0	0	0
Ed Geth	1-3	0-0	2	0	2
Larry Davis	1-1	2-4	0	0	4
T. Stephenson	0-0	0-0	0	0	0
Team			4		
Totals	35-69	23-31	49	22	100
N.C. State	**FG**	**FT**	**R**	**A**	**TP**
Mark Davis	3-10	1-2	5	0	8
Migjen Bakalli	4-12	4-7	4	2	14
Kevin Thompson	2-6	7-8	4	1	11
Lakista McCuller	2-7	1-2	1	2	5
Curtis Marshall	3-10	0-0	5	4	9
Marcus Wilson	3-4	0-0	0	0	7
Victor Newman	1-4	0-0	0	1	2
Todd Fuller	1-2	1-3	3	0	3
Marc Lewis	2-2	4-4	3	0	8
Team			4		
Totals	21-57	18-26	29	10	67

Three-point goals: Carolina 7-15 (Brian Reese 1-2, Henrik Rodl 1-2, Derrick Phelps 0-2, Donald Williams 5-8, Scott Cherry 0-1); N.C. State 7-27 (Mark Davis 1-4, Migjen Bakalli 2-9, Lakista McCuller 0-4, Curtis Marshall 3-7, Marcus Wilson 1-1, Victor Newman 0-2).
Turnovers: Carolina 13, N.C. State 15

KEYS TO THE GAME: Carolina took away N.C. State's 3-point attack by playing aggressive defense on the perimeter...Carolina did not encourage the Wolfpack. The Tar Heels jumped to a 6-0 lead and never trailed. That helped take the capacity crowd out of the game...When N.C. State tried to clog the middle on defense, Carolina again showed a versatile offense.

DEAN SMITH COMMENT: "What a great game Derrick Phelps played tonight, and you can see how much we need him. This was a great road victory in the ACC, and we're happy to have it. Our defense has been active all year and it's encouraging to see that we could do it on the road in the ACC. I don't think that N.C. State ran very much of what it wanted to tonight, and that's part of good defense."

COACH LES ROBINSON COMMENT: "We played a heck of a team tonight. They're good. Carolina's defense got after us tonight, and we didn't adapt well to their pressure. We looked to score rather than looking to run our offense. Carolina's defense really comes after you, and they're so fluid. North Carolina is better than last year. There's no question, they are better. They're more confident and they shoot the ball well."

Inside-Outside Attack Pushes UNC Past Terps

Carolina went for the knockout punch early against Maryland in the Smith Center on Jan. 9, and the plan worked. Carolina jumped to a 10-2 lead after fast starts by Eric Montross and George Lynch, never trailed in the game and went on to win convincingly, 101-73.

101-73

It was an impressive showing by Carolina, which had its third game in five days since returning from Hawaii's Rainbow Classic. Carolina struck inside and outside, putting four players in double figures. Guards Donald Williams (20 points) and Derrick Phelps (10) took care of the outside, while Eric Montross (17) and George Lynch (16) took the fight to Maryland on the inside.

Williams was again hot from 3-point range, hitting 5-8 from that distance. Carolina dominated Maryland on the backboards, getting 50 rebounds to Maryland's 30, and 21 offensive rebounds to Maryland's 11. Montross led with 13 rebounds and Lynch had eight and Phelps seven.

Carolina improved to 12-1, 2-0 in the ACC, and Maryland fell to 8-3, 0-2.

"We're very pleased with a win over what I think is a very good Maryland team," Carolina coach Dean Smith said. "We made the 'threes' and we played very well defensively. I thought our defense was very active, and still

"

I kept waiting for them to give a pump fake or something, but they kept coming right back up (in regard to his career-high six blocked shots). They just kept shooting the close-range jump shot. I thought that pretty soon they were going to start taking it to the basket and try to draw some fouls, but they never did.

"

Kevin Salvadori

(Maryland guard) Kevin McLinton put his head down and got in there and made some baskets (21 points)."

Montross scored six of the Tar Heels' first 12 points, thereby establishing Carolina's inside game. UNC led 12-4, and after Maryland made a run to close the gap to 18-14, the Tar Heels went on a 10-0 spurt and eventually built that lead to 53-31 at halftime.

Carolina shot 52.5 percent in the first half to Maryland's 43.3 percent, and finished the game with a 55.7 field goal percentage. UNC only shot 28.6 percent in 3-pointers in the first half, but hit a sizzling 62.5 percent of the long bombers in the second half, led by Williams' 5-8.

"They're better than they were last year," Maryland coach Gary Williams said of the Tar Heels. "They generate an awful lot of their offense off their defense, which might be one thing that is different from last year's team."

UNC forced 23 Maryland turnovers, which led to easy baskets, but the Tar Heels committed 23 turnovers, 13 in the second half, against the Terps' pressure defense. "It looked for a time there in the second half as if we had never practiced our press offense," Coach Smith said.

Carolina's Williams scored 14 of his 20 points in the second half. Carolina needed that because Maryland's defense created some problems for the Tar Heels early in the second half. With 15:23 left in the game, the Terps cut Carolina's lead to 62-48. But UNC answered with an 11-0 run and built its lead to 73-48. A blocked shot by Kevin Salvadori that led to a Pat Sullivan dunk ignited that rally. Lynch scored on a dunk and Williams knocked in a 3-pointer during that flurry.

UNC's defense, which has been good all season, dictated the tempo in this game. Salvadori had six blocked shots and Montross had five. Maryland was held to 41.7 percent shooting and the Tar Heels outrebounded the Terps, 50-30.

Phelps, who was listed as doubtful before the game because of a slight concussion suffered in the N.C. State game on Jan. 7, had six assists and seven rebounds. Salvadori might have played his best game of the season, finishing with eight points on 3-4 shooting, five rebounds and a career-high six blocked shots.

Carolina played every man on its bench.

Carolina	FG	FT	R	A	TP
Brian Reese	3-6	0-2	3	2	6
George Lynch	7-11	2-4	8	4	16
Eric Montross	6-9	5-8	13	1	17
Henrik Rodl	1-2	0-0	0	4	3
Derrick Phelps	3-12	4-5	7	6	10
Pat Sullivan	4-5	0-0	6	3	8
Donald Williams	7-13	1-2	3	4	20
Kevin Salvadori	3-4	2-2	5	0	8
Dante Calabria	1-1	2-2	1	1	5
Matt Wenstrom	1-2	0-0	2	0	2
Scott Cherry	1-1	0-2	0	0	2
Larry Davis	1-2	0-0	0	0	2
T. Stephenson	0-1	0-0	0	0	0
Ed Geth	1-1	0-0	1	0	2
Team			1		
Totals	39-70	16-27	50	25	101
Maryland	FG	FT	R	A	TP
Exree Hipp	2-5	1-2	1	2	6
Evers Burns	7-17	0-0	7	2	14
Chris Kerwin	3-5	0-2	2	0	6
Johnny Rhodes	6-15	0-0	3	2	13
Kevin McLinton	8-15	5-5	5	6	21
John Walsh	0-2	2-2	1	1	2
Duane Simpkins	2-5	0-0	3	2	4
Mario Lucas	1-4	2-2	1	1	4
Wayne Bristol	0-0	0-0	0	0	0
N. Petrovic	0-0	0-0	0	0	0
Kurtis Shultz	0-1	0-0	2	0	0
Mike Thibeault	1-3	0-0	3	0	3
Team			2		
Totals	30-72	10-13	30	16	73

Three-point goals: Carolina 7-15 (Brian Reese 0-1, Henrik Rodl 1-2, Derrick Phelps 0-2, Pat Sullivan 0-1, Donald Williams 5-8, Dante Calabria 1-1); Maryland 3-15 (Exree Hipp 1-2, Johnny Rhodes 1-8, Kevin McLinton 0-1, John Walsh 0-1, Duane Simpkins 0-1, Mike Thibeault 1-2).
Turnovers: Carolina 23, Maryland 23.

KEYS TO THE GAME: Carolina got the ball inside early to establish that part of its game, which opened up the outside in the second half...Carolina's defense kept pressure on Maryland all over the court, and the Terps hit only 3-15 from 3-point range...Carolina had good offensive balance with four players in double figures.

DEAN SMITH COMMENT: "Offensively, we were sharp until they pressed us in the second half. We didn't throw it away much at all in the first half, and then in the second half, our press offense looked like we haven't practiced it. We'd either get a layup or we'd throw it away."

COACH GARY WILLIAMS COMMENT: "Their style is particularly effective against a team like ours. They bring Williams, Salvadori and Sullivan off the bench and those guys aren't freshmen. They have a 6-8 forward (Lynch) who is second on the team in steals. That's an impressive team. They have their program where we want ours to get to."

Carolina's Kevin Salvadori shoots jumper over Maryland's Chris Kerwin in easy UNC win.

UNC Gets Ball Inside To Derail The Jackets

80-67

Georgia Tech was riding high when it came to the Smith Center on Jan. 13 to play the Tar Heels. The Yellow Jackets had beaten top-ranked Duke in Atlanta three days earlier and had been impressive in other games.

But the Tar Heels, knowing the importance of this game in the ACC standings, played one of their best games of the still-young season in beating Tech, 80-67, to go 13-1 overall, 3-0 in the ACC. Georgia Tech fell to 9-2, 2-1 in the conference. A crowd of 21,572 watched the game.

While much had been made of Carolina's size, Georgia Tech came to Chapel Hill with a frontline bigger than Carolina's. Tech started Malcolm Mackey, 6-11, James Forrest, 6-8, and Ivano Newbill, 6-10, up front. Rebounding would be a key to the game.

With the home crowd charged, Carolina stormed to an 8-0 lead, but there is no way this game would be a rout, as were UNC's first two ACC games against N.C. State and Maryland. Georgia Tech, a gifted team, didn't panic. It worked its way back and took the lead at 23-22 on Martice Moore's second straight basket. That was the only time Georgia Tech led in the game, though. The Tar Heels used great ball movement in the final seven minutes of the half to lead at halftime, 39-34. UNC shot 48.5 percent in the first half, to Tech's 48.4 percent. Going inside against Tech's big defense wasn't easy in the early going.

That would change in the second half, as Carolina point guard Derrick Phelps had a brilliant game. He passed for six assists and had only one turnover, and he hit 7-8 shots from the field in scoring 20 points.

Carolina carved up Tech's man-to-man defense in the second half and shot 66.7 per-cent from the field. UNC did it by going inside, as it attempted only six shots from 3-point range. The Tar Heels broke the game open in the second half and twice led by 18 points, even though Georgia Tech also had a good shooting half and hit 52 percent from the field in the second half, 50 percent for the game.

Phelps stole the ball and scored to in-crease Carolina's lead to 70-53, and then Eric Montross and Donald Williams scored back-to-back baskets as the Tar Heels went ahead 76-58.

Tech came within 11 before settling for the final score of 80-67.

George Lynch continued his brilliant play with 20 points and 11 rebounds and three steals. Eric Montross and Brian Reese each scored 15 points for the winning Tar Heels.

It was a well-played game. Tech had 18 turnovers, Carolina only 14. Carolina shot 56.7 percent for the game and found a way to get inside against Tech's man-to-man defense in the second half.

Guard Travis Best led Georgia Tech in scoring with 20 points. Carolina had 30 re-bounds to Georgia Tech's 26.

"George is George, and this had to be Derrick Phelps' night," UNC coach Dean Smith said of Lynch and Phelps. "He did everything well--defense, rebounding, passing, scoring."

UNC's Donald Williams scared the crowd when he bruised his knee on a collision in the first half, but he returned to the game and hit a driving jump shot to boost the Tar Heel lead to 55-43 with 13:31 left. Williams finished with six points.

"After the win over Duke, I'm disappoint-ed that we didn't play better," Georgia Tech coach Bobby Cremins said. "I wish we'd had more days to prepare for this game."

> "
> *I think I just had to step my game up to another level. I was penetrating and trying to get the ball inside. If I had the easy layup, then I went ahead and took it. I think I did a good job of doing that.*
> "
>
> *Derrick Phelps*

Carolina	FG	FT	R	A	TP
Brian Reese	7-13	0-0	1	2	15
George Lynch	9-13	2-3	11	1	20
Eric Montross	6-10	3-4	6	0	15
Henrik Rodl	0-2	0-0	1	5	0
Derrick Phelps	7-8	5-5	4	6	20
Pat Sullivan	1-2	0-0	1	3	2
Donald Williams	3-8	0-1	1	1	6
Dante Calabria	0-0	0-0	0	1	0
Kevin Salvadori	0-3	0-1	3	0	0
Matt Wenstrom	1-1	0-0	0	0	2
Scott Cherry	0-0	0-0	0	0	0
Team			2		
Totals	34-60	10-14	30	19	80
Georgia Tech	**FG**	**FT**	**R**	**A**	**TP**
James Forrest	4-10	1-2	8	0	9
Malcom Mackey	5-9	2-3	7	1	12
Ivano Newbill	0-2	1-3	1	0	1
Martice Moore	5-10	0-0	1	2	11
Travis Best	8-14	0-0	2	6	20
Drew Barry	1-4	0-0	5	5	2
Bryan Hill	5-7	0-0	0	0	12
Darryl Barnes	0-0	0-0	0	0	0
Team			2		
Totals	28-56	4-8	26	14	67

Three-point goals: Carolina 2-6 (Brian Reese 1-3, Henrik Rodl 0-1, Derrick Phelps 1-1, Donald Williams 0-1); Georgia Tech 7-15 (Martice Moore 1-4, Travis Best 4-7, Drew Barry 0-2, Bryan Hill 2-2.)

Turnovers: Carolina 14, Georgia Tech 18.

KEYS TO THE GAME: Carolina chased Georgia Tech out of its zone de-fense by jumping to an 8-0 lead, and in the second half, UNC got the ball inside for good shots against Tech's man-to-man defense...Carolina's defense did a good job on Tech's Malcolm Mackey, James Forrest and Drew Barry.

DEAN SMITH COMMENT: "We played a difficult non-conference sched-ule and I think it's remarkable what the players have done. You'll recall that I said before the start of the season that I wasn't worried about our outside shoot-ing and I thought our defense would be good. The defense has been outstand-ing so far. Opponents have an awfully hard time running their offense against our defense, and as much as we gamble on defense, our field goal percentage defense is good."

COACH BOBBY CREMINS COM-MENT: "North Carolina played great. Eric Montross is a man. I knew this would be tough for our young team. (Carolina) took advantage of our turnovers. We had a plan for this game and they took us out of it. They kind of rattled us, whereas in the Duke game, we stayed together. This game, we kind of came apart."

Brian Reese soars over Georgia Tech's Travis Best for two of his 15 points.

Carolina Wins Sloppy ACC Game At Clemson

82-72

Carolina, ranked fifth in the nation when it went to Clemson on Jan. 16 to play the Tigers in Littlejohn Coliseum, was not looking for an easy game. That's good, because in a ragged affair, one in which Carolina shot only 34.4 percent in the first half, the Tar Heels survived, 82-72.

UNC improved to 14-1 overall, 4-0 in the ACC, and Clemson dropped to 9-3, 0-3.

In a game that threatened to never end, there were 39 turnovers and 45 fouls between the two teams. Two things saved Carolina from losing this game: Its defense and George Lynch.

Carolina's defense forced 21 turnovers and held Clemson to 44.3 percent shooting from the field, and only 6-21 from 3-point range. But it was Lynch who kept the Tar Heels unbeaten in the ACC. He scored 17 points, but his major contribution was in getting 13 rebounds, five of them off the offensive glass.

The game had no rhythm from the beginning. Clemson led 7-2 and got the crowd of 11,000 very much into the game. Carolina eventually built a 28-18 lead, even though the Tar Heels handled the ball at times as if it were a live hand grenade. Carolina's lead at halftime was 31-24--and it was not a delay game.

Clemson, with exceptional quickness, did spread the court and make Carolina chase, but

"

We rebounded better, defended better, were better in transition. Some people think the team we played today is the best team in the country.

"

Clemson Coach Cliff Ellis

it wasn't holding the ball.

"This isn't one they are going to save and replay on TV," UNC coach Dean Smith quipped after the game.

Psychologically, this was not the best of times for the Tar Heels. They had beaten Georgia Tech in an emotional game three days earlier, while Clemson was embarrassed, humiliated by a loss at Duke. The Tigers were anxious to rebound and the Tar Heels were on automatic pilot. That's a dangerous way to play a basketball game.

Clemson got a great game from Devin Gray, who scored 16 points, and guard Chris Whitney, another excellent talent, had 17 points. Carolina held center Sharone Wright to two points.

Clemson always uses gimmicks on defense against Carolina. This game was no exception.

Gimmick No. 1: When Montross and Williams were in the game at the same time, the Tigers played three men in a zone and two man-to-man on Montross and Williams, a triangle-and-two.

Gimmick No. 2: When only one of those two Tar Heels was on the floor, Clemson went box-and-one. Carolina loves to play against junk defenses, but in this game, the basket looked about as big as a needle's eye. It would be interesting to know what Carolina shot in the layup line in pregame warmups.

UNC did wake up some in the second half and shot 51.6 percent. The Tar Heels led by 13 at one point, and while Clemson closed to within 58-53, Henrik Rodl nailed a 3-point basket for UNC to give the Tar Heels some breathing room. When you examine the overall play of this game, you can bet Carolina was happy to leave Clemson with an 82-72 win.

Take it and get out of town.

In addition to Lynch, Carolina got 13 points from Montross and Donald Williams. Henrik Rodl had 10, Brian Reese nine. Montross added 10 rebounds, as UNC outrebounded the Tigers, 45-33.

"We were much better (than in losing to Duke), no doubt," Clemson coach Cliff Ellis said. ⬤

Carolina	FG	FT	R	A	TP
Brian Reese	3-10	2-6	0	2	9
George Lynch	7-11	3-6	13	1	17
Eric Montross	5-7	3-4	10	2	13
Henrik Rodl	2-8	4-5	3	3	10
Derrick Phelps	5-11	1-3	3	2	11
Pat Sullivan	1-3	4-6	2	1	7
Donald Williams	4-7	3-4	3	0	13
Dante Calabria	0-3	0-0	1	0	0
Kevin Salvadori	0-3	2-2	6	1	2
Matt Wenstrom	0-0	0-0	0	0	0
Larry Davis	0-0	0-0	0	0	0
Scott Cherry	0-0	0-0	0	0	0
Team			4		
Totals	27-63	22-36	45	12	82
Clemson	**FG**	**FT**	**R**	**A**	**TP**
Devin Gray	7-9	1-2	1	1	16
Kevin Hines	5-9	2-4	3	0	12
Sharone Wright	1-4	0-0	5	1	2
Lou Richie	0-1	0-0	0	3	0
Chris Whitney	5-12	4-4	4	3	17
Andre Bovain	4-12	3-4	5	6	13
W. Buckingham	5-8	0-2	9	0	10
Bruce Martin	0-5	2-2	0	2	2
Andy Kelly	0-1	0-0	1	1	0
Team			5		
Totals	27-61	12-18	33	17	72

Three-point goals: Carolina 6-24 (Brian Reese 1-5, Henrik Rodl 2-7, Derrick Phelps 0-2, Pat Sullivan 1-2, Donald Williams 2-5, Dante Calabria 0-3); Clemson 6-21 (Devin Gray 1-2, Chris Whitney 3-8, Andre Bovain 2-5, Bruce Martin 0-5, Andy Kelly 0-1).
Turnovers: Carolina 18, Clemson 21.

KEYS TO THE GAME: George Lynch. Carolina wouldn't have won without him...Defense. It kept UNC in the game until the offense woke up in the second half.

DEAN SMITH COMMENT: "Defense kept us in this game, along with our rebounding, which was also very valuable."

GEORGE LYNCH COMMENT: "When our offense is struggling, we come up with a big play defensively. We're all doing that defensively, including our bench. Kevin Salvadori, Donald Williams, those guys are playing well, and they deserve a lot of credit. We knew that this would be a contest if they got their shooting going. We weren't as aggressive offensively or defensively as we should have been, but we did play well enough to win the game. We should have played better."

George Lynch's 13 rebounds save Tar Heels in a sloppy battle at Clemson.

Second-Half Fireworks Hand Cavs First Loss

Carolina broke Virginia's 16-game winning streak on Jan. 20 in the Smith Center, blowing the Cavaliers away in the second half for an 80-58 ACC victory. The Tar Heels improved to 15-1 on the season, 5-0 in the ACC. UVa, which had won the NIT the year before and beat Duke in Durham in its previous game, fell to 11-1, 4-1.

80-58

The Cavaliers were ranked seventh in the nation coming into this game, which drew a crowd of 21,572.

Carolina got balanced scoring inside and a hot outside shooting game from Henrik Rodl to stop Virginia's win streak. Carolina's defense was spectacular, especially in the second half, when it held Virginia to 38.2 percent shooting from the field.

"North Carolina did nothing tonight to disprove to me that they're the best team in the country," said Virginia coach Jeff Jones.

Carolina, ahead 32-25 at halftime, led 48-36 when it went on a 10-0 run to lead 58-36 and break the game open with 8:50 left to play. The Tar Heels twice led by 29 in the second half, and coach Dean Smith played everybody on his bench.

After a poor shooting first half, UNC shot 56.7 percent in the second half in breaking the game open. Carolina won the rebounding battle, 43-29.

George Lynch, whose home is Roanoke, Va., had 12 points, 11 rebounds, three steals and no turnovers. Eric Montross had 12 points, and Kevin Salvadori, in an excellent game off the bench, scored 14 points and got five rebounds. With Donald Williams hitting only 1-8 from the field, Carolina got outside shooting from Rodl, who didn't miss a shot in scoring 11 points, including 3-3 from 3-point range.

> "
> *North Carolina did nothing tonight to disprove to me that they're the best team in the country.*
> "
>
> *Virginia Coach*
> *Jeff Jones*

Carolina played brilliantly in the second half in building the 29-point lead. The Tar Heels rebounded, ran the break, played solid defense, hit the outside shot.

Virginia doesn't put much pressure on the ball. It plays a sagging man-to-man defense that is very physical, especially on the inside. The scheme worked in the first half, but as Carolina showed more patience in moving the ball in the second half, it broke the defense down for some good shots. Montross got 10 of his 12 points in the second half.

"We decided to force-feed Montross in the second half, hoping we'd get the fouls called," UNC coach Dean Smith said.

Carolina shot 47.6 percent for the game, which is pretty good against Virginia's defense. Derrick Phelps held Virginia's talented point guard, Cory Alexander, to 11 points on 4-12 shooting.

In a matter of days, Carolina had taken care of Georgia Tech and Virginia, two Top 10 teams that came into the Carolina game with a lot of momentum. ●

Kevin Salvadori cuts through the Virginia defense on his way to the basket.

Carolina	FG	FT	R	A	TP
Brian Reese	3-6	3-4	3	2	10
George Lynch	5-12	2-4	11	3	12
Eric Montross	5-8	2-3	6	1	12
Henrik Rodl	4-4	0-0	1	3	11
Derrick Phelps	2-7	2-2	5	5	7
Pat Sullivan	2-5	0-0	2	0	5
Donald Williams	1-8	1-1	5	5	3
Kevin Salvadori	6-10	2-3	5	0	14
Dante Calabria	0-0	0-0	0	0	0
Matt Wenstrom	1-1	0-0	2	0	2
Scott Cherry	0-0	2-2	1	1	2
Ed Geth	1-1	0-0	1	0	2
Larry Davis	0-1	0-0	0	0	0
T. Stephenson	0-0	0-0	0	0	0
Team			1		
Totals	30-63	14-19	43	20	80
Virginia	**FG**	**FT**	**R**	**A**	**TP**
Cornel Parker	2-5	1-2	6	3	5
Junior Burrough	5-17	0-0	5	1	10
Ted Jeffries	1-3	0-0	4	0	2
Jason Williford	2-6	2-2	1	1	6
Cory Alexander	4-12	2-2	5	3	11
Yuri Barnes	2-5	0-1	4	0	4
Doug Smith	6-8	0-0	1	1	16
Shawn Wilson	1-1	0-0	0	0	2
Chris Havlicek	0-2	0-2	0	0	0
Chris Alexander	1-1	0-0	2	0	2
Team			1		
Totals	24-60	5-9	29	9	58

Three-point goals: Carolina 6-12 (Brian Reese 1-2, Henrik Rodl 3-3, Derrick Phelps 1-1, Pat Sullivan 1-2, Donald Williams 0-4); Virginia 5-14 (Jason Williford 0-2, Cory Alexander 1-6, Doug Smith 4-5, Chris Havlicek 0-1).
Turnovers: Carolina 17, Virginia 18.

KEYS TO THE GAME: Defense kept Carolina ahead in the first half...The offense got good shots in the second half in building a 29-point lead...Rodl hit all four of his field goals to make Virginia play him on the perimeter...Montross got 10 points in the second half, and Lynch maintained his terrific rebounding with 11...Salvadori was excellent off the bench.

DEAN SMITH COMMENT: "George Lynch does everything. Our defense was good for most of the game. But we'll have a very difficult time trying to beat them up there (in Charlottesville). We competed hard on defense. We improved tonight and now we must build on this."

COACH JEFF JONES COMMENT: "North Carolina showed why they are a great team. They forced us to do a lot of things poorly. It's hard to come down here and slug it out with a team with that much size and depth. We can find out a lot about ourselves in the way we handle this setback. North Carolina did a great job of going to the offensive boards. We couldn't get in transition because they did such a good job of keeping us from getting the defensive rebounds. Their half-court defense is great, and they don't foul a lot in it."

Eric Montross and George Lynch scrap with Virginia's Cornel Parker for rebound.

Long Pass Seals Road Win Over Seton Hall

70-66

Carolina, which likes a tough basketball schedule, went to the Meadowlands on Jan. 24 and beat Seton Hall, the eventual champions of the Big East, 70-66, in a game that was shown on national television.

It was Carolina's second straight victory over a Top 10 team. The Tar Heels beat seventh-ranked Virginia earlier in the week in Chapel Hill.

This was a tough assignment for Carolina. The Tar Heels routed Seton Hall 83-54 in the Meadowlands the previous year, and the Pirates were seeking revenge.

Carolina won this game despite shooting only 30 percent in the first half and getting outrebounded, 35-26. The Tar Heels improved to 16-1. Seton Hall, which had a 10-game Meadowlands winning streak stopped, fell to 15-3.

Carolina's defense came to the rescue again. It forced 23 Seton Hall turnovers.

UNC, which missed a lot of easy shots in the first half, led for most of the first 20 minutes in a close game. However, Seton Hall got a late push to lead 32-30 at halftime.

The second half didn't start out real well for Carolina, either. Eric Montross, who had been frustrated with his play in the first half, missed a layup on UNC's first possession of the half and got his third personal foul with 19:50 left in the game.

Carolina's offense really came on in the second half, as the team got good shots and made them in shooting 63.6 percent in the period. After Carolina led 44-42, the Pirates ran off seven straight points to lead 49-44.

The game was back and forth from that point. Carolina would pull to within one or two points, but Seton Hall would build its lead back to five. Carolina's spurt came with Seton Hall leading 55-53. Brian Reese scored on a follow shot to tie the game, then Montross scored and made the ensuing foul shot, followed by a Derrick Phelps basket. That was a 7-0 run and resulted in a 60-55 Carolina lead.

Seton Hall never led again, but with 27 seconds left, the Pirates got a 3-point field goal from John Leahy to cut Carolina's lead to 68-66. Seton Hall called timeout to set its defense against Carolina's inbounds play in the backcourt.

Carolina coach Dean Smith, a man not afraid to take risks, went for the knockout in his huddle. He drew up a set of screens and sent Phelps breaking for the basket. The long pass was completed, the play worked to perfection, and Phelps dunked to put Carolina ahead 70-66.

"Coach Smith set up that play in the huddle and it worked," Phelps said.

This was a physical battle between two excellent teams, both of which were virtually certain of going to the NCAA tournament.

Lynch was sensational with 25 points on 9-15 shooting, seven rebounds and three steals. Montross added 13 points and Phelps finished with 12 points, six assists and four steals.

Seton Hall packed back inside on Carolina defensively in a sagging man-to-man, and it entered the game holding its opponents to 39 percent shooting. UNC shot 44.2 percent for the game. Carolina's defense limited Seton Hall to 48.1 percent shooting, and held star guard Terry Dehere to just 4-12 shooting for 10 points. Henrik Rodl guarded Dehere for most of the game. 🏀

"

North Carolina is a good team and they have a great coach. They executed well down the stretch. What more can you say? Defense dominates big games and I think you saw that today.

"

Terry Dehere

Carolina	FG	FT	R	A	TP
Brian Reese	2-6	2-4	3	1	6
George Lynch	9-15	7-8	7	0	25
Eric Montross	3-11	7-10	4	0	13
Pat Sullivan	1-3	4-4	2	1	6
Derrick Phelps	5-7	2-4	3	6	12
Henrik Rodl	1-1	0-0	1	3	2
Scott Cherry	0-0	0-0	0	1	0
Donald Williams	1-6	0-0	2	0	3
Kevin Salvadori	1-2	1-2	1	0	3
Matt Wenstrom	0-1	0-0	0	0	0
Team			3		
Totals	23-52	23-32	26	12	70
Seton Hall	**FG**	**FT**	**R**	**A**	**TP**
Jerry Walker	5-6	0-0	7	3	10
A. Karnishovas	5-9	2-2	4	2	15
Luther Wright	4-8	3-5	14	0	11
Danny Hurley	0-4	0-0	0	2	0
Terry Dehere	4-12	2-2	1	2	10
Adrian Griffin	2-3	1-2	4	0	5
Bryan Caver	2-5	0-1	3	7	4
John Leahy	3-4	2-2	1	1	11
Tchaka Shipp	0-1	0-0	1	0	0
Team			0		
Totals	25-52	10-14	35	17	66

Three-point goals: Carolina 1-5 (Brian Reese 0-1, Derrick Phelps 0-1, Donald Williams 1-3); Seton Hall 6-13 (Arturas Karnishovas 3-3, Terry Dehere 0-4, Bryan Caver 0-2, John Leahy 3-4). **Turnovers:** Carolina 9, Seton Hall 23.

KEYS TO THE GAME: UNC used defense, guts and poise to win on a day when many good shots weren't falling...Eric Montross, who didn't have a field goal in the first half, came alive late in the game and finished with 13 points. George Lynch was superb with 25 points. With the game on the line and UNC ahead 68-66 with 27 seconds left, coach Dean Smith mapped out a long pass to Phelps that worked like a charm.

GEORGE LYNCH COMMENT: "We've been playing with a lot of character the entire season. We have a lot of experience, not only with the starters but the guys on the bench, also. We're ready for big games like this. We've had some close games this season and they've been going in our favor, except for Michigan (in the Rainbow Classic)."

ERIC MONTROSS COMMENT: "I was able to get position inside today, but I just wasn't able to put the ball in the hole. There were a lot of things underneath that were escaping the eye of the officials, and that got frustrating at times. But I couldn't do anything about that and I'm not going to worry about it."

Miracle Comeback Gets UNC Past Florida State

"What do you say after that?" asked Carolina coach Dean Smith.

For sure, words can't describe what went on at the Smith Center on the night of Jan. 27, when North Carolina trailed Florida State by 21 points with 11:48 left in the game, by 20 with 9:36 left and by 19 with 9:02 remaining, only to come back and win, 82-77.

82-77

It has to rank as one of the greatest comebacks in the history of college basketball, not only because Carolina came from so far back to win, but also because of how quickly it did it and against an opponent that was one of the most talented teams in the nation.

Florida State strutted into the Smith Center and took the fight to the Tar Heels. Fresh off a win over Duke, the Seminoles took the court, confident of victory. Some of them sang a little song, saying they were going to do it again, meaning they would beat Carolina just as they did a year ago in Chapel Hill.

They made good on their word for most of the night. FSU dominated this game for 31 minutes. They led 45-28 at halftime, and in the locker room, FSU guard Sam Cassell said he was embarrassed that Carolina thought "Henrik (bleeping) Rodl or Donald (bleeping) Williams could guard me."

Florida State put on a clinic in the first half. It beat Carolina's traps for good shots, and when shots missed, FSU got the offensive rebound.

FSU chose the same strategy it used in beating UNC twice during the regular season the previous year. It spread the court on offense and tried to beat the Tar Heels with its quickness. On defense, the Seminoles played a diamond-and-one on Donald Williams when he was in the game, and always, they packed their defense back on Carolina's inside game.

All of it worked like a dream. Douglas Edwards, FSU's inside star, scored on a layup to put his team ahead 65-44 with 11:48 left. The capacity crowd at the Smith Center just sat there, stunned by this basketball game they were seeing.

Knowing it would take desperate measures to change the course of this game, Carolina coach Dean Smith went to his hurry-up game with more than nine minutes to play. Rodney Dobard scored for Florida State to

push its lead to 71-51, but then Henrik Rodl hit a 3-pointer for the Tar Heels to make it 71-54 with 9:21 left.

Timeout, Carolina. Why? Smith wanted his own team to believe that the rally had begun, and he wanted to send a message to Florida State that the Tar Heels still thought they could win. Smith told his players on the bench to think back to a year earlier, when UNC overcame a 20-point Wake Forest lead in the second half to win.

Carolina's defense suddenly became frenzied. The traps were furious and crisp. The shots, which had not fallen all night, were finding the mark. The crowd, tabbed a wine-and-cheese crowd by Sam Cassell the year before, made so much noise that the building shook.

Edwards scored to put FSU back up by 19, but George Lynch and Donald Williams hit 3-pointers for the Tar Heels to make it 73-60 with 8:38 left.

"Coach Smith smiled at us in the huddle at that point," Eric Montross said, "and we believed it would happen."

Rodl hit another 3-pointer out of this timeout, and then he stole the ball and fed Derrick Phelps for a layup. Florida State took another timeout with 7:37 left. Its lead was down to 73-65. The crowd was wild. FSU was doubting and Carolina was believing.

Carolina trapped FSU's Bob Sura and forced an errant pass. Montross was fouled underneath and FSU coach Pat Kennedy was called for a technical. Williams hit two free throws and then a basket, and Florida State's lead, which was 20 points a few minutes earlier, was down to four with 6:52 left.

UNC could have grown discouraged on its next possession. Lynch's shot in the lane was blocked by Dobard, but Lynch got the carom and fed Montross for an easy one. Montross missed and Dobard rebounded, but Lynch stole the ball and missed a layup. Then Phelps rebounded and missed an easy one.

That could have done it, but Carolina just reached a little deeper. Cassell hit two free throws and Brian Reese one and the score was 75-70.

Lynch, the ultimate competitor, was feeling it. He made a move down the right baseline to score, reducing FSU's lead to 75-72. There was so much noise in the building that

Carolina	FG	FT	R	A	TP
Pat Sullivan	0-3	0-0	0	1	0
George Lynch	5-14	3-4	10	3	14
Eric Montross	7-10	1-2	8	1	15
Henrik Rodl	4-9	0-0	5	2	11
Scott Cherry	0-0	0-0	2	0	0
Derrick Phelps	1-8	2-2	3	7	4
Brian Reese	2-9	1-2	1	1	5
Kevin Salvadori	3-4	0-2	5	0	6
Donald Williams	5-12	8-8	1	0	19
Matt Wenstrom	4-5	0-1	3	0	8
Dante Calabria	0-1	0-0	0	0	0
Team			2		
Totals	31-75	15-21	40	15	82
Florida State	**FG**	**FT**	**R**	**A**	**TP**
Bob Sura	6-18	2-2	6	1	15
Rodney Dobard	8-12	1-4	10	2	17
Doug Edwards	6-13	3-4	12	5	16
Sam Cassell	5-18	2-2	2	4	15
Charlie Ward	2-4	0-0	6	5	5
Byron Wells	0-0	0-0	1	0	0
Derrick Carroll	0-0	0-0	1	0	0
M. Robinson	4-6	1-1	5	0	9
Team			2		
Totals	31-71	9-13	45	17	77

Three-point goals: Carolina 5-20 (George Lynch 1-1, Henrik Rodl 3-6, Derrick Phelps 0-4, Brian Reese 0-3, Donald Williams 1-6); Florida State 6-25 (Bob Sura 1-7, Doug Edwards 1-3, Sam Cassell 3-12, Charlie Ward 1-3).
Turnovers: Carolina 14, Florida State 23.

KEYS TO THE GAME: After Carolina got behind by 21 in the second half, Dean Smith ordered up some zone defense. FSU took quick shots against it, which fueled Carolina's rally...Carolina's defense in the last nine minutes did not yield easy shots...The Smith Center crowd, the wine-and-cheese bunch, contributed to the win.

DOUGLAS EDWARDS, COMMENTING ON UNC'S CROWD REACTION: "They're acting like they won the national championship or something."

DOUGLAS EDWARDS COMMENT: "They impressed me. They kept playing hard, regardless of how far they were behind. I know what their tradition is all about now."

Derrick Phelps scores over FSU's Sam Cassell in Carolina's miracle comeback.

Kennedy couldn't be heard as he shouted instructions to his players. Reese made a steal, fed Phelps, who was fouled by FSU's Charlie Ward. Phelps made both foul shots. Florida State led 75-74 with 3:15 left.

Edwards picked up a loose ball in his own lane and scored, giving FSU a 77-74 lead. Montross answered with a jump hook to make it 77-76 with 1:59 left.

Rodl and Phelps trapped Ward at the 10-second line on the right side. Ward, a football quarterback, tried to heave a pass across court, but Lynch read it all the way, intercepted at midcourt and took it for a dunk. Carolina had come all the way back and led, 78-77, with 1:41 left.

Carolina rebounded a missed FSU shot and Dean Smith held up four fingers in front of the Tar Heels' bench. UNC went to its Four Corners offense, and the man in the middle was Donald Williams. He was being guarded by Cassell. Williams took him on the dribble, penetrating and drawing the foul. Williams made two foul shots to give Carolina an 80-77 lead with 37.7 seconds left.

Edwards missed a 3-pointer, Kevin Salvadori rebounded, fed Williams, who was fouled with 11 seconds left. Williams made two more foul shots.

This one was history. Carolina's comeback was in the books. The Tar Heels won it, 82-77.

"I certainly admire the competitiveness of our players," Dean Smith said.

Said Derrick Phelps: "It's incredible what Coach Smith can bring out in a team. He got the best out of us, and he just kept telling us to be patient."

Carolina's record went to 17-1, 6-0 in the ACC. FSU fell to 5-2 in the ACC.

Of all the great victories that Carolina basketball teams have recorded in the Dean Smith era, this is one that will be talked about for years to come.

George Lynch lays one in and North Carolina is on its way to an unbelievable comeback win.

Anatomy Of A Comeback

North Carolina, down 20 points to Florida State with 9:24 to play and by 19 with 9:02 left, staged a miraculous rally in the Smith Center on Jan. 27 to win, 82-77.

The Comeback, as it shall be known, happened this way:

• Henrik Rodl hits a 3-pointer to cut the lead to 71-54, and coach Dean Smith uses his first timeout. He wanted his team to know that the rally had begun, and he wanted to plant a seed in Florida State's mind that it could actually lose this game. 9:24 left.

• Douglas Edwards answers with a follow shot inside, which could have easily stopped UNC's rally. FSU leads 73-54. 9:02 left.

• George Lynch nails a 3-pointer from the top of the key, only the second one of his career, to trim the lead to 16, 73-57. 8:51 left.

• Derrick Phelps draws a charge on FSU point guard Charlie Ward, Ward's second foul of the game. 8:43 left.

• Donald Williams makes a 3-pointer. FSU's lead is down to 13, 73-60. FSU calls its first timeout. The Smith Center is rocking. No wine and cheese tonight, Mr. Cassell. 8:38 left.

• Rodl hits another 3-pointer. FSU's lead is 73-63. 8:06 left.

• Rodl steals a pass at midcourt and lobs to Phelps, who scored on a driving layup. 73-65. FSU calls timeout No. 2. It is so loud in the Smith Center that it's impossible to be heard. 7:42 left.

• Edwards is called for a foul after he pushes Eric Montross to the floor to prevent a layup. FSU coach Pat Kennedy, who had been flirting with a technical, finally gets one. Donald Williams hits both technical foul shots. FSU leads 73-67. 7:09 left.

• Williams leans in for a 10-footer. It's down to four, 73-69. 6:52 left.

• Rodl fouls FSU guard Sam Cassell, after Carolina missed three layups with a chance to cut it to two. Cassell makes both foul shots. FSU leads 75-69. 5:21 left.

• FSU forward Rodney Dobard picks up his fourth foul when Brian Reese glides to the basket. Reese misses the first, makes the second free throw. It's FSU, 75-70. 4:39 left.

• Lynch scores on a baseline drive. UNC is within three, 75-72. 3:36 left.

• Ward tackles Phelps on a drive to the basket. Phelps hits both free throws. It's a one-point game, 75-74 FSU. 3:15 left.

• Florida State calls its last timeout when Edwards is trapped on the right sideline and can't find a receiver. Score is still 75-74. 2:56 left.

• Edwards scores on a follow shot, a big basket, one that could have been the killer. The Seminoles lead 77-74. 2:28 left.

• Eric Montross, just back in the game after a breather, hits a jump hook. FSU 77, UNC 76. 1:59 left.

• The play that made all the highlights. Rodl and Phelps trap Ward at midcourt. Ward, in trouble and no timeouts left, tries to lob the ball to his left to Bob Sura, but Lynch reads the play, intercepts and takes it in for a dunk. CAROLINA LEADS for the first time since the 16:50 mark of the first half, and the crowd is literally jumping. UNC 78, FSU 77. 1:41 left.

• After a miss by FSU, Dean Smith signals Four Corners. He puts the ball in the hands of sophomore guard Donald Williams. All those fans who wondered about Smith playing Williams at point last season...well, question no more. The shot clock runs down and Williams takes Cassell to the basket and is fouled. Williams hits both free throws. Make that 80-77, Carolina. 37.7 seconds left.

• Douglas Edwards fires a 3-pointer over UNC's Kevin Salvadori. Big Sal rebounds the miss, gets it to Williams, who is fouled in the backcourt by Bob Sura. Williams makes both free throws. 82-77, Carolina. 11.2 seconds left.

• Florida State misses, the ball goes out of bounds to Carolina. The pass in, with two seconds left, goes to Brian Reese, who hurls the ball high into the air. When it comes down, The Comeback is complete.

• Zero seconds left. Dean Smith and his gutsy Tar Heels stun the nation by outscoring Florida State 31-6 in the game's last 9:24, and win the game, 82-77.

"I admire the competitiveness of our players," Coach Smith said.

As for Carolina's Hall of Fame coach, well, let's just say he gets better with age. Last year it was a win over Wake Forest after being down by 22. This year, Florida State. Wonder what the coaching genius has in stock for next season?

"Coach is something," point guard Derrick Phelps said. "It's incredible what he can get out of a team."

Childress, Deacons Go On Tear To Rout Heels

Carolina, fresh off that scintilating comeback win over Florida State, went to Winston-Salem on Jan. 30 to take on Wake Forest, a team it had beaten 23 times in the previous 24 games between the two schools.

62-88

A combination of Wake Forest playing a great game and Carolina being flat resulted in an embarrassing 88-62 loss for the Tar Heels, one that served as a wakeup call and helped the team regain its focus and its edge for the second half of the season.

There was nothing much unusual about the first half. Wake Forest did get hot late to take a 33-30 lead to the locker room, but Carolina had to feel that it could play a lot better in the second half.

However, it took Wake Forest virtually no time in the second half to break this game into a million pieces. Rodney Rogers and Randolph Childress got baskets to make it 39-30, and after Donald Williams scored for Carolina, Childress went on a tear that would bury the Tar Heels. He hit three straight 3-pointers to give the Deacons a 48-32 lead. Then, after Eric Montross scored for UNC, Childress hit two more from 3-point range to make it 54-34. And one minute later, Childress hit another 3-pointer and Wake Forest led, 59-36. Childress had 20 points in the first 6:50 of the second half.

The closest Carolina came after that was 15 points, but the Deacons were not to be denied on this afternoon on their homecourt.

Wake Forest played almost the perfect game in the second half. The Deacs hit 68 percent from the field in the second half to Carolina's

> *To be able to play that way against any team would thrill a coach, but to play that way against what I think is the best team in the country is inexplicable.*
>
> Wake Forest Coach
> Dave Odom

32.5 percent. Childress ended up with 27 points, Rogers had 17, Trelonnie Owens 16 and Derrick Hicks 15.

Carolina's players said the blowout loss got their attention. UNC was gracious in its praise of Wake Forest, which was an excellent team having a great day, but privately, Carolina's players were disappointed in their effort. Many, including team leader George Lynch, felt the effort was not there.

The loss gave Carolina a 17-2 record, 6-1 in the ACC. Wake Forest, which won its fifth straight, improved to 13-3, 5-2.

How dominant were the Deacons? Wake shot 60 percent for the game. The Deacons hit 6-7 from 3-point range in the second half. The capacity crowd at Joel Coliseum had a wonderful afternoon.

"The tendency after something like this is to talk about what North Carolina did wrong," UNC coach Dean Smith said. "Well, North Carolina did do many things wrong, but the credit should go to Wake Forest for doing so much right."

After the game, the Wake students stormed the court in celebration, the long drought to the Tar Heels finally over.

"We're overflowing with joy," said Wake Forest coach Dave Odom, who got his first-ever victory over Carolina as a head coach. "To be able to play that way against any team would thrill a coach, but to play that way against what I think is the best team in the country is inexplicable."

It was apparent, even in the first half, that perhaps the comeback against Florida State had taken its toll on the Tar Heels physically and emotionally. UNC had nine turnovers in the first half, 17 for the game. Wake went with a diamond-and-one defense on Donald Williams in the first half, and when Williams was out of the game, the Deacs went to a sagging man-to-man and bottled up Eric Montross inside.

Though Carolina led for most of the first half, the Deacs surged ahead late in the half, and Brian Reese's 3-pointer at the buzzer brought the Tar Heels to within 33-30.

But this day belonged to Wake Forest. It was a thorough whipping. Carolina didn't enjoy it, but the players did learn something from it that would help during the second half of the season.

Carolina	FG	FT	R	A	TP
George Lynch	5-13	1-1	9	0	12
Brian Reese	7-12	0-0	1	2	16
Eric Montross	1-5	2-2	1	0	4
Derrick Phelps	4-4	0-0	4	4	8
Henrik Rodl	0-4	0-0	2	1	0
Pat Sullivan	3-6	0-0	3	1	7
Scott Cherry	0-2	2-2	2	1	2
Donald Williams	4-9	0-0	1	1	9
Kevin Salvadori	1-4	0-0	2	0	2
Matt Wenstrom	0-2	0-0	2	0	0
T. Stephenson	0-0	0-0	0	0	0
Larry Davis	1-3	0-0	2	0	2
Team			2		
Totals	26-64	5-5	31	10	62
Wake Forest	**FG**	**FT**	**R**	**A**	**TP**
Rodney Rogers	6-12	5-7	4	3	17
Trelannie Owens	8-15	0-0	6	2	16
Derrick Hicks	3-3	9-14	8	0	15
R. Childress	9-13	2-3	5	3	27
Charlie Harrison	0-3	2-2	2	7	2
Travis Banks	1-1	0-0	0	0	2
Marc Blucas	2-2	0-1	1	1	6
Stacey Castle	1-1	0-0	0	0	2
Rusty LaRue	0-0	0-0	0	0	0
D. Rasmussen	0-0	0-0	0	0	0
B. Fitzgibbons	0-0	0-0	0	0	0
Stan King	0-0	1-2	1	0	1
Team			5		
Totals	30-50	19-29	32	16	88

Three-point goals: Carolina 5-18 (George Lynch 1-2, Brian Reese 2-3, Henrik Rodl 0-4, Pat Sullivan 1-2, Scott Cherry 0-1, Donald Williams 1-4, Matt Wenstrom 0-1, Larry Davis 0-1); Wake Forest 9-14 (Rodney Rogers 0-2, Randolph Childress 7-9, Charlie Harrison 0-1, Marc Blucas 2-2).
Turnovers: Carolina 17, Wake Forest 13.

KEYS TO THE GAME: Not many teams would have beaten Wake Forest on this day. Childress couldn't miss from outside, and the Tar Heels weren't emotionally ready to play. UNC had won 11 straight from Wake Forest, 23 of the last 24, and that could have had an impact. Still, Wake Forest deserved this game. No doubt about that.

DEAN SMITH COMMENT: "We'll see if we can learn from this and improve. Wake Forest is very good and I prefer to give them credit. They had a great win. I know it's a very good win for Coach Odom and his program. They certainly outplayed us and deserved to win."

COACH DAVE ODOM COMMENT: "I grew up in this state. I've never been one of those who hated North Carolina. It seems that North Carolina is the kind of school that you're either for or against. They were not my favorite team growing up, but I was right in the middle."

Coach Dean Smith hopes that Henrik Rodl has answer for hot Demon Deacons.

Duke Plays Well Late To Beat Visiting UNC

It was a lousy night for Carolina's shooting to go cold. Playing at Duke before the loud and partisan Blue Devil fans, the Tar Heels got some good shots but could hit only 37.9 percent of them, as Duke won, 81-67.

67-81

It was Carolina's second straight loss in the ACC, dropping the Tar Heels into a first-place tie in the conference with Florida State with records of 6-2. Carolina's overall record was 17-3. Duke, the preseason favorite to win the ACC regular season, was one game back at 5-3.

The Tar Heels were in a shooting slump when they went to Durham for this game, and that didn't change against the Blue Devils. UNC hit only 2-15 from 3-point range, and guard Donald Williams was 3-15 from the floor.

Still, Carolina had every chance to win this one until the very late stages.

"We're disappointed with the loss," UNC coach Dean Smith said, "but we saw some positive things. Duke competed hard, but so did we. It was a well-played game and they pulled it out at the end."

Carolina outrebounded the Blue Devils 40-36 and held Duke to 46.4 percent shooting from the floor. When these two teams meet, defense is almost always the key. Both teams pride themselves on playing good defense, and when they play each other, the intensity seems to go up a couple of notches.

The Tar Heels were led by Eric Montross' 22 points and 13 rebounds. George Lynch finished with 17 points and eight rebounds, as the Tar Heels were very effective inside.

Duke charged ahead 28-17 with five minutes left in the first half. But the Tar Heels battled back to take the lead at 30-29, only to trail 34-32 at halftime.

Montross played brilliantly early in the

"
This is definitely a learning experience for us. It's something I think we can look back on and learn from.
"

Eric Montross

second half, but he was slowed considerably when he was called for his fourth foul with 11:21 to play and the Tar Heels leading 47-44. Montross had scored nine points, gotten five of his 13 rebounds and intercepted a pass in the first eight minutes of the second half.

Lynch hit two free throws to give Carolina a 52-50 lead. Then Duke's Bobby Hurley went to the basket, some bodies collided, the ball came loose and Duke's Thomas Hill picked it up and scored to tie the game at 52 with 7:10 remaining.

Duke's Grant Hill got two foul shots and a field goal before Lynch scored on a follow to make it 56-54, Duke. Thomas Hill made one free throw to give Duke a three-point lead, and then Montross scored and was fouled. Montross missed the free throw, but Lynch rebounded and Pat Sullivan missed a close-range jumper.

Then, Antonio Lange scored for Duke, Williams missed for Carolina and Lang scored to give Duke a 61-56 lead with 3:13 left. Coach Smith called timeout and the Cameron Indoor Stadium crowd was up and screaming. Williams scored out of the timeout, but UNC had gotten its 10th foul of the half by this point, which meant Duke would shoot two free throws on each foul the rest of the way. UNC went zone and Hurley accepted the challenge and nailed a 3-pointer to make it 64-58. Montross was fouled while shooting, and made one of his two free throws to make the score 64-59 with 2:12 left.

A big play came on Duke's next possession. Lang moved out of the left corner and lost the ball going to the basket. Duke's Cherokee Parks grabbed the loose ball, scored and was fouled. That gave Duke a 67-59 lead with 1:55 remaining, and the Blue Devils held on to win.

"We're proud of our guys," Duke coach Mike Krzyzewski said. "It was an outstanding effort on their part. We shot a little better than they did. The final score was not an indication of the closeness of the game. It was really a one- or two-possession game. It's the way teams of this caliber should play."

UNC's Derrick Phelps held Hurley to 4-12 shooting from the floor, but the ones he made were 3-pointers. The Tar Heels also did a nice defensive job on Duke star Grant Hill, holding him to 5-12 shooting.

Carolina	FG	FT	R	A	TP
Brian Reese	3-6	0-0	2	0	6
George Lynch	7-15	3-4	8	3	17
Eric Montross	8-15	6-11	13	0	22
Henrik Rodl	1-2	0-1	1	4	2
Derrick Phelps	1-5	1-2	3	2	4
Pat Sullivan	2-5	5-5	3	1	9
Donald Williams	3-15	0-1	4	2	7
Kevin Salvadori	0-1	0-0	2	0	0
Matt Wenstrom	0-1	0-0	0	0	0
Dante Calabria	0-1	0-0	1	0	0
Team			3		
Totals	25-66	15-24	40	12	67
Duke	**FG**	**FT**	**R**	**A**	**TP**
Grant Hill	5-12	5-6	8	3	15
Marty Clark	1-3	0-0	4	2	2
Cherokee Parks	6-7	2-3	9	0	14
Bobby Hurley	4-12	8-8	4	7	20
Thomas Hill	6-12	4-7	4	2	16
Antonio Lang	3-6	4-4	5	1	10
Kenny Blakeney	0-1	0-0	0	0	0
Erik Meek	1-1	2-3	0	1	4
Chris Collins	0-2	0-0	0	1	0
Kenney Brown	0-0	0-0	0	0	0
Team			2		
Totals	26-56	25-31	36	17	81

Three-point goals: Carolina 2-15 (Brian Reese 0-1, George Lynch 0-2, Henrik Rodl 0-1, Derrick Phelps 1-1, Pat Sullivan 0-1, Donald Williams 1-8, Dante Calabria 0-1); Duke 4-15 (Marty Clark 0-2, Bobby Hurley 4-8, Thomas Hill 0-3, Chris Collins 0-2).

Turnovers: Carolina 15, Duke 12.

KEYS TO THE GAME: Carolina's shooting touch wasn't there for this game...While Duke guard Bobby Hurley hit only 4-12 from the field, all of his baskets were 3-pointers...UNC's Eric Montross was having a monster second half until personal fouls slowed him.

DEAN SMITH COMMENT: "We did some good things defensively. We got the ball to (Montross) in the second half and he did something with it when we did. We will shoot better on open 3-pointers. You have to talk about Lynch's competitiveness on the backboard. There's a long way to go in the season. We hope we can regroup."

COACH MIKE KRZYZEWSKI COMMENT: "They know how to use Montross so well. We seemed to find open people tonight. We attacked. Bobby Hurley was more alert tonight. Our half-court offense was as good as it's been. We were as patient as we've been on offense."

Eric Montross gets between Cherokee Parks and Bobby Hurley to score at Duke.

N.C. State Pummeled As UNC Stops Losing Streak

104-58

After losing to Wake Forest and Duke, Carolina wasted no time in breaking that losing streak. N.C. State paid the price for Carolina's frustration, as the Tar Heels overwhelmed the Wolfpack 104-58 in the Smith Center on Feb. 6.

UNC improved to 18-3, 7-2 in the ACC, while N.C. State fell to 5-12, 1-8.

Coach Dean Smith's goal for his team in this game was to play hard for 40 minutes. The Tar Heels granted him that wish. They played perhaps their best basketball since the early part of the season. UNC shot 51.9 percent from the floor, held State to just 40.3 percent, and the Wolfpack hit only 2-15 from 3-point range. UNC outrebounded the Wolfpack 45-36 and forced a whopping 30 N.C. State turnovers. Carolina held State scoreless for nearly seven minutes in the first half and led 43-23 at the half. Smith put in his reserves with 10:22 left in the game, pulled off his pressure defense and went to a zone, in an attempt not to run up the score.

"Our defense was outstanding," Smith said. "State's plan was sound and it could have caused us some problems."

That plan was to spread the Tar Heels out and take advantage of the Wolfpack's quickness. N.C. State was coming off two good performances--a win over Clemson and an 11-point loss to Wake Forest, in a game that was much closer than that score indicated. So, the Pack had some confidence. But the Tar Heels, determined to play better than the previous two games, jumped on State early, forced the Wolfpack out of its offense, contested just about every pass and dominated offensively and defensively.

Carolina played without Brian Reese, who pulled a muscle in his upper back. George Lynch led a balanced Tar Heel attack with 14 points, five rebounds, five assists, one blocked

"
I'm not going to hit all of my shots. I just have to continue to shoot.
"

Donald Williams

shot and three steals. Eric Montross had 13 points and eight rebounds. Henrik Rodl, Pat Sullivan and Donald Williams each had 12 points and Derrick Phelps had 10 points, nine assists and three steals.

"It hurts to lose to anyone," said N.C. State coach Les Robinson, "but it especially hurts to lose to Carolina. We rejoiced last year."

With Carolina leading 12-7, the Tar Heels turned up the defensive pressure and held State scoreless for the next seven minutes. By the time State finally scored again, Carolina led 24-9.

N.C. State got within 17 early in the second half, but then the Tar Heels blew the Pack away. When Coach Smith put his reserves in with 10:22 left in the game, they outscored State 32-13 the rest of the way. Freshman Larry Davis scored eight points and got four rebounds. Freshman Ed Geth had six points, three rebounds and two steals in six minutes. On one of Geth's buckets, he intercepted a pass at midcourt and took it the distance for a slam.

Donald Williams, who was only 3-15 in the previous game against Duke, hit 5-9 from the floor, 2-6 from 3-point range. 🏀

Carolina	FG	FT	R	A	TP
Pat Sullivan	6-13	0-0	3	2	12
George Lynch	6-10	2-5	5	5	14
Eric Montross	6-10	1-1	8	1	13
Henrik Rodl	4-8	4-4	5	4	12
Derrick Phelps	4-9	0-1	4	9	10
Donald Williams	5-9	0-0	1	0	12
Kevin Salvadori	2-4	2-4	4	0	6
Matt Wenstrom	1-5	1-2	5	0	3
Dante Calabria	1-2	0-1	1	2	3
Scott Cherry	2-2	0-0	2	3	5
Larry Davis	1-3	6-7	4	0	8
Ed Geth	2-2	2-2	3	0	6
T. Stephenson	0-0	0-0	0	2	0
Team			0		
Totals	40-77	18-27	45	28	104
N.C. State	**FG**	**FT**	**R**	**A**	**TP**
Mark Davis	3-8	1-2	6	1	8
Marc Lewis	6-13	1-3	7	0	13
Kevin Thompson	7-9	1-2	14	2	15
Lakista McCuller	2-10	1-2	3	5	5
Curtis Marshall	1-4	0-0	1	0	2
Todd Fuller	4-8	0-0	3	1	8
Marcus Wilson	1-5	2-2	1	0	4
Victor Newman	1-5	0-1	0	1	3
Team			1		
Totals	25-62	6-12	36	10	58

Three-point goals: Carolina 6-18 (Pat Sullivan 0-3, Henrik Rodl 0-3, Derrick Phelps 2-2, Donald Williams 2-6, Dante Calabria 1-1, Scott Cherry 1-1, Larry Davis 0-2); N. C. State 2-15 (Mark Davis 1-3, Lakista McCuller 0-4, Curtis Marshall 0-1, Marcus Wilson 0-2, Victor Newman 1-5).
Turnovers: Carolina 16, N.C. State 30.

George Lynch goes in for two in a one-sided game against the Wolfpack.

KEYS TO THE GAME: Carolina's defense held N.C. State scoreless for seven minutes in the first half to take a commanding lead...UNC had six players score in double figures...N.C. State had to rely on its 3-point shooting to pull an upset, but the Wolfpack hit only 2-15 from long distance, as Carolina pressured the perimeter...Carolina's bench played brilliantly.

DEAN SMITH COMMENT: "We might have beaten a lot of teams today. We played well. We have a group of good competitors. Now, we're in the second half of the ACC season and we hope to do better than the first half, but it will be hard to accomplish that."

COACH LES ROBINSON COMMENT: "We showed a little spurt there at the start of the second half, but Carolina got tougher at that point, which is the sign of a good team. This will make us tougher and a better team next year. We're looking to next year right now, already talking about coming here to play next year."

Matt Wenstrom hooks over N.C. State's Kevin Thompson, as UNC rebounds with big win.

UNC's Zone Handcuffs Cold-Shooting Terps

The Tar Heels, ranked sixth in the country, overcame a slow start to pick up another key ACC road win by beating Maryland 77-63 on Feb. 9 at Cole Field House. Carolina improved to 19-3 overall, 8-2 in the ACC.

77-63

Maryland coach Gary Williams, who pressed the Tar Heels in Chapel Hill and lost big, decided to go with what a lot of UNC's opponents tried on defense--pack in the middle and try to make Carolina shoot outside. Maryland's plan was to keep Carolina's Eric Montross and George Lynch from beating them. It gave the rest of the Tar Heels some easy shots, but Carolina threw the ball away early and fell behind 17-6 and 19-10.

Carolina played much better in the last 10 minutes of the first half and led 30-23 at halftime. The Tar Heels had that lead at halftime even though they shot only 38.7 percent in the first 20 minutes. Again, UNC could thank its defense, which held Maryland to 29 percent shooting in the first half.

Carolina was efficient in the second half; not spectacular, but very business-like. The Tar Heels maintained the lead throughout the second half and were never seriously threatened. Maryland never got closer than 10 points after UNC went ahead 35-25 with 17:43 left in the game, and Carolina's biggest lead of

"

This team is going to rise to the occasion and do what it has to do to win. It is unfortunate that teams are going to put that many defenders down low, but we've got good and capable outside players who are going to penetrate, get them off of us and allow us to get the dish. Our plays will still work.

"

Eric Montross

the game was at 59-41 with 8:39 left.

The Tar Heels shot 61.5 percent in the second half and 49.1 percent for the game, and outrebounded the Terps 44-30. Derrick Phelps and friends hit enough from the outside to open up things for Montross and George Lynch inside. Montross led the Tar Heels with 17 points and seven rebounds. Lynch had 12 points and 12 rebounds. Phelps added 11 points and eight rebounds, and Pat Sullivan finished with 10 points.

"We gambled defensively early in the game and hoped that they wouldn't shoot well and they didn't," Coach Williams said. "But then we quit hitting our shots and couldn't maintain the lead."

A capacity crowd of 14,500 watched at Cole Field House.

"Maryland has a good zone offense," UNC coach Dean Smith said, "but they're just not hitting their shots. We played more zone tonight than we have in years."

Still, Maryland stayed in this game and played hard. Gary Williams' teams always play hard.

One of the game's best plays came with the Tar Heels running the shot clock down to six seconds, leading 65-53, with about three minutes to play. UNC had the ball out of bounds near midcourt. Phelps took it, and with a burst of speed, drove through the Maryland defense for a layup and a 67-53 advantage. The closest Maryland would get after that would be 11 points.

Brian Reese returned to Carolina's lineup after sitting out the N.C. State game with a pulled back muscle. He had some excellent moments in scoring six points in 20 minutes. This was the first time in many games that Reese felt injury-free.

Carolina forced 20 Maryland turnovers in the game, but committed 22, which was source of concern for Coach Smith.

The victory over Maryland tied Dean Smith with Ed Diddle, who coached at Western Kentucky, for third place on the all-time Division 1 men's basketball victory list with 759 wins, all of them at UNC. "Let's not get started on that," Smith told a reporter. "I usually say that I've coached a long time and we've had some good teams. I'm more excited about winning tonight. Let's focus on this team and what it has done."

Carolina	FG	FT	R	A	TP
Pat Sullivan	4-6	2-4	2	0	10
George Lynch	4-10	4-4	12	1	12
Eric Montross	7-8	3-5	7	0	17
Henrik Rodl	0-3	2-2	1	6	2
Derrick Phelps	5-8	0-0	8	2	11
Donald Williams	2-9	5-5	5	2	9
Brian Reese	3-7	0-0	1	2	6
Kevin Salvadori	2-5	0-1	6	0	4
Dante Calabria	1-1	2-2	0	1	5
Matt Wenstrom	0-0	0-0	0	0	0
Scott Cherry	0-0	1-2	0	0	1
Team			2		
Totals	28-57	19-25	44	14	77
Maryland	**FG**	**FT**	**R**	**A**	**TP**
Exree Hipp	7-13	0-0	6	4	16
Evers Burns	3-13	4-4	4	1	10
Chris Kerwin	1-5	2-2	2	0	4
Johnny Rhodes	5-12	0-0	4	4	13
Kevin McLinton	0-7	4-4	7	6	4
Mario Lucas	4-6	1-2	3	1	10
Duane Simpkins	1-2	0-1	0	1	2
Kurtis Shultz	0-0	0-0	0	0	0
Wayne Bristol	1-4	2-2	3	1	4
John Walsh	0-0	0-0	0	0	0
Team			1		
Totals	22-62	13-15	30	18	63

Three-point goals: Carolina 2-7 (Henrik Rodl 0-2, Derrick Phelps 1-2, Donald Williams 0-1, Brian Reese 0-1, Dante Calabria 1-1); Maryland 6-15 (Exree Hipp 2-3, Johnny Rhodes 3-9, Mario Lucas 1-1, Wayne Bristol 0-2).
Turnovers: Carolina 22, Maryland 20.

KEYS TO THE GAME: Carolina solved Maryland's packed-in defense with some timely second-half shooting, which opened up Montross and Lynch inside. Carolina's zone stopped Maryland cold after the Terps broke to a 17-6 lead.

DEAN SMITH COMMENT: "I think we played much better in the second half than we did in the first, when I thought Maryland was more active than we were. I'm sure that Gary Williams is disappointed, but he is a tremendous coach. He has a young team that is going to keep getting better."

COACH GARY WILLIAMS COMMENT: "George Lynch didn't shoot the ball well tonight, but he had 12 rebounds and does all the things he needs to do to help Carolina win games. The effort was there for us. I think we did okay defensively. I thought we had some good shots in the game, shots that we wanted, that didn't go down."

Eric Montross concentrates on a free throw attempt which would help the Tar Heels to victory in Cole Field House.

UNC Has Late 13-0 Run To Defeat Georgia Tech

One of the key games in North Carolina's drive to the NCAA championship came on Feb. 14 in Atlanta. Georgia Tech, a talented team with national hopes of its own, hosted the Tar Heels in Alexander Coliseum.

77-66

North Carolina had beaten the Yellow Jackets in 12 of the last 15 meetings between the two teams, most recently on Jan. 13 in Chapel Hill, and coach Bobby Cremins and his team were thinking payback.

But the Tar Heels, down 36-31 at halftime, played a sparkling second half on offense and defense to win, 77-66. The victory, televised nationally on ABC, put Carolina's record at 20-3 overall, and kept it tied for first in the ACC with Florida State, each with 9-2 league marks. It also became the 23rd straight season that Dean Smith's Carolina program had won 20 or more games, a remarkable record in consistency, as well as an NCAA record.

This was an up and down season for Georgia Tech. The Yellow Jackets beat Duke in Alexander earlier in the season, and had other impressive wins. However, Tech had also slipped against some teams it was expected to beat, and when Carolina came calling, the men from Atlanta needed a win over a top opponent to help its NCAA tournament hopes. Tech's record fell to 12-8 overall, 5-6 in the ACC, with the loss.

Carolina trailed 36-27 late in the first half before cutting the deficit to five at halftime. The Tar Heels scorched Georgia Tech at the start of the second half, outscoring the home team 10-2 to take a 41-38 lead.

But the Tar Heels were a long way from victory. Forward George Lynch got his fourth foul with 16:30 left in the game and Georgia Tech regained the lead at 42-41 a minute later. UNC's Pat Sullivan picked up his fourth foul with 13:40 left.

Still, Carolina led most of the second half, and was in front 64-63 when Lynch fouled out with 4:51 to play.

This was a Carolina team that almost always played well at crunch time. Donald Williams, who scored 15 points in the second half, hit one of his baskets to make the score 66-63. Then Brian Reese scored, followed by a Derrick Phelps steal and dunk, and then out of the Four Corners, Williams scored, and then Montross. From a 64-63 game, the Tar Heels turned up their defensive pressure and scored 13 straight points to crack it open and win by 11.

Carolina shot 64.3 percent in the second half while holding Tech to 37.5 percent. Williams led Carolina with 21 points.

"I kidded Donald at halftime," Coach Smith said. "I came up to him and said, 'It's time for you to come on, young man.' He smiled and I smiled. I hope it worked."

Carolina's offense sputtered and stalled in the first half, when it hit only 33 percent from the field against Tech's packed-in zone. Eric Montross was held to two points in the first half, but he was much more active in the second half, when he scored 10 points. Point guard Derrick Phelps was the catalyst with 13 points, seven assists, one turnover, four steals.

James Forrest lead Georgia Tech with 18 points and Travis Best had 17. ●

Derrick Phelps looks for some help.

Carolina	FG	FT	R	A	TP
Henrik Rodl	1-2	0-0	1	5	3
George Lynch	3-8	1-2	4	0	7
Eric Montross	4-8	4-5	9	1	12
Derrick Phelps	5-8	2-2	2	7	13
Brian Reese	4-9	0-0	3	1	9
Pat Sullivan	0-4	4-6	4	1	4
Donald Williams	8-15	2-4	1	2	21
Kevin Salvadori	4-7	0-0	6	1	8
Matt Wenstrom	0-0	0-0	1	0	0
Dante Calabria	0-0	0-0	0	0	0
Scott Cherry	0-0	0-0	0	0	0
Team			3		
Totals	29-61	13-19	34	18	77
Georgia Tech	**FG**	**FT**	**R**	**A**	**TP**
Martice Moore	2-9	0-0	6	2	4
James Forrest	7-12	4-5	13	1	18
Malcolm Mackey	2-7	3-3	5	0	7
Travis Best	6-12	3-3	2	1	17
Drew Barry	4-7	2-2	3	6	13
Bryan Hill	1-4	3-4	1	3	5
Ivano Newbill	1-2	0-0	1	0	2
Rod Balanis	0-0	0-0	0	0	0
Todd Harlicka	0-0	0-0	0	0	0
Team			2		
Totals	23-53	15-17	33	13	66

Three-point goals: Carolina 6-13 (Henrik Rodl 1-2, Derrick Phelps 1-1, Brian Reese 1-2, Pat Sullivan 0-1, Donald Williams 3-7); Georgia Tech 5-13 (Martice Moore 0-3, Travis Best 2-3, Drew Barry 3-4, Bryan Hill 0-2, Ivano Newbill 0-1.)
Turnovers: Carolina 11, Georgia Tech 18.

KEYS TO THE GAME: Carolina did it again down the stretch. Leading 64-63, and with George Lynch out of the game on fouls, UNC outscored Tech 13-0 to win the game.

DEAN SMITH COMMENT: "I'm really proud of the way we played. I think this is the best we've played all year. I'm impressed with Georgia Tech and I've been impressed with them all year long. We did some really nice things in the second half. We caused some turnovers to start the half and that made it easier on us."

COACH BOBBY CREMINS COMMENT: "I thought we played a pretty good game. They just beat us in the end. We had a key possession with about three minutes left when we turned the ball over. The key to the game was turnovers."

Eric Montross finishes off a dunk in Carolina's win at Georgia Tech.

UNC Survives Whitney's Clinic On 3-Pointers

Sooner or later, the law of averages is going to catch up with the Tar Heels. After all, Clemson has never beaten Carolina in basketball in Chapel Hill. Never.

80-67 That was very much on the mind of the Tigers when they came to the Smith Center on Feb. 17. Clemson, behind superlative performances by guard Chris Whitney and center Sharone Wright, came close. In fact, the Tar Heels had to play one of their finest games to win, 80-67.

"I want our players to be proud of beating a very good Clemson team that was having a good night," coach Dean Smith said.

The win improved UNC's record to 21-3, 10-2 in the ACC, while the Tigers dropped to 12-9, 2-9. Carolina was still tied with Florida State for first place in the ACC.

Carolina led by 10 at halftime, but the Tigers shot a blistering 57.7 percent, 72.7 from 3-point range, in the second half. After some of Clemson's shots, it seemed that fate was going to get the Tigers over the hump in this game.

Carolina actually played well to begin the second half, well enough to break open many games. But Clemson guard Chris Whitney, who had only three points in the first half, suddenly found the range. No matter how closely he was guarded or how far he was from the basket, Whitney became deadly from 3-point range.

Whitney had three baskets from 3-point range in the first seven minutes of the second half, as Carolina led 49-39. The game was one of swapping baskets in the second half, but with eight minutes to play, Carolina didn't appear to be in much trouble as it led 66-53.

Then the drama began. Whitney hit a 3-pointer, Devin Gray made two foul shots, Sharone Wright got a dunk. Carolina's lead was down to 66-60 with just under seven minutes to play. The crowd of 21,147 at the Smith Center began to buzz like a hive of bees.

Whitney, well covered and far from the basket, nailed another 3-pointer with 4:04 left to cut Carolina's lead to 70-65. But then Clemson's Wayne Buckingham turned it over and Carolina, again playing well down the stretch, scored nine straight points to lead 79-65 and clinch the victory.

The game was much closer than that. After Whitney hit the "three" to bring his team within 70-65, Carolina double-teamed him every time he touched the ball, forcing him to pass it. Whitney scored 24 points, 21 of them in the second half, and he hit 8-10 from 3-point range. Wright, meanwhile, was also sensational. He scored 20 points, got 12 rebounds and blocked seven shots.

Eric Montross led Carolina with 22 points and Brian Reese, coming on strong after recovering from injuries, had 18. Derrick Phelps had 12 points and eight assists, and George Lynch had five steals.

Carolina had to shoot the ball well to win this game, and it did. The Tar Heels hit 55 percent from the field. Clemson shot 57.7 percent in the second half, 47 percent for the game.

At one point in the second half, Carolina's Phelps said to the hot-shooting Whitney: "Cool it, you're embarrassing me out here."

Clemson is now 0-39 against Carolina in basketball in Chapel Hill. Clemson coach Cliff Ellis said that streak had "absolutely nothing to do with the outcome of this game." ✸

Derrick Phelps drives to the basket for an easy two.

Carolina	FG	FT	R	A	TP
George Lynch	4-11	0-0	5	2	8
Eric Montross	9-15	4-6	7	1	22
Brian Reese	8-11	0-0	4	1	18
Derrick Phelps	6-12	0-0	6	8	12
Henrik Rodl	1-2	0-0	2	6	2
Dante Calabria	2-3	0-0	0	0	4
Pat Sullivan	1-1	0-0	0	1	3
Donald Williams	1-4	6-8	1	2	8
Kevin Salvadori	1-1	0-0	2	0	2
Matt Wenstrom	0-0	1-2	1	0	1
Ed Geth	0-0	0-0	0	0	0
Scott Cherry	0-0	0-0	0	0	0
Larry Davis	0-0	0-0	0	0	0
Team			1		
Totals	33-60	11-16	29	21	80
Clemson	FG	FT	R	A	TP
Jeff Brown	4-13	0-0	4	0	10
W. Buckingham	1-3	0-0	1	1	2
Sharone Wright	8-12	4-6	12	0	20
Chris Whitney	8-11	0-0	4	6	24
Andre Bovain	1-1	0-0	1	0	2
Devin Gray	2-8	3-4	5	0	7
Bruce Martin	0-3	0-0	2	0	0
Frank Tomera	0-1	0-0	0	0	0
Lou Richie	1-1	0-0	2	3	2
Team			2		
Totals	25-53	7-10	29	14	67

Three-point goals: Carolina 3-10 (Brian Reese 2-3, Derrick Phelps 0-2, Henrik Rodl 0-1, Dante Calabria 0-1, Pat Sullivan 1-1, Donald Williams 0-2); Clemson 10-19 (Jeff Brown 2-5, Chris Whitney 8-10, Devin Gray 0-1, Bruce Martin 0-3). **Turnovers:** Carolina 14, Clemson 22.

KEYS TO THE GAME: With Clemson's Whitney lighting it up from 3-point range, Carolina's offense kept producing good shots. It was as if Carolina was getting two points to Clemson's three in the second half...UNC again was excellent at "winning time." After Clemson came within 70-65, the Tar Heels scored nine straight points.

DEAN SMITH COMMENT: "I'm proud of the way our team reacted when Clemson cut our lead to five. Many teams would have folded there, but our players seemed to get even more resolve."

COACH CLIFF ELLIS COMMENT: "It was a hard-fought effort on our part. We showed courage, we played extremely well. Montross down low got some big buckets. Whitney hit his 'threes' in the second half. We gave it a heck of an effort. It was a battle, a big battle."

Brian Reese slams one home as Clemson's Wayne Buckingham watches.

First-Half Defense Silences UVa Crowd

78-58

North Carolina, playing maybe its best defensive half of the season, held Virginia to 25.8 percent field goal shooting in the first half in Charlottesville on Feb. 21, built a 42-22 halftime lead and went on to win a key ACC game, 78-58, before 8,864 fans at University Hall.

"We're trying to improve, because we must if we expect to contend in the NCAA tournament," UNC coach Dean Smith said after the game.

Carolina improved to 22-3, 11-2 in the ACC, still tied with Florida State atop the ACC standings. UVa dropped to 16-6, 8-5 in the ACC.

Virginia's sagging man-to-man defense was designed to keep opponents from getting the ball inside for high percentage shots. Nevertheless, Carolina's offense got the ball down low for a 50 percent field goal percentage in the decisive first half.

Carolina put Virginia on its heels by storming to a 15-5 lead in the game's first six minutes. Carolina's defense was all over the Cavaliers, seldom giving the team in orange a decent look at the basket. When television stopped the game for a timeout with 7:55 left in the first half, Carolina was ahead 31-13. The Virginia crowd was stunned and pretty much taken out of the game by Carolina's overpowering beginning.

The Tar Heels led 39-15 with 3:22 left in the half only to see Virginia score seven straight points. UNC got the last three points of the half to lead 42-22.

The game never got close in the second half. The Tar Heels led by 26 on several occasions before clearing the bench and settling for a 78-58 road victory.

"The lion's share of the credit goes to North Carolina's defense," said Virginia coach Jeff Jones. "They took us out of everything that we wanted to do on offense, and they got much of their offense from their defense. Their defense is by far better than any team we've faced."

Meanwhile, on offense, Carolina used sharp passing, crisp cuts, good screens and patience to get the ball inside. Eric Montross and George Lynch each had 17 points for UNC, Brian Reese had 11, and Pat Sullivan and Derrick Phelps 10 each.

Montross scored eight of UNC's first 15 points as the Tar Heels got the inside game established early.

Virginia made a brief rally in the second half, cutting UNC's lead to 42-26. Carolina scored four straight points to silence the crowd and bury any hopes Virginia might have entertained about coming back.

UNC continued to show that it was an excellent road team. Hostile surroundings did not intimidate the Tar Heels. 🏀

> "This could be the best Carolina team I've played on. Of course, I did play on the team that went to the Final Four two years ago, but I don't believe it was as strong as this year's team."
>
> George Lynch

Carolina	FG	FT	R	A	TP
Brian Reese	4-8	2-4	6	2	11
George Lynch	6-11	5-5	11	3	17
Eric Montross	7-13	3-4	7	1	17
Derrick Phelps	3-8	3-3	7	5	10
Donald Williams	1-4	0-0	2	1	2
Henrik Rodl	0-1	4-4	2	2	4
Pat Sullivan	3-3	4-4	0	0	10
Kevin Salvadori	0-2	0-0	1	0	0
Matt Wenstrom	1-3	0-0	1	0	2
Dante Calabria	1-2	0-0	0	2	2
Scott Cherry	0-0	1-2	0	0	1
Ed Geth	0-1	0-0	1	0	0
Larry Davis	1-1	0-0	0	0	2
T. Stephenson	0-0	0-0	0	0	0
Team			2		
Totals	27-57	22-26	40	16	78
Virginia	**FG**	**FT**	**R**	**A**	**TP**
Junior Burrough	7-15	5-6	9	0	19
Jason Williford	1-1	0-0	0	1	2
Ted Jeffries	2-8	4-4	6	0	8
Cornel Parker	1-11	1-2	5	2	4
Cory Alexander	4-14	0-1	3	6	10
Doug Smith	2-7	2-2	3	2	8
Yuri Barnes	1-2	0-0	5	0	2
Chris Havlicek	0-3	0-0	2	1	0
Shawn Wilson	2-3	1-2	4	0	5
Chris Alexander	0-0	0-0	1	0	0
Bobby Graves	0-0	0-0	0	0	0
Team			1		
Totals	20-64	13-17	39	12	58

Three-point goals: Carolina 2-8 (Brian Reese 1-2, Derrick Phelps 1-2, Donald Williams 0-2, Henrik Rodl 0-1, Dante Calabria 0-1); Virginia 5-18 (Cornel Parker 1-5, Cory Alexander 2-6, Doug Smith 2-7).
Turnovers: Carolina 12, Virginia 16.

Brian Reese

KEYS TO THE GAME: Carolina's defense in the first half would not allow Virginia to run its offense. And by jumping to a 20-point lead at halftime, the Tar Heels took Virginia's capacity crowd out of the game...Derrick Phelps held Virginia point guard Cory Alexander to 4-14 shooting...UNC was able to get the ball inside, even though Virginia's defense was designed to keep it from doing so.

DEAN SMITH COMMENT: "Fortunately, Virginia didn't shoot well. Our defense did some good things. Derrick Phelps did a great job on Cory Alexander, who can get it going and often does. This is a great win for us. We've played awfully well the last four or five games. Brian Reese, after being hurt since the N.C. State game, has played very good basketball the last couple of games."

COACH JEFF JONES COMMENT: "North Carolina was very, very good. I cannot think of one aspect of their play that I wouldn't term as outstanding or excellent. We didn't have the right answer to the way they were playing. Their defense was exceptional. They were definitely ready to play. They came out and played extremely well. They jumped on us early and we were not able to keep up, and things just got bigger and bigger for them. I really think they fed on that."

Notre Dame No Match For High-Flying UNC

85-56

One of the most impressive things about North Carolina's basketball team was its ability to focus on the task at hand and not get too far ahead of itself.

When Notre Dame came to Chapel Hill with a 9-14 record on Tuesday night, Feb. 23, there is no doubt that the Tar Heels were thinking just a little into the future, to Saturday when they would travel to Tallahassee to play Florida State for first place in the ACC standings.

Carolina knew, however, that before it could play Florida State, it had to take care of Notre Dame. The Irish defeated UNC the previous season, and a loss at home to Notre Dame, which had played a tough schedule, could hurt Carolina's NCAA tournament seeding. In other words, it was a game Carolina could not afford to lose.

This would be the last out-of-conference game for Carolina before the NCAA tournament. The Tar Heels concentrated on the business at hand and won easily over the Irish, 85-56 in the Smith Center. Carolina didn't run away and hide from the game's outset. When Joe Ross scored for the Irish with 5:30 left in the first half, Carolina's lead was only 28-23. Notre Dame was doing a good job of controlling tempo and was not turning the ball over much against Carolina's traps.

Pat Sullivan stole a Notre Dame pass and fed Donald Williams for a basket just before the horn as UNC led 40-27 at halftime.

Carolina built the lead to 52-31 early in the second half and Notre Dame never challenged. Coach Dean Smith cleared his bench midway through the second half, and when freshman

> *Playing against a non-conference team at this stage of the season will help prepare us for some of the teams we might see in the NCAA tournament.*
>
> *George Lynch*

Ed Geth hit a foul shot with 6:14 left, the Tar Heels led 70-33.

"I am very, very impressed with North Carolina," said Notre Dame coach John MacLeod, whose team had played Indiana, Kentucky, Michigan, Duke, Marquette, UCLA and New Orleans before coming to Chapel Hill. "Their defense would not let us run an offense. They pressed us, trapped us, chased us out of our offense."

Carolina held the Irish to 38.2 percent shooting for the game, outrebounded them 47-24, created 19 turnovers and finished with 12 steals. The Tar Heels, meanwhile, shot 49.2 percent, even though they hit only 1-11 from 3-point range.

"North Carolina is right up there with the best, with the top six or seven that have the best chance of winning it all," MacLeod said. "They are as good as anybody. Dean Smith has done a great job with this squad. This team has improved significantly over last year's team. They are a fun team to watch and I'm sure it's fun to coach them. I'm impressed. They look good. They have tremendous team play, very unselfish. They're strong, rangy and athletic, and they have good depth."

Eric Montross led UNC with 19 points. George Lynch and Brian Reese had 11 points and eight rebounds each, and Kevin Salvadori had another impressive showing with eight points, six rebounds and two blocked shots.

"It was a sound strategy," UNC coach Dean Smith said of Notre Dame's plan to slow tempo. "It caused us to chase and gamble."

Carolina seemed to get a spark when Notre Dame star Monty Williams started "wolfing" at George Lynch. Reese and Montross came to Lynch's defense, and the crowd of 21,572 finally got into the game. Lynch turned up his defense another notch and the Tar Heels outscored Notre Dame 12-4 the rest of the first half and led 40-27 at intermission.

Everybody in uniform played for Carolina, including Pearce Landry, the leading scorer on the Tar Heel junior varsity team. No Tar Heel played more than 24 minutes in this lopsided victory.

Carolina improved to 23-3, while Notre Dame's record became 9-15.

Carolina	FG	FT	R	A	TP
Brian Reese	3-7	5-6	8	4	11
George Lynch	3-7	0-0	8	2	6
Eric Montross	6-9	7-11	4	0	19
Donald Williams	3-8	0-0	3	1	7
Derrick Phelps	1-3	4-8	3	4	6
Pat Sullivan	3-6	1-1	0	2	7
Henrik Rodl	1-2	0-0	0	1	2
Kevin Salvadori	3-6	2-2	6	0	8
Matt Wenstrom	2-3	0-0	4	0	4
Dante Calabria	0-1	0-0	2	1	0
Scott Cherry	2-4	2-3	3	1	6
Larry Davis	1-3	0-2	1	0	2
Ed Geth	1-1	1-2	2	0	3
T. Stephenson	2-2	0-0	1	0	4
Pearce Landry	0-1	0-0	1	1	0
Team			1		
Totals	31-63	22-35	47	17	85
Notre Dame	**FG**	**FT**	**R**	**A**	**TP**
Billy Taylor	2-6	1-2	1	0	5
Monty Williams	8-21	4-4	5	1	20
Jon Ross	2-4	0-0	5	1	4
Lamarr Justice	1-4	0-0	1	3	3
Ryan Hoover	4-11	2-2	2	2	12
Brooks Boyer	0-2	0-0	1	1	0
Malik Russell	1-1	2-4	3	1	4
Joe Ross	2-3	0-0	2	2	4
Sean Ryan	0-0	1-2	0	0	1
Matt Adamson	1-3	0-0	1	0	3
Patrick Keaney	0-0	0-0	0	0	0
Team			3		
Totals	21-55	10-14	24	11	56

Three-point goals: Carolina 1-11 (Brian Reese 0-1, Donald Williams 1-5, Derrick Phelps 0-1, Pat Sullivan 0-1, Henrik Rodl 0-1, Dante Calabria 0-1, Larry Davis 0-1); Notre Dame 4-16 (Monty Williams 0-3, Jon Ross 0-1, Lamarr Justice 1-1, Ryan Hoover 2-8, Brooks Boyer 0-1, Matt Adamson 1-2).

Turnovers: Carolina 13, Notre Dame 19.

KEYS TO THE GAME: Carolina kept its eyes on the target, which was Notre Dame. UNC's defense made Notre Dame play at a faster pace than the Irish wanted.

DEAN SMITH COMMENT: "We played hard defensively in the first half. We have to get it out of our mindset that we're supposed to win games like this. I was impressed with George Lynch's play. For those of you who are so hung up on points scored, look at Lynch's game tonight. He rebounded, played defense, hustled for loose balls."

COACH JOHN MACLEOD COMMENT: "North Carolina does a good job of getting the ball inside to Montross. We couldn't handle that big bear once he got it."

Senior reserve Scott Cherry beats Notre Dame's Ryan Hoover in the open court.

Tar Heels Overcome Odds To Beat FSU On The Road

Set the scene when Carolina went to Tallahassee on Feb. 27 to play Florida State:

-The Seminoles had a 21-point lead in the second half at Chapel Hill, only to see the Tar Heels rally and win. They were still angry about that.

86-76

-Florida State coach Pat Kennedy later said that the game had been taken out of the hands of the players in the last nine minutes, a not-so-subtle criticism of the officiating.

-Kennedy was upset that Carolina's crowd rushed the court after the game in Chapel Hill.

-Florida State, the previous Wednesday, had been humiliated at Duke. The Seminoles needed a win over Carolina to make things right.

-It was Senior Day at Tallahassee, the last home game for stars such as Douglas Edwards and Sam Cassell.

-Carolina and Florida State were playing for first place in the ACC standings.

A perfect setting for Carolina basketball on the road, wouldn't you say?

This game had it all from the very beginning. Neither team could build a working margin. Carolina led for most of the way in the first half, but only by margins ranging from one to three points. FSU's Maurice Robinson scored just before the halftime horn to tie the game at 33 at the half.

Carolina shot 40 percent in the first half to FSU's 53.8 percent. Carolina got the backboards, 21-15, and had seven turnovers to Florida State's 10.

The second half was tense and highly

> *What a great basketball game...You saw two teams out there today that tried very hard. I didn't know if we could win even if we played well.*
>
> North Carolina Coach
> Dean Smith

competitive. Carolina worked its way to a 54-47 lead, only to see FSU tie the game at 56 on a Sam Cassell 3-pointer.

Carolina, leading 61-58, had one of its crucial spurts. Brian Reese, who had a sensational game, scored in the lane to give Carolina a 63-58 lead with 6:09 left. Then Reese scored on a follow shot, Donald Williams made two foul shots, and UNC's lead was 67-58 with 5:17 left. Carolina then trapped Cassell, drawing a charge. Out of the Four Corners, Derrick Phelps passed to Eric Montross for a basket and a 69-58 Carolina lead with 4:46 left.

Rodl stole the ball, passed to Phelps going to the basket, who was hit hard from behind and knocked down by FSU's Rodney Dobard. Donald Williams shot Phelps' free throws, made them both and UNC led 71-58 with 4:34 left. That was a 10-0 Carolina spurt.

Carolina went to its Four Corners offense the rest of the way to win, 86-76. It was one of the best wins of the season.

"What a great basketball game," coach Dean Smith said. "You saw two teams out there today that tried very hard. I didn't know if we could win even if we played well."

Brian Reese, healthy and on the top of his game, had a career-high 25 points on 11-18 shooting. George Lynch had 16 points, 10 rebounds and five steals. Eric Montross added 15 points and Donald Williams had 13. Derrick Phelps had 10 assists.

Henrik Rodl hit two 3-point baskets in the first half that were big for the Tar Heels. Lynch's 12 points and 10 rebounds in the first 20 minutes kept the Tar Heels in the game.

The victory clinched at least a tie for first place in the ACC standings for the Tar Heels. Their record went to 24-3, 12-2 in the ACC. Florida State's ACC mark was 11-4.

As Carolina's players filed towards the bus waiting to take them to the airport for the charter flight back to Chapel Hill, one FSU fan said to another: "They're used to winning games like this."

Dean Smith didn't return to Chapel Hill with the team. He and wife Linnea spent the night in Florida, to celebrate his 62nd birthday.

Carolina	FG	FT	R	A	TP
Eric Montross	5-10	5-5	5	1	15
Derrick Phelps	2-2	0-2	6	10	4
Donald Williams	3-12	6-6	1	0	13
Brian Reese	11-18	2-3	6	1	25
George Lynch	7-14	2-2	10	1	16
Pat Sullivan	0-2	2-2	3	1	2
Henrik Rodl	2-2	0-2	0	2	6
Dante Calabria	1-1	1-2	2	1	3
Kevin Salvadori	1-4	0-0	3	0	2
Team			4		
Totals	32-65	18-24	40	17	86
Florida State	FG	FT	R	A	TP
Sam Cassell	5-11	6-7	4	5	18
Bob Sura	6-17	1-3	3	5	14
Doug Edwards	9-13	5-6	10	4	23
Byron Wells	3-8	0-0	5	1	6
Rodney Dobard	4-6	1-2	3	0	9
Lorenzo Hands	0-1	0-0	0	0	0
M. Robinson	3-6	0-1	3	0	6
Team			3		
Totals	30-62	13-19	31	15	76

Three-point goals: Carolina 4-11 (Donald Williams 1-6, Brian Reese 1-3, Henrik Rodl 2-2); Florida State 3-21 (Sam Cassell 2-5, Bob Sura 1-12, Doug Edwards 0-1, Byron wells 0-3).
Turnovers: Carolina 15, Florida State 18.

KEYS TO THE GAME: Carolina's 10-0 run late in the game took its lead from 61-58 to 71-58. Again, the Tar Heels were at their best when the game was on the line...Brian Reese had 25 points.

DEAN SMITH COMMENT: "We got a little conservative in our press offense and we certainly don't want that to happen. Ideally, we wanted this game to be in the 60s, and that's hard to tell a team that is averaging almost 90 points a game, but we thought we needed some form of tempo in this game. I think Brian Reese did some excellent driving against their zone defense. It was his coming out party offensively. His injuries are behind him now and he's playing well."

Brian Reese steps in to make it tough on Florida State's Bob Sura in Tallahassee.

UNC Beats Deacs To Win ACC Regular Season Race

83-65

The lowest point in Carolina's season was in Winston-Salem on Jan. 30 when Wake Forest blasted the Tar Heels, 88-62.

So, when Wake Forest came to the Smith Center on March 3 for a rematch, Carolina didn't need any additional incentives--but it had one, anyhow.

A Carolina win would give the Tar Heels the outright ACC regular season championship, which was one of the team's goals in the preseason.

North Carolina, which won the game 83-65, wasted no time in establishing its superiority. After Randolph Childress, who tortured Carolina in Winston-Salem with his outside shooting, hit a 3-pointer to make the score 19-15 in UNC's favor, the Tar Heels got balanced scoring and outscored the Deacons 19-1 to lead 38-16 with 5:35 left in the first half.

Wake Forest cut that Carolina lead to 45-27 at the half, but the Tar Heels appeared to be completely in charge of the game. UNC hit

61 percent of its field goals in the first half to 43 percent for the Deacons. Wake Forest had no offensive rebounds at the half and eight turnovers.

Carolina was clicking inside and out. Brian Reese had 13 points, George Lynch 12 and Eric Montross 10 at halftime for the Tar Heels, while Donald Williams had six points, on two 3-point baskets.

Wake Forest, a team that would finish tied with Duke for third place in the ACC standings, and would also advance to the NCAA Final 16, could get no closer than 10 points in the second half.

Carolina put four players in double figures, dominated the backboards, had six fewer turnovers than the Deacons. Derrick Phelps continued his excellent assist-error ratio with seven assists and only one turnover.

It was a big night for Carolina basketball. The Tar Heels clinched the ACC regular season championship, and it was the 16th time in 32 years that Dean Smith's teams have either tied for this honor or won it outright, an amazing achievement.

UNC improved to 25-3 with the win, 13-2 in the ACC, while Wake slipped to 18-7, 9-6. Smith now has 19 seasons when his teams have won 25 or more games, the most of any coach in the history of major college basketball. Former Las Vegas coach Jerry Tarkanian had 14 such seasons and UCLA legend John Wooden had 11.

"This was a well-played game," UNC coach Dean Smith said. "There were not many turnovers and the shooting was excellent. Our rebounding in the first half was a key. We gave them no second shots."

Carolina's first-half assault was impressive, both inside and on the perimeter. When the Deacons bunched their zone around Eric Montross, then Brian Reese and Donald Williams stepped outside to hit 4-4 from 3-point range. And when Wake had to go outside to cover the perimeter, Montross and Lynch dominated inside.

"North Carolina played awfully well," Wake coach Dave Odom said. "That's as good as I've seen them play this year, especially in the first half."

Brian Reese scores an easy bucket against the Wake Forest defense.

Carolina	FG	FT	R	A	TP
Brian Reese	6-11	1-2	3	4	16
George Lynch	9-16	0-0	7	4	18
Eric Montross	7-8	3-4	6	0	17
Donald Williams	4-9	3-4	1	0	13
Derrick Phelps	2-5	0-0	5	7	4
Pat Sullivan	1-3	0-0	0	1	2
Henrik Rodl	2-4	0-0	2	2	4
Kevin Salvadori	1-2	5-6	7	0	7
Dante Calabria	0-1	0-0	1	0	0
Larry Davis	0-0	0-0	0	0	0
Scott Cherry	0-0	0-0	0	1	0
Ed Geth	0-0	0-0	0	0	0
Matt Wenstrom	1-1	0-0	0	0	2
Team			1		
Totals	33-60	12-16	33	19	83
Wake Forest	**FG**	**FT**	**R**	**A**	**TP**
Trelonnie Owens	3-11	0-0	3	2	6
Rodney Rogers	4-12	4-6	8	3	12
Derrick Hicks	3-3	0-0	5	3	6
R. Childress	5-10	2-2	1	4	16
Charlie Harrison	2-4	0-0	0	4	4
Marc Blucas	4-7	2-2	2	1	14
Travis Banks	1-1	1-1	0	0	3
D. Rasmussen	1-2	0-0	3	0	3
Stacey Castle	0-0	1-2	0	0	1
Rusty LaRue	0-1	0-0	0	0	0
B. Fitzgibbons	0-0	0-0	0	0	0
Barry Canty	0-0	0-0	0	0	0
Team			0		
Totals	23-51	10-13	22	17	65

Three-point goals: Carolina 5-9 (Brian Reese 3-3, Donald Williams 2-3, Derrick Phelps 0-1, Henrik Rodl 0-1, Dante Calabria 0-1); Wake Forest 9-18 (Trelonnie Owens 0-1, Rodney Rogers 0-2, Randolph Childress 4-6, Marc Blucas 4-6, David Rasmussen 1-2, Rusty LaRue 0-1).
Turnovers: Carolina 9, Wake Forest 15.

KEYS TO THE GAME: Carolina dominated the backboards in the first half and allowed Wake Forest no second shots...George Lynch's defense against Wake star Rodney Rogers was excellent, as Rogers hit only 4-12 from the field...Eric Montross was 7-8 from the field...Derrick Phelps had seven assists and four rebounds...Trelonnie Owens, who hurt Carolina in Winston-Salem, was only 3-11 from the field .

DEAN SMITH COMMENT: "Our rebounding in the first half was a key. We gave them no second shots. Reese's 3-pointer when Wake cut the lead to 10 in the second half was a big play. I think our players were confident in the second half. We were getting good shots, and when you continue to do that, you usually come out ahead."

COACH DAVE ODOM COMMENT: "Anytime North Carolina shoots like they did tonight, and us not being able to convert our shots, it's difficult to beat them. I challenged our team to compete in the second half, and they did. I'm proud of them for that. We competed hard for 40 minutes and especially in the second half."

Donald Williams takes aim against Deacons, as Brian Reese gets rebounding position.

Carolina's 16-1 Spurt Keys Emotional Victory

83-69

A lot is usually at stake when North Carolina plays Duke in basketball, especially when it comes as the last game of the regular season.

But when the Blue Devils visited the Smith Center on March 7, there was only one thing on the line--pride. These two programs, located only eight miles apart, don't like to lose to each other, so you never have to worry about the intensity level when they play each other. It is high.

Carolina had the ACC regular season championship locked up before the game with Duke ever tipped off. Duke could have taken third place in the conference outright with a win in Chapel Hill, but that wasn't seen as crucial to Duke's postseason chances.

This was Senior Day in Chapel Hill. Carolina fans were saying goodbye to five seniors who were among the best leaders ever to play for Dean Smith at Carolina. George Lynch, Henrik Rodl, Scott Cherry, Matt Wenstrom and Travis Stephenson had their families at courtside as they were introduced to the home crowd for the last time.

Dean Smith started those five seniors in this game, and they played well while they were in there together. But it was a sophomore by the name of Donald Williams, who hit only 3-15 shots when Carolina lost at Duke in February, who had the most to prove.

"That first Duke game was like a bad dream," Williams said. He was ready for this one.

In a game between two rivals, you don't look for one to take the lead early and keep it. These games aren't usually played that way. More likely, they go back and forth, the lead switching hands, the tension high.

This game was different in that regard. Duke freshman Chris Collins hit a 3-pointer to give Duke a 3-0 lead, but when Williams scored to put Carolina ahead 4-3, Duke never led again in the game, nor was it ever tied.

Before 21,572 fans in the Smith Center on Senior Day, this was Carolina's afternoon.

Williams hit a 3-pointer over Collins to make Carolina's lead 11-6. Then Eric Montross scored on a dunk, and Williams on back-to-back 3-pointers to make it 19-8 with 11 :30 left in the half.

Duke made defensive switches in an attempt to slow down Williams and the Tar Heels, but there would be no stopping them in this game.

Carolina's attack was working inside and out, and while UNC was hitting 58 percent of its shots in the first half, defensive ace Derrick Phelps was doing a number on Duke star point guard Bobby Hurley, who hit only 2-12 from the floor.

Carolina also took care of the rebounding in the first half, getting 18 to Duke's 12, and guard Phelps led Carolina with five. The Tar Heels also had four fewer turnovers than the Blue Devils in the first half.

North Carolina came out of its halftime meeting in a nasty mood and jumped all over Duke. Carolina scored the first 10 points of the half to lead, 50-30. The capacity crowd rocked the Smith Center, wanting revenge for the loss in Durham.

Duke was not about to quit, however. Good competitors don't, and Duke is certainly that. After trailing 59-36 with 14:15 left in the game, Duke went on a tear of its own. Duke hit three baskets from 3-point range as it outscored Carolina 18-5 to pull within 64-54 with 8:50 left.

But Carolina got going again behind Williams, Lynch and Montross and built the lead back to 76-58 with five minutes left. Duke would not be able to come back from that deficit.

"We're very happy for our seniors to go out this way," UNC coach Dean Smith said. "But this is just the end of the regular season. Now, we look forward to the ACC tournament."

Carolina's defense held Duke without a field goal for nearly six minutes to start the second half, as the Tar Heels outscored the visitors 16-1 to build a commanding lead. Montross was a horse during that run, scoring five straight times and blocking a shot, which helped give Carolina a 56-31 lead at that point, the biggest of the game.

Duke fired 26 shots from 3-point range and made nine. Duke was forced into the long distance offense to try to make up the big deficit. After Duke rallied to within 69-57, a big sequence occurred.

Montross got loose on the inside, but before he could score, Duke's Antonio Lang

Carolina	FG	FT	R	A	TP
George Lynch	6-10	0-3	11	1	12
T. Stephenson	1-1	0-0	0	0	2
Matt Wenstrom	0-0	0-0	1	0	0
Henrik Rodl	0-1	0-2	0	3	0
Scott Cherry	1-2	0-0	0	0	2
Derrick Phelps	3-6	2-2	9	7	8
Eric Montross	6-9	6-11	7	1	18
Donald Williams	10-15	2-2	1	1	27
Brian Reese	4-8	2-4	4	3	10
Pat Sullivan	1-3	0-0	2	0	2
Kevin Salvadori	1-3	0-0	3	1	2
Larry Davis	0-1	0-0	0	0	0
Dante Calabria	0-0	0-0	0	1	0
Ed Geth	0-1	0-0	1	0	0
Team			4		
Totals	33-60	12-24	43	18	83
Duke	**FG**	**FT**	**R**	**A**	**TP**
Thomas Hill	4-13	4-4	2	1	13
Antonio Lang	1-6	3-4	9	0	5
Cherokee Parks	3-6	1-1	2	0	7
Chris Collins	4-10	3-4	4	5	15
Bobby Hurley	2-12	1-3	4	6	6
Marty Clark	4-6	1-2	2	2	12
Kenny Blakeney	2-4	1-1	2	1	5
Erik Meek	2-4	0-0	3	1	4
Kenney Brown	0-0	2-3	2	0	2
Stan Brunson	0-1	0-0	1	0	0
Team			0		
Totals	22-62	16-22	31	16	69

Three-point goals: Carolina 5-12 (Derrick Phelps 0-2, Donald Williams 5-8, Brian Reese 0-2); Duke 9-26 (Thomas Hill 1-5, Antonio Lang 0-1, Chris Collins 4-8, Bobby Hurley 1-7, Marty Clark 3-3, Kenny Blakeney 0-2).
Turnovers: Carolina 15, Duke 13.

KEYS TO THE GAME: Donald Williams got hot from outside and made Duke alter its defensive rotation... Carolina took care of the backboards in both halves... UNC's defense kept Duke from getting decent shots...Carolina kept its emotions in check on Senior Day and stayed focused...The Tar Heels outscored Duke 16-1 to start the second half.

DEAN SMITH COMMENT: "Our traps were good. We put good pressure on them. We also limited them to three offensive rebounds in the first half, which is uncanny against Duke. We've improved. We need to keep improving. We're playing our best basketball of the season, but I don't buy the momentum theory. You build your own momentum. We could have a bad game."

COACH MIKE KRZYZEWSKI COMMENT: "Carolina played hard for 40 minutes and we played fairly hard. We didn't value the ball enough and gave them too many easy shots before our defense could get set. Our guys came back well and put us in a position to cut their lead to single digits in the second half, and if we'd done that, you never know what would have happened."

*The defense of Derrick Phelps holds Duke's
Bobby Hurley to 2-12 shooting.*

Fans celebrate the end of the regular season after routing Duke.

fouled him, sending him careening across the floor. An intentional foul was called and with 6:13 left in the game, Montross hit one foul shot. Then, as the teams came back to play, Hurley walked up to official Lenny Wirtz and started clapping in his face. Wirtz had no choice but to call the technical on Hurley, and Williams made both free throws. Reese then scored on a goaltending to make it 74-57 with 6:01 left.

"We wanted to come over here and play well," Duke coach Mike Krzyzewski said. "We played well for about five minutes in the first half and for about five minutes in the second half. You have to be pretty tough for 40 minutes to beat them and we weren't."

Carolina's defense dominated the game. Carolina shot 55 percent to Duke's 35.5 percent. Williams made up for his poor game in Durham. He hit 10-15 from the field, 5-8 from 3-point range, and scored 27 points. Lynch closed out his Smith Center career with 12

points and 11 rebounds. Montross had 18 points and Brian Reese 10.

Duke played the game without star Grant Hill, who was out with a toe injury.

As the game neared its end, Dean Smith took his seniors out for one more ovation. It was an emotional moment, especially when Lynch, the unquestioned team leader, left the home floor for the last time.

Carolina finished a magnificent regular season with a record of 26-3, 14-2 in the ACC. Duke, the preseason favorite to win the ACC regular season, was 23-6, 10-6 in the league.

The final score was 83-69 in Carolina's favor.

***Five Tar Heel seniors huddle before their
last game at Smith Center.***

Terps Can't Run Offense Against UNC's Defenders

102-66

Carolina was ranked No.1 in the nation, had a nine-game winning streak and was playing its best basketball of the season when it went to Charlotte to open the ACC tournament against Maryland on March 12.

The Tar Heels continued their stylish play by blasting Maryland, 102-66. The Terps earned the right to play Carolina by beating N.C. State the night before in the game between the eighth-and ninth-seeded teams.

Carolina didn't mess around with coach Gary Williams' team, and it was defense that broke the game open after the teams were tied at 16 in the first half. The Tar Heels held the Terrapins to 28.2 percent shooting in the first half in building a 51-34 halftime lead. Maryland was able to shoot only 35.6 percent for the game, had 17 turnovers and was outrebounded, 57-33.

It was the third win of the season for the Tar Heels over the Terps. Carolina, which shot 49.3 percent from the field, improved to 27-3, and advanced to meet Virginia, a winner over Wake Forest in the quarterfinals, in the semifinal round on March 13. Maryland ended its season at 12-16.

Carolina, seeded No. 1 in the tournament, was serious about this opening game. After all, Maryland gave the Tar Heels a battle in the first half in College Park on Feb. 9 and led 17-6. Maryland, though the decided underdog, also had everything to win and nothing to lose in this game, which is a nice psychological position to be in, especially when a team is coached by a competitor such as Gary

> "
> *I'm glad Coach Smith had the confidence in me to call on me when Derrick Phelps had three fouls in the first half. He called on me to go in and give a few minutes and everything worked out pretty well for me.*
> "
>
> *Scott Cherry*

Williams.

"I told our team before the game that if we could shoot 60 percent for the game, we had a chance to beat North Carolina," Coach Williams said. "But we made some mistakes, and North Carolina is the kind of team that makes you pay for mistakes."

Carolina's George Lynch, who was now in the homestretch of his college career, was certainly at the top of his game to start the ACC tournament. Lynch had 22 points, 15 rebounds and three steals. Brian Reese, a junior, added 16 points, three assists and six rebounds, and junior Eric Montross finished with 11 points and eight rebounds.

Montross and Reese, waiting for a slow hotel elevator, were 80 seconds late for the pregame meal, so coach Dean Smith, in keeping with his team rule of being on time, didn't start them. In their place, Smith started Kevin Salvadori and Pat Sullivan. Point guard Derrick Phelps picked up his third foul with 8:52 left in the first half, so Smith used freshman Dante Calabria and senior Scott Cherry to fill in at the point.

Carolina broke from that 16-16 tie game to slowly pull away. Lynch had eight of UNC's first 18 points. The Tar Heels led 46-34 with a minute left in the first half, and Cherry hit a 3-pointer and two free throws to boost that lead to 17 at halftime. That was a key run, because Maryland never recovered from it.

The Tar Heels were all business to start the second half. Reese hit back-to-back baskets, then sophomore Donald Williams hit his only 3-pointer of the game and Sullivan scored on a feed from Lynch to give UNC a 59-36 lead. Carolina led 72-48 on a Montross layup with 10:03 left. Coach Smith started putting the reserves in with eight minutes to go, and the reserves played well, building on the lead. Senior Matt Wenstrom had six points, and freshmen Larry Davis and Ed Geth had seven each.

There were some moments of concern for Carolina. Lynch hurt his ankle while chasing a loose ball in the second half and came out of the game for several minutes, but he returned and did not seem hampered. Phelps banged a knee, also in the second half, and limped out of the game, but he, too, was able to return.

Cherry had five points and played well when Phelps was on the bench in foul trouble.

Carolina	FG	FT	R	A	TP
Pat Sullivan	3-3	1-1	2	1	7
George Lynch	9-15	4-5	15	1	22
Kevin Salvadori	2-5	2-2	5	0	6
Derrick Phelps	1-5	0-0	3	4	2
Donald Williams	2-7	2-2	1	3	7
Eric Montross	4-6	3-3	8	0	11
Brian Reese	5-11	6-7	6	3	16
Henrik Rodl	1-3	2-2	1	7	4
Dante Calabria	1-6	0-0	3	3	2
Scott Cherry	1-1	2-2	0	1	5
Matt Wenstrom	2-2	2-2	1	1	6
Ed Geth	3-4	1-1	5	0	7
Larry Davis	3-6	1-2	2	0	7
T. Stephenson	0-1	0-0	0	0	0
Team			5		
Totals	37-75	26-29	57	24	102
Maryland	FG	FT	R	A	TP
Exree Hipp	7-15	3-4	0	2	19
Evers Burns	6-18	2-6	11	2	14
Chris Kerwin	0-2	0-0	2	1	0
Johnny Rhodes	6-12	0-1	5	3	15
Kevin McLinton	2-9	0-0	6	3	4
Duane Simpkins	3-8	1-2	1	6	8
Mario Lucas	1-3	1-2	2	1	3
John Walsh	0-1	0-0	1	0	0
Kurtis Shultz	0-0	0-0	0	0	0
Wayne Bristol	1-4	1-2	3	0	3
Mike Thibeault	0-1	0-0	0	0	0
Team			2		
Totals	26-73	8-17	33	18	66

Three-point goals: Carolina 2-8 (Donald Williams 1-4, Brian Reese 0-1, Henrik Rodl 0-1, Dante Calabria 0-1, Scott Cherry 1-1); Maryland 6-19 (Exree Hipp 2-5, Johnny Rhodes 3-7, Duane Simpkins 1-3, John Walsh 0-1, Wayne Bristol 0-3).
Turnovers: Carolina 17, Maryland 18

KEYS TO THE GAME: Carolina's defense. The Terps, a young team, could have made this an interesting game, if Carolina had given them any encouragement. UNC did not. Its defense swarmed all over Maryland in the first half and made it virtually impossible for Maryland to run its offense.

DEAN SMITH COMMENT: "We didn't look sharp until Scott Cherry went in. He knows what we want defensively. Our man defense was much better than our zone, but we played some zone against them (in the regular season) and had success, so we tried it some today."

COACH GARY WILLIAMS COMMENT: "Carolina certainly is as good as anybody in the country, and they're playing as good as anybody. But a team could get hot in one game and knock them out of the ACC tournament or NCAA tournament. Any team can be beaten in college basketball. If somebody shoots the ball exceptionally well against Carolina, they could beat them in one game, but probably not in a best of seven (game series)."

Henrik Rodl squeezes way to basket against Maryland in ACC tournament game.

Phelps Hurt As Heels Top Cavs In Semifinals

Carolina beat Virginia 74-56 in the semifinals of the ACC tournament in Charlotte, but it was the team's most costly victory of the season.

74-56 With just over two minutes to play and Carolina protecting a big lead, UNC point guard Derrick Phelps fielded a long pass, broke open for a layup and was fouled by Virginia's Jason Williford. Phelps hit the floor hard and stayed there for some 12 minutes while doctors saw to him. Phelps felt numbness in his legs immediately after the fall and was taken from the Charlotte Coliseum court on a stretcher. X-rays at Carolinas Medical Center revealed no broken bones, but Phelps had a severely bruised tailbone. He returned to the team hotel on Saturday night but would not be able to play in the ACC tournament championship game the next afternoon.

It was a weird day. A blizzard hit Charlotte at midday on March 13. So bitter was the weather that the P.A. announcer at the Coliseum warned on many occasions that the power could go out during the game. Workers from Duke Power Co. were standing by in the building in the event of a power shortage.

Virginia, an excellent team in its own right, was fired up for this game because it had lost two times by routs to the Tar Heels during the regular season--80-58 and 78-58. Also, while Virginia, with 19 wins, including two victories over Duke, figured to have clinched a bid to the NCAA tournament, it knew that a win over No. 1 ranked North Carolina would bring with it a high tournament seeding.

With Virginia playing its sagging man-to-man defense and clogging up the middle against Carolina's power game, the first half was competitive and intense. Carolina had a 13-0 spurt late in the half and broke from an 18 tie to lead 31-18 with 3:30 remaining. But then the Tar Heels got sloppy and careless, and Virginia took advantage to get back in the game. Cory Alexander, UVa's talented point guard, had two 3-pointers in a Cavalier run that cut Carolina's lead to 35-30 at halftime.

Phelps led the Tar Heels with eight points in the first half, and UNC hit 9-10 from the free throw line.

In the second half, Carolina led 43-39 when, with 16:36 left in the game, the Coliseum lights dimmed and then faded to black. The two teams stood in front of their respective benches waiting for the lights to come back on, which they did after about a seven-minute delay, only to quickly go out again. The teams then returned to their dressing rooms to wait it out. The lights stayed off for 28 minutes. The teams were summoned from their dressing rooms and given two minutes to warm up before play resumed.

Carolina made good use of the delay. Eric Montross scored inside for Carolina on its first possession after the lights came on. Reese then penetrated the Virginia zone and scored, and then Montross scored on a turnaround. The Tar Heels led 49-39 before UVa's Alexander scored, but then UNC reeled off eight straight points in a 14-2 spurt that resulted in a 57-41 lead with 11:09 to play. Virginia would get no closer than 12 the rest of the way.

Again, this was a game that showed that Carolina could beat good teams even when the Tar Heels were not playing their best. UNC shot only 37.9 percent from the field, and Lynch was only 1-11 shooting. Of course, Lynch helped in other ways, such as his 11 rebounds. Carolina owned the backboards, 43-21.

Montross, who was Virginia's target on defense, still managed 14 points and seven rebounds. Reese continued his improved play with 16 points, and Pat Sullivan came off the bench to score 11 points. The Tar Heels were led in scoring by Donald Williams with 19 points.

Carolina went to 28-3 on the season and advanced to the ACC tournament championship game against Georgia Tech, a team that was on a roll. The Cavaliers fell to 19-9 but would get a bid to the NCAA tournament the next day.

The victory was Dean Smith's 768th as the Tar Heels' head coach, which put him second behind the late Kentucky coach Adolph Rupp on the all-time victory list for Division 1 men's basketball coaches. ❂

Carolina	FG	FT	R	A	TP
Brian Reese	5-10	6-8	5	2	16
George Lynch	1-11	2-2	11	3	4
Eric Montross	3-5	8-8	7	0	14
Derrick Phelps	3-7	2-2	3	3	8
Donald Williams	5-13	6-8	3	0	19
Pat Sullivan	4-6	3-4	5	0	11
Kevin Salvadori	0-3	0-0	3	0	0
Scott Cherry	1-1	0-0	1	0	2
Henrik Rodl	0-0	0-0	1	0	0
Dante Calabria	0-1	0-0	0	0	0
Ed Geth	0-1	0-0	1	0	0
Larry Davis	0-0	0-0	1	0	0
Matt Wenstrom	0-0	0-0	0	0	0
T. Stephenson	0-0	0-0	0	0	0
Team			2		
Totals	22-58	27-32	43	8	74
Virginia	**FG**	**FT**	**R**	**A**	**TP**
Junior Burrough	4-12	1-2	4	1	9
Jason Williford	2-6	0-0	4	1	4
Ted Jeffries	4-8	0-2	3	1	8
Cornel Parker	3-6	0-0	7	3	7
Cory Alexander	9-18	1-3	1	2	22
Doug Smith	2-6	0-0	3	2	6
Yuri Barnes	0-1	0-0	3	0	0
Shawn Wilson	0-0	0-0	2	0	0
Chris Havlicek	0-0	0-0	0	0	0
Rahsaan Mitchell	0-1	0-0	0	0	0
Team			3		
Totals	24-58	2-7	30	10	56

Three-point goals: Carolina 3-8 (Brian Reese 0-1, Donald Williams 3-6, Pat Sullivan 0-1); Virginia 6-19 (Jason Williford 0-1, Cornel Parker 1-3, Cory Alexander 3-8, Doug Smith 2-6, Rahsaan Mitchell 0-1).
Turnovers: Carolina 12, Virginia 17.

KEYS TO THE GAME: Carolina, not shooting well from the field, continued its stingy defensive play and dominated the backboards.

DONALD WILLIAMS COMMENT: "I had the ball a lot at the end because I was the one Coach Smith wanted on the free throw line. I like that role."

Georgia Tech Edges UNC For ACC Tourney Title

75-77

Carolina, playing without injured point guard Derrick Phelps, lost 77-75 to talented Georgia Tech, the sixth seed, in the ACC tournament championship game in Charlotte on March 14.

Phelps, who severely bruised his tailbone against Virginia the previous day, had trouble walking on the morning of the championship game and sat on Carolina's bench in street clothes.

Carolina, which hit just 37.9 percent from the field in beating Virginia in the semifinals, had another poor shooting day against Georgia Tech's zone--hitting just 39.4 percent. Donald Williams, who would later grab headlines for his hot shooting in the NCAA Final Four, made only 4-18 shots against Georgia Tech and was an anemic 11-38 in the three ACC tournament games.

Meanwhile, Carolina, which used Henrik Rodl, Scott Cherry and Dante Calabria at the point, missed Phelps more on defense than on offense. UNC was unable to stop Georgia Tech point guard Travis Best from penetrating, and while Best hit only 3-14 from the field, he frequently broke down Carolina's defense and gave baskets to James Forrest, who had 27 points, and Martice Moore, who had 10.

"This was Georgia Tech beating North Carolina," UNC coach Dean Smith said after the game, refusing to make excuses. "There will be no asterisk by it because Derrick Phelps was injured. He was in pain and couldn't walk very well, much less run and jump."

Carolina, which was ranked No. 1 in the country going into the game, fell to 28-4. Georgia Tech, which went into the ACC tournament not at all certain that it would get an NCAA tournament invitation, got the ACC's automatic bid by virtue of winning the tournament championship. The Yellow Jackets improved their record to 19-10 and were seeded fourth in the NCAA West.

Brian Reese led Carolina with 24 points, Eric Montross had 19 points and a brilliant 17 rebounds, and Donald Williams had 11 points. George Lynch had his second poor shooting game in a row, as he hit only 4-12.

UNC led the game 20-13 and was playing well defensively, but then the Tar Heels went cold from the floor and the Yellow Jackets outscored them 16-2 to take a 29-22 lead late in the first half. Forrest scored 10 straight points during that stretch. Carolina fought back late in the half to trail by only 31-27 at halftime.

Carolina had an 11-0 run in the second half to grab a 48-43 lead. Montross scored inside, Reese got five straight points and Henrik Rodl, who started in Phelps' place, scored his only two points of the game on a drive down the lane. After Montross blocked a Tech shot, Reese scored again and UNC led 48-43.

Carolina led 50-45 when things started turning sour for the regular season ACC champs. George Lynch, who had nine points and eight rebounds, got his fourth foul with 13:33 left in the game when he fouled Forrest inside. Forrest made both free throws and Tech's Drew Barry later scored on a follow shot, cutting UNC's lead to 50-49. On Carolina's next possession, a technical foul was called on a reserve player on Carolina's bench. Best made one of the two free throws to tie the game.

Carolina got a 3-pointer from Williams and a basket and foul shot by Reese to lead 58-55 with 10:24 left, but the Tar Heels went cold again. Tech scored 11 straight points to lead 66-58 with just more than six minutes to play. Carolina rallied down the stretch, but couldn't quite make up the difference.

After Tech's Barry made two foul shots to give his team a 72-66 lead, Brian Reese hit a 3-pointer for the Tar Heels to make it 72-69 with 53 seconds left. Best answered with two more foul shots and then Reese hit another 3-pointer to make it 74-72 with 38 seconds remaining. Forrest made one of two free throws to make it 75-72, but Reese missed a 3-pointer, as Tech held on to win, 77-75.

Montross and Reese were named first-team All-Tournament. Lynch and Williams made second team.

The Tar Heels, disappointed in the outcome of this game, decided to bury it quickly and look ahead. The NCAA tournament was next, and when the Carolina bus pulled into the Smith Center parking lot early Sunday evening after the trip home from Charlotte, the team learned that it had been seeded first in the NCAA East.

A new season was about to begin.

Carolina	FG	FT	R	A	TP
Brian Reese	8-18	6-7	6	0	24
George Lynch	4-12	0-1	9	2	8
Eric Montross	6-11	7-9	17	1	19
Henrik Rodl	1-1	0-2	0	6	2
Donald Williams	4-18	0-0	2	1	11
Pat Sullivan	3-5	0-0	3	2	7
Scott Cherry	0-2	0-0	1	2	0
Kevin Salvadori	2-4	0-0	1	0	4
Dante Calabria	0-0	0-0	0	0	0
Team			4		
Totals	28-71	13-19	43	14	75
Georgia Tech	FG	FT	R	A	TP
Martice Moore	2-7	4-4	3	1	10
James Forrest	11-19	5-6	10	0	27
Malcolm Mackey	2-5	0-1	6	1	4
Travis Best	3-14	8-9	3	6	14
Drew Barry	4-9	2-2	9	6	11
Bryan Hill	2-5	2-2	1	2	7
Ivano Newbill	1-1	2-2	5	0	4
Team			2		
Totals	25-60	23-26	39	16	77

Three-point goals: Carolina 6-21 (Brian Reese 2-5, George Lynch 0-1, Donald Williams 3-12, Pat Sullivan 1-2, Scott Cherry 0-1) Georgia Tech 4-16 (Martice Moore 2-3, Travis Best 0-7, Drew Barry 1-4, Bryan Hill 1-2).
Turnovers: Carolina 15, Georgia Tech 14.

KEYS TO THE GAME: Carolina shot poorly against Georgia Tech's zone, and the UNC defense could not stop Best from penetrating and dishing.

DEAN SMITH COMMENT: "Do not be deceived by Tech's sixth-place finish in the ACC. They are very talented and could win the national tournament. They did not play like a sixth-place team today. We couldn't seem to contain Travis Best. We're disappointed with the loss, but we're happy we still have some season left."

Eric Montross gets all ball against Georgia Tech's James Forrest in ACC tourney.

Excellent 64-Team Field Seeks The Pot Of Gold

The 64-team NCAA tournament field consisted of many teams that had a good chance of putting together a six-game winning streak and taking college basketball's top prize.

Carolina, the regular season champions of the ACC, had a record of 28-4 after it completed play in the conference tournament. The Tar Heels were the No. 1 seed in the East.

They were joined as No. 1 seeds by three other college basketball powers. Kentucky, a 3-point shooting team that liked to pressure on defense, was playing sensational basketball at the end of the season and earned top billing in the NCAA Southeast. Indiana, the champions of the Big Ten, went to No. 1 in the nation when Carolina lost to Georgia Tech in the ACC tournament finals, and coach Bob Knight's team was seeded No. 1 in the Midwest. And the top seed in the West was a team well known by the Tar Heels--the Michigan Wolverines. Michigan, while not a conference champion, earned a top seed with a sparkling record against a tough schedule. Its victories included back-to-back wins over Carolina and Kansas in the Rainbow Classic back in December.

Another thing that stood out about this tournament field was the excellent teams ranked as No. 2 seeds in the four regions. Kansas, the best team in the tough Big Eight, was seeded second in the Midwest. The Jayhawks already had a regular season win over the region's top seed, Indiana. Cincinnati, the No. 2 seed in the East, made it to the Final Four the previous year and felt that this year's team was better. The No. 2 seed in the West was Arizona, the Pac-10 champions, a team that thought it deserved top billing in the West. And the No. 2 seed to Kentucky in the Southeast was Seton Hall, champions of the Big East, a loser to Carolina in the regular season, and a team that was on top of its game heading into the NCAA tournament.

While some basketball people doubted the ACC's strength back in early December, the conference had one of its strongest years ever. Six teams from the league made it to the NCAAs. In addition to Carolina, Florida State, which finished second in the conference, was the No. 3 seed in the Southeast. Wake Forest and Duke tied for third in the conference. Duke, after losing its last regular season game to Carolina and then dropping its first game in the ACC tournament to Georgia Tech, was a third seed in the Midwest. Wake Forest was the fifth seed in the Southeast. Virginia, which lost to the Tar Heels in the semifinals of the ACC tournament, was seeded sixth in the East. And Georgia Tech, the league's tournament champion and automatic qualifier, was the fourth seed in the West.

There were some intriguing matchups in first-round games. College basketball's rules are designed to favor the underdog team, and in the NCAA tournament, where it is one loss and out, there is often great pressure in the early rounds on the highly seeded teams. Arizona, for instance, while having excellent teams, had had trouble surviving early NCAA games in recent years. The Wildcats lost again in the first round, this time to Santa Clara, the 15th seed in the West.

Georgia Tech, thinking it had momentum after winning the ACC tournament, lost in the NCAA first round to Southern University, the 13th seed in the West.

Carolina, meanwhile, was assigned the East's 16th seed, East Carolina. Many people had predicted a Carolina-ECU matchup. When the pairing was announced, the East Carolina campus, located in Greenville, N.C., was thrilled and excited about the possibility.

Kareem Richardson, a guard on East Carolina's team, said: "To look at the other bench and see Dean Smith, the second winningest coach in college basketball, will be unbelievable. It's something that will be nice to tell my kids and grandkids about. But we have to play basketball and not look at the North Carolina on their jerseys. We can't get caught up in their mystique."

East Carolina coach Eddie Payne said "it's a big thrill for the guys who grew up in North Carolina to play this game. It's going to be a basketball game. That's what we have to get our guys to think about. We have to think just about the game, not the event. North Carolina is the best team in the country right now. We just have to play smart."

The NCAA basketball tournament represents one of the most exciting times in the entire sports year. It is indeed "March Madness." It is routine to see so-called upsets in every round of the tournament. Teams like East Carolina have a chance. Favored teams, knowing the consequences of not being at their best, sometimes play tentatively. The underdog team, with little to lose and operating with a significant psychological advantage, often plays inspired basketball.

Nobody said the single-elimination tournament was fair. But it certainly is exciting.

The ACC's six teams all had a chance to win the tournament. Teams take these games one at a time, or else they pack for a quick trip home and an end to their season.

Carolina knew how excited East Carolina was about playing this game. To UNC's credit, it approached it the same way it would a game against Indiana or Michigan. Carolina would either get the right to keep on playing, or East Carolina would enjoy the biggest win in its basketball history.

There's one thing for sure about this NCAA tournament: Every team in the field knows exactly what is at stake. ✺

Inside Game Clicks As Tar Heels Nail Pirates

85-65

The NCAA tournament selection committee, in making its pairings for first round games, obviously saw a potentially attractive matchup in pitting North Carolina, the No. 1 seed in the East, against East Carolina, a team that won its way into the tournament by getting three straight upset victories in the Colonial Athletic Association tournament.

The East Carolina campus was thrilled about the game's possibilities. The Tar Heels and Pirates don't play each other in the regular season, and quite frankly, this was a dream game for ECU. Just think what it would do for the university and the basketball program if it could upset the mighty Tar Heels. Or even if it could make it a close game.

East Carolina had more than a psychological advantage coming into this game. The Tar Heels were not sure of the status of their point guard and defensive leader, Derrick Phelps. Phelps bruised his tailbone in the semifinals of the ACC tournament and had to miss the tournament championship game. UNC coach Dean Smith did not start Phelps against East Carolina, but Phelps would get some playing.

The plans for both teams were easy to anticipate. East Carolina started a frontline of 6-8, 6-8, 6-4, which made it pretty obvious that the Tar Heels were going to try to go inside to Eric Montross, 7-0, and George Lynch, 6-8. ECU coach Eddie Payne, on the other hand, was going to jam the middle and try to make Carolina shoot outside.

East Carolina, which came into the NCAA tournament with a 13-16 record, had quickness. Payne, fearing Carolina's pressure defense, had his regulars practice against seven and eight men, trying to simulate UNC's trapping defenses. Payne also hoped to shorten the game, to milk the shot clock, to take advantage of the TV timeouts to rest his team against Carolina's depth. And to pull the upset, he knew his team had to shoot well from 3-point range.

Carolina, to its credit, did not overlook this game or take it for granted. The Tar Heels played hard from the outset. Carolina, getting the ball inside with relative ease, led 26-12, but the Pirates would not let loose of their dream. ECU guard Lester Lyons, an erratic shooter coming into the game, was anything

but in the first half. He hit 5-6 shots from the field in the first half, 3-4 from 3-point range, as East Carolina trailed by only 45-34 at halftime.

Carolina's plan was working. Montross was 5-6 from the field in the first half and Lynch hit all five of his shots. East Carolina did a good job of taking care of the ball in the first half and had only five turnovers against Carolina's pressure.

Phelps entered the game for Dante Calabria with 11:49 left in the first half, and exactly two minutes later, as ECU's Lyons was speeding to the basket under a full head of steam, Phelps stepped in front of him to draw the charge. It brought UNC coach Dean Smith off the bench, holding his head. Phelps got up slowly but stayed in the game. He was back.

East Carolina got within 49-40 with 17:41 left in the game, but the Pirates would get no closer. It was far from a rout, however. Carolina led by only 13 with 13:14 left in the game.

While ECU came into this game dreaming of an upset, Carolina had a dream of its own--to win six games in a row and capture the national championship. East Carolina became the biggest game of the season in the eyes of the Tar Heels, and they weren't about to overlook it.

Carolina's inside game was excellent. Montross finished with 17 points and nine rebounds and blocked two shots. Lynch had 15 points and eight rebounds. Phelps played 14 minutes and got back into the groove.

After two poor shooting games in the ACC tournament, Carolina got excellent shots against ECU and nailed 54.7 percent of them. Still, the Tar Heels were only 5-16 from 3-point range, and its chief outside threat, Donald Williams, hit only 3-9.

It was a well-played game. ECU had only 11 turnovers and North Carolina had eight.

One of Carolina's strengths all season long had been its ability to focus and concentrate. It got the job done against East Carolina, an in-state rival who came into the game loose and played well.

One down and five to go. Before Carolina defeated East Carolina in the late game in Winston-Salem's Lawrence Joel Coliseum, Rhode Island, a dangerous team from the Atlantic 10, defeated Purdue of the Big Ten. The Rams would be Carolina's next opponent in round two. 🏀

Carolina	FG	FT	R	A	TP
Brian Reese	3-7	5-6	2	5	11
George Lynch	7-9	1-2	8	2	15
Eric Montross	6-9	5-7	9	2	17
Donald Williams	3-9	0-0	2	0	9
Henrik Rodl	3-5	3-3	0	4	10
Pat Sullivan	0-0	4-4	1	1	4
Dante Calabria	0-1	0-0	0	1	0
Kevin Salvadori	2-4	4-4	4	0	8
Derrick Phelps	3-6	0-1	2	0	6
Larry Davis	1-1	0-0	0	0	3
Scott Cherry	1-1	0-0	0	0	2
T. Stephenson	0-0	0-0	0	0	0
Matt Wenstrom	0-1	0-0	1	0	0
Team			5		
Totals	29-53	22-27	34	15	85
East Carolina	**FG**	**FT**	**R**	**A**	**TP**
Curley Young	5-13	0-0	4	1	10
Anton Gill	3-10	0-1	5	1	6
Ike Copeland	0-2	1-2	7	2	1
Lester Lyons	8-11	6-6	2	4	27
K. Richardson	4-9	0-0	1	3	10
Ronnell Peterson	2-5	0-0	2	1	6
James Lewis	1-3	2-4	5	0	4
Wilburt Hunter	0-3	1-2	1	0	1
Team			4		
Totals	23-56	10-15	31	12	65

Three-point goals: Carolina 5-16 (Brian Reese 0-2, Donald Williams 3-9, Henrik Rodl 1-2, Dante Calabria 0-1, Derrick Phelps 0-1, Larry Davis 1-1); East Carolina 9-21 (Curley Young 0-4, Anton Gill 0-2, Lester Lyons 5-6, Kareem Richardson 2-4, Ronnell Peterson 2-4, Wilburt Hunter 0-1).
Turnovers: Carolina 8, East Carolina 11.

KEYS TO THE GAME: Carolina was able to take advantage of its size and got the ball inside. Lynch and Montross were a combined 13-18 from the field.

DEAN SMITH COMMENT: "We played well offensively and certainly it's hard to chase them defensively. I respect their quickness and the job that Eddie Payne has done coaching them. Our players did a tremendous job at the beginning of the second half."

COACH EDDIE PAYNE COMMENT: "We had to give up something on defense, but even with our emphasis on the inside, we couldn't keep them from getting the ball in the paint."

Eric Montross converts during a first round win over the ECU Pirates.

UNC Has 55-10 Rally To Rip Rhode Island

112-67

Rhode Island guard Carlos Cofield would have been better off if he had just called in sick.

Talking to the media the day before Rhode Island and Carolina were to play in round two of the NCAA East subregional in Winston-Salem, Cofield, who grew up in Charlotte, said he had never liked Carolina. He didn't like the Tar Heels growing up, he said, and he doesn't like them now. Furthermore, Cofield said the Rams would knock Carolina out of the NCAA tournament and "send them packing."

Rhode Island, the second-place finisher in the Atlantic 10 Conference, was no slouch. The Rams beat Purdue, and its star Glenn Robinson, in the first round of the NCAA tournament. During the regular season, Rhode Island lost by only four to Wake Forest in this same building. In the Atlantic 10, the Rams beat NCAA tournament teams Temple, Massachusetts and George Washington during the regular season.

But on this afternoon in Joel Coliseum, before a crowd of 14,366, the Tar Heels would not have lost to many teams. From a 22-16 lead with just over eight minutes left in the first half, Carolina went on a tear that sent shock waves reverberating throughout the entire NCAA tournament field, en route to a smashing 112-67 victory.

Playing defense in a frenzy, UNC chased Rhode Island completely out of its offense and forced a tempo that the Rams did not want--fast and furious. From that 22-16 lead, Carolina outscored Rhode Island 28-5 over the last eight minutes of the first half to lead 50-21 at halftime.

To be sure, Carolina was close to perfect in the last eight minutes of the first half. The Tar Heels had five players with seven points or more at halftime. In that eight-minute rampage, Brian Reese slammed home a dunk off a fastbreak, Henrik Rodl got a backdoor layup off a screen by Eric Montross, Pat Sullivan got a steal and layup, and Derrick Phelps, who hit all seven of his shots, went coast-to-coast for a layup. Donald Williams, rediscovering his shooting eye, hit a 3-pointer. And with the seconds ticking down in the first half, Reese, operating out of the Four Corners, penetrated and pitched to George Lynch for a dunk.

The game was over at halftime, but Carolina was taking no chances. The first eight minutes of the second half looked to be a replay of the last eight minutes of the first period. Carolina outscored the Rams 27-5 to lead 78-31.

In a 16-minute period, Carolina, the top seed in the East, outscored Rhode Island, the eighth seed, 55-10. That is hard to believe, even in retrospect.

Carolina coach Dean Smith, who said it was the best his team had played to that point in the season, substituted for his starters with 13 minutes left in the game. George Lynch played 24 minutes, Eric Montross 20, but no other Tar Heel played as much as 20 minutes in the game.

Phelps, still recovering from the tailbone injury suffered in the ACC tournament semifinals, played 19 minutes and scored 15 points. Williams had 17 points for Carolina, Montross 15, Kevin Salvadori 11 and Matt Wenstrom 14.

"North Carolina was tremendous this afternoon," said Rhode Island coach Al Skinner, whose team dropped to 19-11. "They showed why they are the No. 1 seed in the East."

North Carolina, in that outstanding display of basketball in the first half, held Rhode Island to a shooting percentage of 22.9. The Rams were able to hit only 31.9 percent for the entire game, while Carolina had its second straight excellent shooting game, hitting 56.8 percent from the field.

The 112-67 win by the Tar Heels put them in the NCAA Final 16 for the 13th straight year, only one short of UCLA's record of 14 straight.

Meanwhile, Rhode Island's Carlos Cofield, the young man who grew up a Duke fan in Charlotte, scored three points and was 1-10 from the field. But he was right about one thing: The Tar Heels were sent packing. Not to go home, but for a trip to the Meadowlands for the NCAA East Regionals.

Arkansas, a tremendous team out of the Southeastern Conference and the East's fourth seed, won two games in Winston-Salem for the right to play Carolina in New Jersey. Nolan Richardson, the Arkansas coach, had an ominous and not-so-subtle forecast, when he said: "I'd hate to be a team with hopes of winning the national championship that had to play Arkansas."

The battle was engaged.

Carolina	FG	FT	R	A	TP
Brian Reese	3-8	0-0	4	6	7
George Lynch	4-7	1-2	7	1	9
Eric Montross	5-7	5-5	9	2	15
Donald Williams	7-11	0-0	2	0	17
Derrick Phelps	7-7	0-1	2	2	15
Pat Sullivan	2-4	5-6	5	5	9
Henrik Rodl	2-2	0-0	1	5	4
Kevin Salvadori	4-7	3-5	5	1	11
Dante Calabria	0-2	0-0	1	1	0
Larry Davis	1-8	1-2	2	1	3
Scott Cherry	1-2	3-4	1	3	6
T. Stephenson	0-1	0-0	1	0	0
Matt Wenstrom	5-7	4-5	3	1	14
Ed Geth	1-1	0-0	0	0	2
Team			7		
Totals	42-74	22-30	50	28	112
Rhode Island	**FG**	**FT**	**R**	**A**	**TP**
Mike Brown	5-18	1-2	6	2	15
Andre Samuel	7-16	3-4	8	0	17
Rafael Solis	1-5	3-8	5	0	5
Carlos Cofield	1-10	0-0	0	3	3
C. Easterling	1-1	2-2	1	1	5
Damont Collins	0-0	1-2	1	1	1
Abdul Fox	5-11	0-0	1	0	10
Kyle Ivey-Jones	3-6	0-0	3	1	7
Matt Keebler	0-1	0-0	2	0	0
John Cowie	0-0	0-0	1	0	0
Mike Moten	0-4	4-4	4	0	4
Team			2		
Totals	23-72	14-22	34	8	67

Three-point goals: Carolina 6-14 (Brian Reese 1-2, Donald Williams 3-5, Derrick Phelps 1-1, Pat Sullivan 0-1, Dante Calabria 0-1, Larry Davis 0-2, Scott Cherry 1-1, Travis Stephenson 0-1); Rhode Island 7-21 (Mike Brown 4-9, Andre Samuel 0-2, Carlos Cofield 1-6, Carlos Easterling 1-1, Abdul Fox 0-1, Kyle Ivey-Jones 1-1, Matt Keebler 0-1)).
Turnovers: Carolina 11, Rhode Island 15

KEYS TO THE GAME: Carolina's defense keyed a 55-10 rout in the last eight minutes of the first half and the first eight minutes of the second half.

DEAN SMITH COMMENT: "We were sharp offensively. We're delighted to win this subregional and now we move on to the next tournament."

COACH AL SKINNER COMMENT: "It was another level that we attempted to achieve today, but we didn't do it. North Carolina has answers to all the questions. If they shoot the ball the way they did today, they will be hard to defend."

Donald Williams gives Rhode Island's Carlos Cofield a shooting clinic.

Tar Heels Put The Hogs Out By Way Of Backdoor

With North Carolina leading Arkansas 75-74 and 52 seconds left in the game, Tar Heel coach Dean Smith called timeout to set strategy for the final seconds.

First, Smith made two substitutions--Donald Williams for Henrik Rodl and Eric Montross for Kevin Salvadori. Then, with the game and the season on the line, Smith told his players that they were going to run a backdoor cut. It's part of Carolina's regular offense, but with so much on the line, assistant coaches Bill Guthridge and Phil Ford persuaded Smith to diagram the play, which Smith did.

Smith deployed Montross, Brian Reese and Derrick Phelps left of the foul circle. Senior George Lynch was at the top of the key, shaded to the right, and Williams was on the right wing.

Smith knew that Williams would be guarded by Corey Beck, one of Arkansas' most aggressive and daring defenders. His style was to overplay his man, deny him the ball.

Lynch got the ball at the top of the key, and as he was doing a reverse pivot, Williams broke sharply towards the ball, Beck with him step for step. Lynch faked a pass to Williams, enticing Beck even more, and Williams suddenly screeched to a halt and broke back towards the basket. Lynch fed the wide-open Williams for a layup and a 77-74 UNC lead.

Still, 42 seconds remained, plenty of time for Arkansas to tie or even win this game. Lynch, one of Carolina's great all-time competitors, had fought hard and encouraged his team the entire game. He had one more big play left in his defensive repertoire. Arkansas looked for a 3-point shot to tie as Carolina pressured the perimeter. Robert Shepherd, who had hit 3-4 from 3-point range for the Hogs, got the ball left of the circle. But as Shepherd left his feet, Lynch got a hand on the ball and forced a traveling violation.

Carolina got the ball back with 23 seconds to play. Williams hit a foul shot with 21.5 seconds left, missed the second one, which was rebounded by Brian Reese. Williams was fouled again with 16.8 seconds left, made both shots this time, and Carolina beat Arkansas, the fourth seed in the East, 80-74.

The game was extremely well played, competitive and emotionally charged. Both teams knew what was at stake and stood up to the pressure.

Carolina's record improved to 31-4 and Arkansas fell to 22-9. Arkansas coach Nolan Richardson did a brilliant job of playing the underdog role to the hilt. He had his team loose and psychologically ready to take on the powerful Tar Heels.

In fact, it took one of Carolina's finest performances of the season to survive this game and advance in the NCAA tournament. UNC got hold of an Arkansas team that played one of its finest games of the season. The Hogs were a team of speed and quickness and defensive ingenuity.

Carolina learned from the outset that it would take its best effort to win. The season's high for 3-point field goals in a game for Arkansas had been seven. Well, the Hogs hit 8-16 from 3-point range in the first half alone. The scouting report on Arkansas indicated that it was an extremely difficult team to defend when it was hitting from outside.

Carolina, maybe a little tight in the role of the favorite, began the game tentative against Arkansas' pressure defense. The Hogs brimmed with confidence, hit inside and out, and when Clint McDaniel buried a 3-pointer, Arkansas led 25-14 with 9:49 left in the first half. It was dangerous to get behind a team this talented, even early in the game. After all, Coach Richardson called his defense "40 Minutes of Hell."

Meanwhile, UNC coach Smith took point guard Derrick Phelps out of the game for a talk and a rest, and when Phelps went back in, he handled the Arkansas pressure brilliantly.

Carolina didn't mess around. In a furious rally, the Tar Heels got a steal and dunk from Lynch, two Montross foul shots, a Williams 3-pointer and a follow shot and foul shot by Lynch on their way to tying the game at 28 with with 6:44 left. That's the way this UNC team responded when backed into a corner. The Tar Heels outscored the Hogs 14-3 in 3:05.

However, Arkansas went back up 38-31 with 3:50 left in the half, but again Carolina rallied to tie the score at 45 at halftime.

The first-half play was fierce on both sides. Arkansas led for 19 minutes of the half and its biggest lead was 11. Carolina led only once, 45-43.

Carolina	FG	FT	R	A	TP
Brian Reese	5-11	3-6	8	4	13
George Lynch	9-13	5-7	10	2	23
Eric Montross	6-8	3-6	8	1	15
Derrick Phelps	2-5	0-1	7	7	5
Donald Williams	7-19	5-6	1	3	22
Pat Sullivan	1-4	0-0	2	0	2
Henrik Rodl	0-1	0-0	1	2	0
Scott Cherry	0-0	0-0	0	0	0
Kevin Salvadori	0-1	0-0	2	0	0
Team			6		
Totals	30-62	16-26	45	19	80
Arkansas	FG	FT	R	A	TP
Darrell Hawkins	2-10	0-0	4	2	5
Scotty Thurman	5-12	0-0	0	1	12
Dwight Stewart	2-3	0-0	1	1	5
Corey Beck	0-2	0-0	2	5	0
Robert Shepherd	5-8	0-0	3	2	13
Warren Linn	0-1	0-0	1	0	0
Clint McDaniel	3-12	3-4	6	1	12
Roger Crawford	1-2	1-2	1	3	4
C. Williamson	7-7	2-3	2	1	16
Elmer Martin	2-4	3-4	5	5	7
Team			6		
Totals	27-61	9-13	31	21	74

Three-point goals: Carolina 4-12 (Brian Reese 0-1, Derrick Phelps 1-1, Donald Williams 3-9, Henrik Rodl 0-1); Arkansas 11-24 (Darrell Hawkins 1-4, Scotty Thurman 2-5, Dwight Stewart 1-1, Robert Shepherd 3-4, Warren Linn 0-1, Clint McDaniel 3-8, Roger Crawford 1-1).
Turnovers: Carolina 12, Arkansas 12.

KEYS TO THE GAME: Carolina's rebounding edge at 45-31 and its ballhandling. UNC had only 12 turnovers against the Arkansas pressure...Lynch had 23 points, 10 rebounds. Montross 15 points, eight rebounds. Reese 13 points, eight rebounds. Williams 22 points. Phelps seven assists and only one turnover.

DEAN SMITH COMMENT: "It was a well-played game between two excellent teams. Their defense made us look bad at times and our defense made them look bad at times. Arkansas has nothing to be ashamed of, nor would I be ashamed had we lost. But we are obviously excited to win. I'm real pleased with the way we played."

COACH NOLAN RICHARDSON COMMENT: "The Tar Heels are excellent. They have the things that I said they had that could take them all the way. They made the plays at the end of the game, which is the difference in a team being good and being real good. Lynch did an excellent job of giving them second chances and stick-backs. I think that was the key to the game."

Arkansas' Corey Beck feels the UNC trap created by Eric Montross (00) and George Lynch.

Eric Montross shoots over Dwight Stewart of Arkansas, as UNC advances to Final Eight.

There was some disturbing news for both teams at halftime. The Tar Heels shot 53.1 percent and were still tied. On the other hand, Arkansas, not known for its 3-point shooting, had eight baskets from 3-point range in the first half and was still in a tie game.

The two teams went back and forth for the first five minutes of the second half. Then, Carolina, leading 56-55, made a little spurt to lead 64-58. Phelps scored against the press on a pass from Henrik Rodl, Reese made a good move inside and Lynch knocked in a 12-footer from the lane in that drive.

The Tar Heels stretched that to 68-61 with 9:11 left, and the Hogs, having trouble against Carolina's zone, called timeout.

Then the Razorbacks rallied behind three baskets by Corliss Williamson on the inside, and with the shot clock down to its last tick, Elmer Martin hit an 18-footer from the right wing, which tied the score at 69. Phelps and Lynch both missed easy shots for Carolina, but the Tar Heel defense held, and then in transition, Reese went all the way for a 71-69 Carolina lead. Williams followed with two foul shots to make it 73-69 with 4:24 left.

Arkansas' Williamson, who would finish 7-7 from the floor, hit another inside shot to make it a two-point game. Then, Williams had a huge play for Carolina. With the shot clock running down, an Arkansas defender reached in and knocked the ball from Williams' hands. The Carolina sophomore regained control, spun and hit a jumper for a 75-71 lead with 1:53 left in regulation.

After another defensive stop, Phelps pitched ahead to Lynch, who chased the ball down on the left baseline. Lynch then hesitated and made a move for the basket. The shot went down, but Lynch was called for charging and the basket was disallowed.

The Razorbacks had the ball back with 1:32 to play, down by only four. The Tar Heels went back into a zone defense. Arkansas got the ball to Darrell Hawkins, who was closely guarded by Rodl, but his 3-pointer was good anyhow. Carolina led 75-74 with 1:06 left, setting up the gutsy and wise backdoor call by Smith and the defensive work by Lynch.

"I don't deserve the credit for that play," said Williams, speaking of the backdoor layup. "The credit goes to Coach Smith for designing it and to George Lynch for making a great pass. All I had to do was lay it up."

The Tar Heels moved on, this time to the Final Eight to face Cincinnati, a Final Four team from last season. More drama ahead.

Carolina Stops Cincy To Earn Spot In Final Four

75-68

The Cincinnati Bearcats, in talking to the media the day before they played North Carolina for the championship of the NCAA East Regionals, seemed to go out of their way to take a verbal crack at the Tar Heels.

Cincinnati coach Bob Huggins, when asked about coaching against Dean Smith, said he'd coached against great coaches before and wasn't worried about it. Besides, Huggins said, if he and Smith were going to be the matchup, "I'd kill him. He's old."

A Cincinnati player laughed derisively when asked about Carolina's basketball tradition. "Michael Jordan can't play for them tomorrow," he said.

That was the table setting for Carolina's date with Cincinnati in the Final Eight in the Meadowlands. The winner would go to New Orleans to play Kansas in the NCAA semifinals the following weekend. The loser would look forward to next year.

It became obvious early in the UNC-Cincy game that the trash-talking had served the Bearcats well. They began the game loose and confident, talking and laughing, playing well. Leading 16-12 at the television timeout with 11:31 left in the first half, Cincinnati made its bid to crack open the game.

Nick Van Exel, the Cincinnati guard and leader, and a player who tried to talk his opponent into submission, led this 13-2 surge that would give the Bearcats a 29-14 lead. Van Exel, shooting from way outside, scored on three 3-point field goals and a regular basket in that spurt to give the Bearcats the 15-point lead with 6:57 left in the first half.

Van Exel nailed yet another 3-pointer with five minutes left in the half to make Cincinnati's lead 33-20. UNC coach Dean Smith had seen enough. He got his defensive ace, Derrick Phelps, off to the side and told him to forget Carolina's help defense. He wanted Phelps on Van Exel at all times, no switching. It was a strategic move that would prove crucial. Van Exel, who had killed the Tar Heels up to this point, would be taken completely out of the game by Phelps.

Meanwhile, Carolina, behind George Lynch's inspirational play, began to rally. Lynch played himself into a state of exhaustion in the last seven minutes of the half. Defiantly shaking his fist in the face of defeat, Lynch rebounded a missed shot, scored and was fouled. Carolina trailed by only 35-31, and Van Exel, with Phelps in his face, was making no noise, not a peep.

Cincinnati's Terry Nelson hit a shot at the buzzer to give his team a 37-36 lead at halftime.

"I would have been happy to have been within seven or eight at halftime," Carolina's Smith said.

Van Exel had 21 of Cincinnati's 37 first-half points, but he didn't score in the last five minutes of the half, which was a good sign for the Tar Heels.

Carolina, the top seed in the East, and Cincinnati, the second seed, slugged it out in the second half. It was a bitter struggle, one that gnawed at emotions on both sides. UNC had the game tied several times early in the second half, and after falling behind 57-52 with 11:02 left, the Tar Heels outscored the Bearcats 9-0 to take a 61-57 lead with 6:11 left. In a game like this one, when most shots were contested, a four-point lead began to look huge. Donald Williams got the 9-0 run started with a 3-pointer.

Then the teams traded rallies. Cincinnati tied it at 62, Carolina went back ahead 66-62 on two Brian Reese foul shots with 1:44 left. Cincinnati had a little push, and when Tarrence Gibson scored on a drive with 35 seconds left, the score was tied at 66.

Carolina's offense produced a great shot inside for Lynch, but the ball rolled off the rim and was knocked out of bounds by Cincinnati with eight-tenths of a second left on the scoreboard clock. Dean Smith diagrammed a play for Eric Montross, but when Cincinnati took timeout after seeing Carolina's offensive set, Smith brought his team to the bench and changed the call. He used Montross as a screener and decoy. The play was designed to go to Brian Reese in the lane, who was told to catch the ball and shoot in one motion.

Smith's play worked beautifully, except for one thing. Instead of catching and shooting in the lane, the wide-open Reese tried to dunk and missed at the buzzer. The Tar Heels seemed stunned by the miss, but they quickly gathered themselves in the huddle, and Smith clapped his hands and said: "This is what we want. We need the practice."

Carolina	FG	FT	R	A	TP
Brian Reese	2-9	4-4	3	3	8
George Lynch	7-14	7-9	14	0	21
Eric Montross	6-8	3-6	7	0	15
Donald Williams	8-17	1-2	1	0	20
Derrick Phelps	0-3	3-4	2	7	3
Pat Sullivan	2-4	0-0	2	2	4
Kevin Salvadori	1-2	0-0	5	0	2
Henrik Rodl	1-1	0-0	0	2	2
Dante Calabria	0-0	0-0	0	0	0
Team			9		
Totals	27-58	18-25	43	14	75
Cincinnati	**FG**	**FT**	**R**	**A**	**TP**
Erik Martin	6-11	4-4	6	2	16
Terry Nelson	2-3	0-0	5	2	4
Corie Blount	3-10	2-2	9	2	8
Tarrance Gibson	5-11	0-0	5	6	13
Nick Van Exel	8-24	1-2	3	5	23
Keith Gregor	1-5	0-1	2	1	2
LaZelle Durden	0-2	0-0	0	0	0
Mike Harris	0-0	0-0	1	0	0
Curtis Bostic	1-3	0-0	3	1	2
John Jacobs	0-1	0-0	0	0	0
Team			5		
Totals	26-70	7-9	39	19	68

Three-point goals: Carolina 3-8 (Brian Reese 0-1, Donald Williams 3-7); Cincinnati 9-24 (Terry Nelson 0-1, Tarrance Gibson 3-8, Nick Van Exel 6-13, LaZelle Durden 0-2)
Turnovers: Carolina 18, Cincinnati 18.

KEYS TO THE GAME: Derrick Phelps shut down Cincinnati's Van Exel during the game's last 30 minutes...Lynch's play inspired the Tar Heels when they were down 15 in the first half...Montross occupied Cincinnati's attention inside, thereby opening up things for other players...Williams knocked in the two big 3-pointers in overtime.

DEAN SMITH COMMENT: "North Carolina defeated an excellent team and a very difficult team against which to play. It was a man's game on the boards. I am real pleased with our second-half defense. (Williams') 3-pointers in overtime were big and Lynch was sensational on the backboards. We're certainly happy to be playing next week."

COACH BOB HUGGINS COMMENT: "We could have won the game. They did a great job and I give them credit for it, but we still could have won the game. Their size probably wore us down at the end. Lynch probably doesn't get the credit that he deserves. Our kids have heart, nobody will blow us out, not even the Boston Celtics. We don't have moral victories. We had our shot to win this game, but we just couldn't get it done."

Cincinnati's Tarrance Gibson pressures Brian Reese in front of UNC's bench.

"three" from the top of the key and the Tar Heels had a 74-68 lead with 1:50 left.

Dean Smith was not happy with the way his team protected that lead, but the defense kept Cincinnati from taking advantage of some Carolina turnovers late in overtime.

The Tar Heels won, 75-68, to advance to the Final Four for the second time in three years.

Carolina had many heroes in this one. Lynch was never better. He had 21 points, 14 rebounds and an astounding six steals. His leadership when Carolina fell behind by 15 in the first half exceeded all of those lofty statistics. Montross was a horse inside. He hit 6-8 from the field, occupied Cincinnati's defense, got seven rebounds. Donald Williams, with the big 3-pointers in overtime, had 20 points and was learning to love these pressure situations.

Then there was Derrick Phelps. He had no field goals, only three points, and one might look at that line in the scorebook and conclude that he had a bad game. Far from it. After Van Exel got his 21st point in the game's first 15 minutes, Phelps took on the defensive challenge. Van Exel could get only two more points in the remaining 30 minutes of regulation and overtime, and against Phelps, he hit only 1-10 field goals. Phelps' defense was decisive, and he chipped in seven assists and three steals.

Carolina's defense held Cincinnati to 37.1 percent shooting.

"We had our chance to win this game," Cincinnati coach Huggins said. "Anybody who doesn't think we are one of the elite programs in the country doesn't understand the game."

Van Exel conceded nothing. "If we played North Carolina 10 times," he said, "we'd beat them more than they'd beat us."

Carolina's Lynch was the NCAA East's MVP. He was joined on the All-Regional team by Montross and Williams. Dean Smith just shook his head in dismay when learning that Phelps had received no such individual honor. Playing against two quick, pressing defensive teams in the Meadowlands, point guard Phelps had 14 assists and four turnovers in two games. That doesn't mention his defense.

The disappointment of Reese's miss was buried by the time the Tar Heels lined up for overtime. Five more minutes of basketball. The pressure was as heavy as morning fog in a swamp.

Cincinnati's Corie Blount hit a jumper to put the Bearcats up, 68-66. Lynch scored inside after a beautiful pass from Reese to tie the game.

After a Cincinnati miss, the Tar Heels had a chance to make some winning plays. First, Eric Montross rebounded his team's missed shot, tossed outside to Donald Williams, who squared up and nailed a 3-pointer to give UNC a 71-68 advantage. After another defensive stop, Williams, who was feeling it now, hit another

As the Tar Heels celebrated the NCAA East championship, workers at the Meadowlands brought out scissors and a ladder. It was a part of the exercise for the winning team to snip the nets.

Carolina's players left them. This was nice, winning to go to the Final Four, but going wasn't the goal. The nets the Tar Heels wanted were hanging on the baskets in the Superdome in New Orleans.

Cincinnati's Van Exel, meanwhile, was defiant to the end. When asked if UNC had a chance to win the national championship, Van Exel shot back: "No."

The Tar Heels left Newark Airport early Sunday night for the trip to Chapel Hill. There was a lot of laughter on the flight, until the five seniors circulated the word to the rest of the team: "We are going to New Orleans to win. We have nothing to celebrate yet."

Kansas, coached by former UNC assistant coach Roy Williams, knocked Carolina out of the Final Four in 1991. The Jayhawks were in Carolina's way again.

Would it be different this time? "We have two more games to win," George Lynch said, "and Kansas is the first of the two."

Eric Montross holds his defensive ground against Bearcats' Erik Martin.

Henrik Rodl looks to pass inside against Cincinnati's LaZelle Durden.

North Carolina Tar Heels
NCAA East Champions

Glamor Field Won Right To Play For Championship

Never in the history of college basketball has there been a Final Four like the one that was going to New Orleans in April 1993 to settle the season-long fight for the national championship. Three of the most famous names in all of basketball--North Carolina, Kentucky and Kansas--were going to be there, along with Michigan, a program that moved comfortably in such circles.

This was the first time that three No. 1 seeds had ever made it to the Final Four. North Carolina was the top seed in the East, Kentucky came as the No. 1 seed from the Southeast, and Michigan was on its way to New Orleans as the highest ranked team from the West Region. Kansas was hardly a dark horse. The Jayhawks were seeded second in the Midwest, but won its ticket to New Orleans by beating the region's top seed, Indiana, for the second time this season.

No doubt, these were the glamor names of college basketball. The team that emerged from this classic field would unquestionably earn the right to be called the best of the best in college basketball for 1992-93.

The most exciting day of the sports year is the Saturday of the Final Four. Four teams and their fans and the nation's media gather in one place to dramatically end the basketball season and officially welcome the coming of springtime. There is nothing like it.

The first game on Saturday would feature North Carolina and Kansas, and all the connecting stories. Kansas coach Roy Williams was a Dean Smith assistant coach for 10 years. Dean Smith played on a national championship team at Kansas and is still one of that state's favorite sons. All of that made good reading, just as it did in 1991 when the same two teams met in the Final Four in Indianapolis, but the players on the two teams didn't care. They had a game to play, period. The coach on the other bench would not be a distraction, not this time.

The second game on Saturday was Kentucky and Michigan. The Wildcats of coach Rick Pitino were winning by outrageous margins over excellent teams. Kentucky went to the Southeast Regional in Charlotte and crushed Wake Forest, 103-69, and then dispatched Florida State, another excellent ACC team, 106-81. Former Kentucky coach Joe B. Hall was quoted in a New Orleans newspaper as saying that the Wildcats would "humiliate Michigan."

Michigan, meanwhile, did not come out of the West by running away with it. The Wolverines had an extremely tough game with UCLA and then hard-fought wins over George Washington and Temple. But Michigan was a strange team at times. It seemed to play to whatever level of competition needed to win and advance. The Wolverines were good and they knew it. They were in the Fi-

nal Four the year before and lost to Duke in the championship game. This was a young, tough and experienced team.

Kansas was playing its best basketball of the season. The Jayhawks beat Ball State by 18, Brigham Young by 14, and after California beat Duke, Kansas smashed the Bears 93-76 to set up a showdown with top seeded Indiana for the right to represent the Midwest in the Final Four. Kansas beat Indiana in the regular season, and it takes a special team to beat the Hoosiers twice in the same season. Kansas did it, beating coach Bob Knight's team, 83-77.

North Carolina was also on a hot streak, winners of 15 of its last 16 games. The Tar Heels, after winning easily over East Carolina and Rhode Island to begin the NCAA tournament, seemed to gain confidence and mental toughness with close wins in the Meadowlands over Arkansas and Cincinnati. The Cincinnati game was probably Carolina's poorest performance in the NCAA tournament, but the Tar Heels were still able to beat a good team to advance to the Final Four.

Dean Smith and Roy Williams, the Kansas coach, are close friends. They already had their first golf date of the spring set for April 26 in California. However, when it was determined that their two teams would meet in the Final Four, both men agreed that they should talk about their teams, not about coaching against each other. "Surely you guys are smart enough to think of something better to write about," Williams admonished the writers.

And there was plenty to write about. At some point during the 1992-93 season, North Carolina, Kentucky, Kansas and Michigan had all been ranked No. 1 in the weekly polls. Indeed, three of the teams--Carolina, Kansas and Michigan--spent the Christmas holidays together in Hawaii, where they all played in the Rainbow Classic. The four teams knew each other well.

The teams arrived in New Orleans on staggered schedules. While some got to town early in the week, North Carolina was the last team to arrive. Smith believes in keeping his team on campus, having the players in class, practice at home, and then go to the tournament site as late as possible.

Ticket scalpers were loving all of this. The dream field pushed ticket prices to a premium. Scalpers would hold up tickets on a street corner and basketball fans would immediately surround them. This was a showcase for college basketball.

While school bands played and thousands of basketball fans converged on New Orleans and reporters asked the players and coaches every question you could imagine, the four basketball teams tried to block all of this out.

"Remember why we're here," Carolina senior George Lynch told his teammates. "We have two more games to win."

UNC's Balanced Attack Too Much For Jayhawks

North Carolina, with its inside-outside combination of Eric Montross and Donald Williams hitting for a combined 16-25 shots from the field and 48 points, beat Kansas 78-68 in the NCAA semifinals in the New Orleans Superdome.

78-68

A crowd of 64,151 crammed into the building to watch Carolina avenge a loss to the Jayhawks and coach Roy Williams in the 1991 NCAA semifinals.

This was a superb basketball game played between two programs that have extremely close connections and the utmost respect for one another. Williams, who finished his fifth season as the Kansas coach, was an assistant to Dean Smith at North Carolina for 10 years and sat on the bench beside Smith in the Superdome when Carolina beat Georgetown for the national championship in 1982. Smith, who recommended Williams for the Kansas job, is a Kansas alumnus and played on the 1952 KU team that won the national championship.

All of that makes good media talk, but it meant nothing to the players on the two teams. They wanted to make their own news, their own mark in basketball history.

North Carolina's defense, which was the team's catalyst all season, stepped up to its highest level in beating Kansas. Many people thought Kansas had the best guard combination in the nation in Adonis Jordan and Rex Walters, two senior veterans, and they certainly played well against the Tar Heels. Walters was 7-15 for 19 points and Jordan was 7-13 for 19 points. Walters got 13 of his points in the first half, and when Carolina put defensive stopper Derrick Phelps on him in the second half, Jordan broke loose for 14 points.

However, Carolina's inside defense, led by Montross, George Lynch and Brian Reese, shut down the Kansas inside game and dominated the backboards, 35-24.

This was a game fitting for Final Four billing. Both teams were emotionally ready, and even though Carolina trailed only once in the entire game--and that at 3-2--it was still anybody's game with less than three minutes to play.

Carolina had many anxious moments, including in the first half when Montross and Phelps each picked up his second personal foul with more than 11 minutes left in the half. Also, forward Brian Reese's vision was hampered in the second half by a migraine headache, and Phelps banged a sore knee and was forced to leave the game for a short period in the second half.

Nevertheless, when Carolina had to make a play to maintain control of the game, the Tar Heels were up to the challenge. Time and again they answered the call.

The first real break in the game came with Carolina leading 21-20. Williams, who had no trouble with depth perception in the spacious Superdome, hit a floating bank shot, and then Montross scored on a follow shot, Lynch on a baseline jumper and then inside on a pass from Henrik Rodl. Carolina led 30-20 with 5:47 left in the first half. But 3-point baskets by Walters and Greg Gurley rallied Kansas late in the half and helped the Jayhawks cut Carolina's lead to 40-36 at halftime.

The early stages of the second half saw Carolina go inside to Montross and Kansas bomb away from 3-point range. Carolina built its lead to 48-41, but Jordan hit a 3-pointer and Richard Scott scored inside to make it 48-46.

Time for another Carolina spurt. Montross scored on a hook shot. Then he got the ball inside, scored and was fouled. He missed the foul shot, but Reese rebounded and scored to boost Carolina's lead to 54-46 with 14:46 to play.

Jordan's 3-pointer sparked a Kansas run that cut Carolina's lead to 56-53 at the TV timeout with 11:54 left in the game. The Tar Heels got two free throws from Williams and a jump hook from Montross to lead 60-53 with the ball. It appeared that a break might be coming. However, Jordan stole the ball from Reese near midcourt and took it for a score, a momentum play.

This one was not going to be easy pickings for either side, but when teams are this good and the season is this far along, you expect a 40-minute struggle.

Carolina's Donald Williams was 5-7 from 3-point range, and one of those "threes" put Carolina ahead 63-55 with 9:35 left.

There was trouble looming for UNC, however. Montross picked up his fourth foul with 8:11 to play. Kansas, seemingly heartened by this turn of events, got an immediate 3-pointer from Jordan to cut Carolina's lead to

Carolina	FG	FT	R	A	TP
Brian Reese	3-5	1-2	4	6	7
George Lynch	5-12	4-6	10	0	14
Eric Montross	9-14	5-8	4	1	23
Derrick Phelps	1-3	1-2	5	6	3
Donald Williams	7-11	6-6	3	0	25
Pat Sullivan	0-2	0-0	1	1	0
Henrik Rodl	0-0	0-0	0	2	0
Kevin Salvadori	3-5	0-0	3	1	6
Dante Calabria	0-0	0-0	0	0	0
Scott Cherry	0-0	0-0	2	0	0
Larry Davis	0-0	0-0	0	0	0
T. Stephenson	0-0	0-0	0	0	0
Ed Geth	0-0	0-0	0	0	0
Matt Wenstrom	0-0	0-0	0	0	0
Team			3		
Total	28-52	17-24	35	17	78
Kansas	**FG**	**FT**	**R**	**A**	**TP**
Darrin Hancock	2-5	2-2	5	1	6
Richard Scott	3-5	2-2	1	1	8
Eric Pauley	2-5	1-1	9	2	5
Rex Walters	7-15	0-0	0	5	19
Adonis Jordan	7-13	0-0	1	4	19
Calvin Rayford	0-0	0-0	0	0	0
Steve Woodberry	2-5	0-0	2	2	4
Patrick Richey	1-4	0-0	2	0	2
Greg Ostertag	0-2	2-2	2	0	2
Greg Gurley	1-2	0-0	0	0	3
Sean Pearson	0-1	0-0	0	0	0
Team			2		
Totals	25-57	7-7	24	15	68

Three-point goals: Carolina 5-7 (Donald Williams 5-7); Kansas 11-20 (Rex Walters 5-9, Adonis Jordan 5-7, Steve Woodberry 0-2, Greg Gurley 1-1, Sean Pearson 0-1)
Turnovers: Carolina 16, Kansas 16

KEYS TO THE GAME: Carolina's defense held Kansas to 43.9 percent shooting...UNC had tremendous balance, able to score inside and outside...Lynch had 10 rebounds for Carolina, as UNC won the battle of the boards, 35-24...Williams' 3-point basket to put Carolina ahead 71-65 was big...UNC's defense shut down Kansas inside.

DEAN SMITH COMMENT: "Our defense on their big people was great. I'm proud of Roy Williams and I'm proud of our team. I am very pleased with our team. We have a chance Monday night. We'll be ready to play. Our goal each year is to win the national championship. I'm concerned for Roy. He is such a competitor, and this is an emotional moment for him."

COACH ROY WILLIAMS COMMENT: "Three hundred teams started in November with a goal to be here. We had a realistic goal to make it. We'll keep knocking on the door and one day we'll knock the sucker down. No coach could be prouder than I am tonight. We put our body and soul into it."

Brian Reese beats Patrick Richey of Kansas to loose ball in the NCAA semifinals.

63-58.

Competitors step up at times like this. Phelps, playing on a hurt knee, drove to the basket for a layup that spun on the rim before falling in with 7:32 left. Carolina led by seven.

Kansas, like Carolina, considers seven minutes a lifetime. Jordan knocked in another 3-pointer to reduce Carolina's lead to 65-61. UNC led 67-63 with 4:36 left when Dean Smith called timeout to get Williams, Montross and Scott Cherry into his lineup.

After Montross made one foul shot for Carolina, Kansas' Darrin Hancock got a loose ball, drove to the basket against Montross and Lynch, and Lynch reached in and fouled him. Lynch asked Montross

why he had not tried to flick the ball from behind, and Montross said he had four fouls and had to be smart. "I want to play on Monday night," Lynch snapped.

Hancock made both foul shots with 2:47 left. Carolina led 68-65. Kansas went with a trap, a defense that Carolina calls 32. Phelps, who was double-teamed, read the sequence perfectly. He got the ball to Williams, who did not hesitate. He got his look at the basket from the right of the key and let it fly. So perfect was the shot that it barely touched any of the net on its way through the basket. Carolina's lead was 71-65 with 2:43 left, and while there was plenty of time for Kansas to change the course of this game, Williams' basket seemed to take something out of the Jayhawks.

"That was a big basket that Donald Williams hit," Kansas coach Williams said afterwards.

Showing that he is much more than just a shooter, Williams stole the ball at his defensive end and later made two foul shots with 1:23 left. Carolina led 73-65 and the defense denied Kansas any good shots in the final seconds.

The Tar Heels prevailed 78-68 to avenge the 79-73 loss to the Jayhawks in the 1991 NCAA semifinals in Indianapolis. Coaches Smith and Williams exchanged handshakes at midcourt and then went their respective ways-- Williams to console his disappointed team and Smith to challenge his to get ready to play one more game.

Lynch and Montross, both tough competitors, came out of a late timeout with their arms around each other. The words they exchanged came in the heat of battle, but each man sought the same goal. Team chemistry remained a Carolina strength, as it had been all season.

And a long season it was. The Tar Heels' record stood at 33-4 with one game to play. The dream was alive.

Kansas coach Williams, a fierce competitor, fought back tears after the game. "Some of you might wonder how it feels to lose to North Carolina, and it still feels crappy," he said. "But I will be pulling like the dickens for North Carolina on Monday night, and if that makes Kentucky and Michigan people

Old habits are hard to break. Kansas coach Roy Williams, a former UNC assistant, chats with George Lynch.

Donald Williams penetrates Kansas defense against Eric Pauley and Richard Scott.

upset, then they don't understand Roy Williams."

Carolina's Smith said his team had to play "maybe our best game of the year to win. That's how well Kansas played."

"Tonight, they were a better team," said Rex Walters of Kansas. "Carolina has a great system. They may be just a little more physical. But they are a classy program, the top program in America, and I think we're up there, too."

All of this began with the start of practice back on Nov. 1. Some 300 Division 1 men's basketball teams had the dream of going to the Final Four and making it to the championship game. Thousands of young men sweated and sacrificed and gave everything they had to make the dream come true.

Now there were two teams left, the best two teams in college basketball. Carolina and Michigan had already played a great game in Hawaii back in December, with Michigan winning, 79-78.

They would do it one more time in the Superdome on Monday night, April 5, 1993, with the biggest prize in all of college athletics at stake. ◉

After having words, George Lynch (34) and Eric Montross are arm-in-arm.

UNC-KANSAS PLAY-BY-PLAY

1993 NCAA Semifinals Play-by-Play
Kansas vs. North Carolina
April 3, 1993
Louisiana Superdome, New Orleans, La.
Kansas Starters: Darrin Hancock, Richard Scott, Eric Pauley, Rex Walters, Adonis Jordan.
North Carolina Starters: Brian Reese, George Lynch, Eric Montross, Derrick Phelps, Donald Williams.

FIRST HALF

19:45: Montross, 6-foot bank shot from the lane (assist Phelps). UNC 2-0.
19:27: Jordan, 3-pointer from 21 feet on the left (assist Walters). KU 3-2.
19:20: Reese, driving layup (assist Phelps). UNC 4-3.
18:43: Reese, backdoor dunk (assist Phelps). UNC 6-3.
17:45: Walters, 3-pointer from 21 feet at the circle (assist Jordan). Tied 6-6.
17:00: Lynch, follow shot. UNC 8-6.
16:04: Montross, alley-oop dunk (assist Phelps). UNC 10-6.
15:50: TV TIMEOUT
15:50: Kevin Salvadori, driving layup (assist Montross). UNC 12-6.
15:22: Montross foul (P1 T1).
14:55: Phelps foul (P1T2).
14:55: Greg Ostertag, made 2 free throws. UNC 12-8.
14:43: Steve Woodberry, foul (P1 T1).
14:43: Salvadori, jump hook from left baseline (assist Reese). UNC 14-8.
13:55: Walters, 9-foot jumper in the lane. UNC 14-10.
13:30: Woodberry, foul (P2T2).
13:30: Lynch, missed 2 free throws.
13:07: Jordan, 10-foot jumper from the right. UNC 14-12.
12:44: Williams, 3-pointer from 21 feet on the left (assist Reese). UNC 17-12.
12:35: Scott, foul (P1T3).
12:22: Pauley, foul (P1T4).
12:22: Montross, made 2 free throws. UNC 19-12.
12:04: Walters, 3-pointer from 21 feet at the circle. UNC 19-15.
11:45: Montross, foul (P2T3).
11:45: TV TIMEOUT
11:16: Henrik Rodl, foul (P1T4).
11:15: Pauley, 12-foot jumper from the left baseline (assist Walters). UNC 19-17.
11:15: Phelps, foul (P2T5).
11:15: Pauley, made 1 of 2 free throws. UNC 19-18.
10:35: Walters, foul (P1T5).
10:24: Lynch, follow shot. UNC 21-18.
10:08: Woodberry, follow shot. UNC 21-20.
9:39: Woodberry, foul (P3T6).
9:22: Williams, 9-foot bank shot from the left. UNC 23-20.
8:20: Montross, follow shot. UNC 25-20.
7:56: TV TIMEOUT
7:12: Lynch, 14-foot jumper from the left baseline (assist Rodl). UNC- 27-20.
6:37: Lynch, layup (assist Rodl). UNC 29-20.
5:47: Ostertag, foul (P1T7).
5:47: Reese, made 1 of 2 free throws. UNC 30-20.
5:21: Walters, 10-foot jumper from the right. UNC 30-22.
4:56: Rodl, foul (P2T6).
4:56: Scott, made 2 free throws. UNC 30-24.
4:26: Williams, 3-pointer from 21 feet on the left (assist Pat Sullivan). UNC 33-24.
4:16: Walters, 3-pointer from 22 feet on the right baseline (assist Jordan). UNC 33-27.
4:01: Lynch, driving layup. UNC 35-27.
3:24: Hancock, follow shot. UNC 35-29.
3:07: TV TIMEOUT
2:08: Williams, 3-pointer from 22 feet on the left (assist Salvadori). UNC 38-32.
1:46: Pauley, layup (assist Hancock). UNC 38-34.
0:07: Salvadori, follow shot. UNC 40-34.
0:01: Hancock, 14-foot jumper from the left baseline. UNC 40-36.
HALFTIME: UNC 40-36

SECOND HALF

19:41: Pauley, foul (P2T1).
19:16: Montross, follow shot. UNC 42-36.
18:54: Walters, 3-pointer from 22 feet on the left. UNC 42-39.
18:14: Montross, layup (assist Phelps). UNC 44-39.
18:13: Pauley, foul (P3T3).
18:13: Montross, missed 1 free throw.
17:57: Montross, 3-foot hook in the lane (assist Reese). UNC 46-39.
17:31: Lynch, foul (P1 T1).
17:23: Sullivan, foul (P1T2).
17:07: Scott, layup (assist Walters). UNC 46-39.
17:01: Scott, foul (P2T3).
17:01: Lynch, made 2 free throws. UNC 48-41.
16:39: Jordan, 3-pointer from 22 feet on the right (assist Scott). UNC 48-44.
16:11: Lynch, foul (P2T3).
16:01: Scott, layup (assist Pauley). UNC 48-46.
15:42: Montross, 8-foot hook in the lane (assist Phelps). UNC 50-46.
15:25: TV TIMEOUT
15:25: Williams, foul (P1T4).
14:51: Montross, layup (assist Reese). UNC 52-46.
14:50: Scott, foul (P3T4).
14:50: Montross, missed 1 free throw.
14:46: Reese, 13-foot bank shot from the left. UNC 54-46.
14:11: Jordan, 3-pointer from 22 feet straight away (assist Walters). UNC 54-49.
13:35: Williams, 6-foot driving jumper in the lane. UNC 56-49.
13:20: Woodberry, 6-foot jumper in the lane. UNC 56-51.
12:47: Scott, 10-foot jumper from the left baseline (assist Jordan). UNC 56-53.
12:46: Ostertag, foul (P2T5).
12:05: Montross, foul (P3T5).
11:53: Hancock, foul (P1 T6).
11:53: TV TIMEOUT
11:43: Walters, foul (P2T7).
11:43: Williams, made 2 free throws. UNC 58-53.
10:56: Montross, 9-foot hook on the left (assist Reese). UNC 60-53.
10:13: Jordan, driving layup. UNC 60-55.
9:35: Williams, 3-pointer from 21 feet on the left. UNC 63-55.
8:11: Montross, foul (P4T6).
8:11: Jordan, 3-pointer from 21 feet on the right (assist Walters). UNC 63-58.
7:32: Phelps, layup. UNC 65-58.
7:16: TV TIMEOUT
6:32: Jordan, 3-pointer from 22 feet on the right (assist Woodberry). UNC 65-61.
6:15: Scott, foul (P4T8).
6:15: Lynch, made 2 free throws. UNC 67-61.
4:49: Patrick Richey, layup (assist Woodberry). UNC 67-63.
4:36: UNC TIMEOUT
4:14: Ostertag, foul (P3T9).
4:14: Montross, made 1 of 2 free throws. UNC 68-63.
2:47: Lynch, foul (P3T7).
2:47: Hancock, made 2 free throws. UNC 68-65.
2:43: Williams, 3-pointer from 21 feet on the right (assist Phelps). UNC 71-65.
1:43: KU TIMEOUT
1:23: Woodberry, foul (P4T10).
1:23: Williams, made 2 free throws. UNC 73-65.
0:44: Scott, foul (P5T11).
0:44: Montross, made 2 free throws. UNC 75-65.
0:29: Jordan, foul (P1 T12).
0:29: Phelps, made 1 of 2 free throws. UNC 76-65.
0:21: Walters, 3-pointer from 21 feet on the left (assist Pauley). UNC 76-68.
0:19: KU TIMEOUT
0:09: Richey, foul (P1T13).
0:09: Williams, made 2 free throws. UNC 78-68.

FINAL SCORE: UNC 78-68.

UNC Outlasts Michigan To Win National Title

Monday, April 5, 1993, was a long day for the North Carolina and Michigan basketball players. The two teams would play for the national championship in the Superdome at 8:22 p.m. New Orleans time.

77-71

Time dragged. It was a typical early spring day in New Orleans. It was cloudy, windy, on the brisk side. Players on both teams did what they could to pass the time. They played cards, visited with family and friends, walked around New Orleans.

The game, though, was seldom out of mind. How could it be? Fans on the street and in the hotel lobbies wore Carolina or Michigan hats and shirts, the pep bands of the two schools broke out in music whenever three or more fans gathered and requested it.

The media was here from all over the United States to cover college basketball's championship game.

Competitors live for moments such as these. It is their chance to perform at the highest level with the most at stake. The anticipation and the waiting is fun on one hand, but it is also mentally exhausting and nerve-wracking.

Carolina's team boarded its bus shortly before 7 p.m. for the 10-minute ride to the Superdome. It was a quiet and reflective ride. Some players wore head phones and listened to music. Others looked out the bus window and thought about the game. There was very little talking.

This was the last time this team would go together to play a game.

Once in the locker room, Carolina's players and coaches did everything they could to treat this as just another game. Pat Sullivan and Scott Cherry did some fancy dribbling and passing, their Harlem Globetrotter imitation. Players get themselves ready to play in different ways. North Carolina's players obviously knew what was at stake. They had worked and competed hard for this moment. They knew this was the biggest game of the season. Still, Carolina's locker room was relaxed and loose, considering what was at stake.

Michigan's team had a reputation of doing a lot of talking on the court. Temple coach John Chaney, whose team lost a hard game to the Wolverines in the NCAA tournament, wasn't complimentary of Michigan's style. Car-

olina and Michigan played in the Rainbow Classic in Hawaii in December, a game won by Michigan 79-78, and Carolina's players recalled that before that game and early on during it, the Wolverines did a lot of talking, were cocky and sure. But as the game went along and Michigan saw first-hand the toughness and competitiveness of the Tar Heels, the talking pretty much stopped.

Jimmy King, an excellent player on the Michigan team, had a feeling back in December that the two teams would meet again. "They are tough," King said then of the Tar Heels, "but if we play them again in the NCAA tournament, we will be improved and we'll beat 'em again."

There was very little talking as the two teams warmed up before the championship game. Michigan's Chris Webber and Carolina's Donald Williams knew each other from high school all-star games, and as they passed during warmups, Webber told Williams "that it was all over." Williams just smiled and went about his business.

The first game between the two teams in Hawaii was a masterpiece. Would this game for the national championship live up to its billing? Many times they don't.

Carolina, loose and extremely aggressive on defense early, broke to a 9-4 lead. But Michigan lost in the championship game the previous season and was determined to win it this time. The Wolverines, playing confidently now, went on a 19-4 run and led 23-13. Michigan did not hit a 3-point field goal in beating Kentucky in overtime in the semifinals, but it hit three straight 3-pointers in this run, two by Rob Pelinka and one by Jalen Rose. Michigan had four 3-point field goals in the first half, plus three earned the old-fashioned way--a basket and a foul shot.

Carolina survived this blitz, just as it had a first-half onslaught by Michigan in Hawaii, and outscored the Wolverines 12-2 to tie the game at 25 with 7:49 left. The play was so intense, so spectacular at times that many of the 64,151 in attendance stood to watch.

UNC took the lead at 33-32 and kept it for the rest of the half. Donald Williams hit a 3-pointer with 49 seconds left in the half to give the Tar Heels a 42-36 lead at halftime.

Very little was decided in the first half, except that this game was going to be bitterly

Carolina	FG	FT	R	A	TP
Brian Reese	2-7	4-4	5	3	8
George Lynch	6-12	0-0	10	1	12
Eric Montross	5-11	6-9	5	0	16
Derrick Phelps	4-6	1-2	3	6	9
Donald Williams	8-12	4-4	1	1	25
Pat Sullivan	1-2	1-2	1	1	3
Kevin Salvadori	0-0	2-2	4	1	2
Henrik Rodl	1-4	0-0	0	0	2
Dante Calabria	0-0	0-0	0	0	0
Matt Wenstrom	0-1	0-0	0	0	0
Scott Cherry	0-0	0-0	0	0	0
Total	27-55	18-23	29	13	77
Michigan	**FG**	**FT**	**R**	**A**	**TP**
Chris Webber	11-18	1-2	11	1	23
Ray Jackson	2-3	2-2	1	1	6
Juwan Howard	3-8	1-1	7	3	7
Jalen Rose	5-12	0-0	1	4	12
Jimmy King	6-13	2-2	6	4	15
Eric Riley	1-3	0-0	3	1	2
Rob Pelinka	2-4	0-0	2	1	6
Michael Talley	0-0	0-0	0	1	0
James Voskuil	0-1	0-0	0	1	0
Team			2		
Totals	30-62	6-7	33	17	71

Three-point goals: Carolina 5-11 (Brian Reese 0-1, Derrick Phelps 0-1, Donald Williams 5-7, Henrik Rodl 0-2); Michigan 5-15 (Chris Webber 0-1, Jalen Rose 2-6, Jimmy King 1-5, Rob Pelinka 2-3)

Turnovers: Carolina 10, Michigan 14

KEYS TO THE GAME: Williams shot extremely well, and Carolina hit 61.9 percent from the field in the second half...Lynch and Montross scored 28 points inside, and Lynch had 10 rebounds against Michigan's athletic frontline.

DEAN SMITH COMMENT: "This was a tremendous win over an outstanding Michigan team that gave a great effort. I do congratulate Michigan on that effort."

COACH STEVE FISHER COMMENT: "I felt we were in much better control in the second half. We had a much better flow to our game in the second half. North Carolina is a very physical team and they got to the free throw line, which is what championship teams do."

Brian Reese unleashes a finger-roll against Michigan's Rob Pelinka and Chris Webber.

The second half was a showcase for college basketball. Two great teams competed at such a high level and neither would flinch. It's a sad commentary on America's sports society that one of these teams would be considered a loser, a failure to win the so-called "big game." Both teams had won big games all season to get to this point, and once here, they played admirably in a situation that was so pressurized that it was stifling.

Carolina's lead in the early second half ranged from four to six points until Williams hit a 3-pointer with 16:28 left to give the Tar Heels a 53-46 advantage. That wouldn't last long. Michigan scored six straight points to cut UNC's lead to 53-52, and with 8:35 left, the Wolverines went ahead 60-58 on a Chris Webber dunk. It was the first time Michigan had led in the game since 32-31.

The game would become one of big plays, each team answering challenges. Williams hit a 3-pointer to put Carolina ahead 61-60. When Jalen Rose hit a 3-pointer to give Michigan a 65-61 lead with 6:06 left, Williams hit off the left baseline to make it 65-63. King hit a jumper to give Michigan a 67-63 lead with 4:31 left, but Williams answered 19 seconds later with a 3-pointer from the right of the key. It was 67-66 Michigan.

Carolina's defense stopped Michigan, and moving out on the fastbreak, UNC's Brian Reese hit Derrick Phelps for a layup. The ball stayed on the rim for a second before falling through, and Carolina led 68-67 with 3:07 left.

After another defensive stop, Carolina coach Dean Smith took timeout and put Pat Sullivan and Henrik Rodl in for Williams and Reese. Twenty-eight seconds remained on the shot clock as Carolina broke its huddle. George Lynch, UNC's brilliant senior, had the ball to the right of the lane with five seconds left on the shot clock. He spun left into the lane, fell backwards slightly and lifted a shot over the arm of Michigan defensive star Juwan Howard, 6-10. The shot, one of the most important Lynch ever took, was good and the Tar Heels led 70-67 with 2:28 left.

Carolina's defense stopped Michigan again and got the ball back with 1:44 left. Michigan, with only three team fouls, could not send UNC to the foul line until it fouled three more times. Fouling quickly, Michigan got its sixth team foul with 1:10 left. But for some reason, it didn't foul as Carolina inbounded the ball, and Lynch fed Eric Montross behind the Michigan defense for a dunk and a 72-67 lead with 1:03 left.

contested for 40 minutes. The end could come down to a last-second shot, just as it had in Hawaii. The only player on either team who had foul trouble at the half was Michigan's Ray Jackson, who had three personals.

Michigan shot a little better than Carolina in the first half--44.8 percent to 41.2 percent--but UNC had only three turnovers to Michigan's 10. Carolina's defense was bothering Michigan. The Wolverines, the first seed and champions of the NCAA West, hit an uncharacteristic 4-8 from 3-point range in the first half. The rebounding was virtually even.

Jackson scored with 48 seconds left to cut Carolina's lead to 72-69 and Michigan took its final timeout. Brian Reese fielded the ball on the inbounds play and stepped out of bounds. Michigan's Webber rebounded a missed shot and scored with 36 seconds left to make it 72-71.

Michigan's Pelinka fouled Pat Sullivan with 20 seconds left, and Sullivan went to the line to shoot one-and-one. "This is for the national championship," a Michigan player reminded Sullivan.

Sullivan made the first foul shot, but when he missed the second one, Webber rebounded. He looked to his right to pass the ball to Rose, but Lynch stepped in to deny that option. Then Webber tried to call a timeout but was ignored by the official, who looked away. And while the official looked away, he missed Webber's obvious travel in front of Carolina's bench.

Michigan's Ray Jackson tries to block shot attempt by Eric Montross.

Michigan player gets in first-half trouble against defensive wizards George Lynch and Derrick Phelps.

Webber dribbled the ball into the corner in front of his bench, where he picked up his dribble and was trapped by Lynch and Phelps. No passing lanes were open, so Webber made a "T" with his hands and called timeout. A timeout Michigan didn't have.

A technical foul was called with 11 seconds left. Dean Smith told Donald Williams to shoot them, and Williams hit both. Then Williams was fouled with eight seconds left and made two more foul shots. The sophomore was at his best. He scored 25 points, hit 5-7 from 3-point range, and was named the Final Four's MVP. Lynch and Montross joined him on the All-Tournament team.

Carolina had its dream, a 77-71 win over Michigan for the national championship. Dean Smith and Michigan coach Steve Fisher shook hands. Smith hugged his players, who celebrated at mid-court.

This time, Carolina did cut down the nets, and the last one on the ladder was Smith. Before he took the net down, he pointed to the players, one at a time, and said, "This is for you and you and you..."

More than an hour after the game ended, the media finally left Carolina's locker room. George Lynch, who had led this team for 38 games, sat in front of his locker. He called for some scissors to cut the tape off his ankles. He hesitated before taking off his Carolina uniform, because he knew he would do it for the last time.

"Here goes," he said, and pulled the sweaty No. 34 jersey over his head.

He and his teammates had been on a mission, one that began in March 1992 after UNC was beaten by Ohio State in the NCAA tournament in Lexington. They worked hard in the offseason, Lynch always leading the way, and once practice began on Nov. 1, the Tar Heels stalked this national championship. There were a few downturns, some moments of doubt, but the objective stayed the same.

As Lynch sat there in front of his locker and tried to absorb it all, he noticed a message scribbled on the chalkboard in the middle of the room: "Congratulations. You are a great team. There will be no practice tomorrow."

Lynch smiled, showered, and left with his teammates for the bus ride back to the hotel.

The North Carolina Tar Heels were the best of college basketball. They were the 1993 NCAA champions.

North Carolina Tar Heels
1993 National Champions

UNC-MICHIGAN PLAY-BY-PLAY

1993 NCAA Finals Play-by-Play
Michigan vs. North Carolina
April 5, 1993
Louisiana Superdome, New Orleans, La.
Michigan Starters: Chris Webber, Ray Jackson, Juwan Howard, Jalen Rose, Jimmy King.
North Carolina Starters: Brian Reese, George Lynch, Eric Montross, Derrick Phelps, Donald Williams.

FIRST HALF
18:57: Phelps, driving layup. UNC 2-0.
18:15: Montross, follow shot. UNC 4-0.
18:15: King foul (P1 T1).
18:15: Montross, made 1 free throw. UNC 5-0.
17:47: Jackson, foul (P1 T2).
17:29: Williams, foul (P1 T1).
17:29: King, made 2 free throws. UNC 5-2.
17:01: Webber, dunk (assist Rose). UNC 5-4.
16:28: Jackson, foul (P2T3).
16:28: Montross, made 2 free throws. UNC 7-4.
16:04: Webber, foul (P1T4).
15:59: Lynch, alley-oop dunk (assist Phelps). UNC 9-4.
15:30: TV TIMEOUT
15:30: Rob Pelinka, 3-pointer from 20 feet at the circle (assist Rose). UNC 9-7.
14:39: Pelinka, 3-pointer from 22 feet on the left (assist Rose). Michigan 10-9.
14:03: Rose, 3-pointer from 22 feet on the left (assist Webber). Michigan 13-9.
13:28: Webber, 7-foot jumper from the left. Michigan 15-9.
13:08: Montross, dunk (assist Williams). Michigan 15-11.
12:49: Webber, follow shot. Michigan 17-11.
12:49: Lynch, foul. (P1 T2).
12:49: Webber, made 1 free throw. Michigan 18-11.
12:33: King, foul (P2T5).
12:22: Reese, 7-foot turnaround jumper in the lane. Michigan 18-13.
12:08: Howard, 4-foot jumper in the lane. Michigan 20-13.
12:07: Kevin Salvadori, foul (P1T3).
12:07: Howard, made 1 free throw. Michigan 21-13.
11:32: Howard, 4-foot jumper in the lane off a fastbreak (assist Michael Talley). Michigan 23-13.
11:12: Howard, foul (P1 T6).
11:12: Salvadori, made 2 free throws. Michigan 23-15.
11:12: TV TIMEOUT
10:40: Lynch, layup (assist Reese). Michigan 23-17.
10:10: Webber, layup (assist Rose). Michigan 25-17.
10:10: Lynch, foul (P2T4).
10:10: Webber, missed 1 free throw.
9:42: Howard, foul (P2T7).
9:42: Phelps, made 1 of 2 free throws. Michigan 25-18.
9:37: Lynch, 8-foot jumper from the right (assist Reese). Michigan 25-20.
8:38: Webber, foul (P2T8).
8:38: Reese, made 2 free throws. Michigan 25-22.
8:02: Williams, 3-pointer from 22 feet on the right baseline. Tied 25-25.
7:49: Pat Sullivan, foul (P1 T5).
7:49: TV TIMEOUT
7:32: King, 3-pointer from 22 feet on the left (assist Jackson). Michigan 28-25.
7:00: Sullivan, 18-foot jumper from the left (assist Salvadori). Michigan 28-27.
5:53: Lynch, layup. UNC 29-28. 5:31: Henrik Rodl, driving reverse layup (assist Phelps). UNC 31-28.
4:52: Rose, 8-foot jumper from the right baseline. UNC 31-30.
4:14: Montross, foul (P1T6).
3:50: King, layup. Michigan 32-31.
3:42: Rose, foul (P1T9).
3:42: Reese, made 2 free throws. UNC 33-32.
3:42: TV TIMEOUT
3:05: Williams, 10-foot driving jumper from the right baseline. UNC 35-32.
2:55: Reese, foul (P1T7).
2:55: Jackson, made 2 free throws. UNC 35-34.

2:22: Phelps, 6-foot jumper in the lane. UNC 37-34.
1:58: Eric Riley, follow shot. UNC 37-36.
1:47: Jackson, foul (P3T10).
1:47: Montross, made 2 free throws. UNC 39-36.
0:49: Williams, 3-pointer from 23 feet on the right. UNC 42-36.

HALFTIME: UNC 42-36

SECOND HALF
19:49: Montross, 8-foot hook in the lane (assist Phelps). UNC 44-36.
19:36: Webber, layup (assist King). UNC 44-38.
19:16: King, 10-foot jumper from the right baseline. UNC 44-40.
18:32: Reese, follow shot. UNC 46-40.
17:57: Montross, hook (assist Phelps). UNC 48-40.
17:34: Rose, 13-foot jumper from the right. UNC 48-42.
17:14: Rose, foul (P2T1).
16:49: Webber, layup (assist Howard). UNC 48-44.
16:28: Williams, 3-pointer from 22 feet on the right (assist Sullivan). UNC 51-44.
16:14: King, 4-foot bank shot in the lane (assist Howard). UNC 51-46.
15:55: TV TIMEOUT
15:55: Williams, 13-foot jumper from the right. UNC 53-46.
15:25: Jackson, 18-foot jumper from the left (assist King). UNC 53-48.
15:16: MICHIGAN TIMEOUT
15:16: Rose, driving jumper. UNC 53-50.
14:41: Webber, dunk off a fastbreak. UNC 53-52.
13:57: Jackson, foul (P4T2).
13:57: Montross, made 1 of 2 free throws. UNC 54-52.
13:42: Lynch, foul (P3T1).
12:07: Montross, foul (P2T2).
11:47: Phelps, driving layup. UNC 56-52.
11:37: Webber, layup (assist Riley). UNC 56-54.
11:18: Riley, foul (P1T3).
11:18: Montross, missed 2 free throws.
10:09: King, dunk off a fastbreak. Tied 56-56.
9:37: Lynch, 16-foot jumper from the circle (assist Phelps). UNC 58-56.
9:16: Webber, reverse layup (assist King). Tied 58-58.
8:35: Webber, alley-oop dunk (assist Howard). Michigan 60-58.
7:37: Williams, 3-pointer from 23 feet on the left. UNC 61-60.
6:59: Howard, 15-foot jumper from the left (assist Pelinka). Michigan 62-61.
6:50: UNC TIMEOUT
6:06: Rose, 3-pointer from 22 feet on the right (assist James Voskuil). Michigan 65-61.
4:45: Williams, 12-foot from the left baseline. Michigan 65-63.
4:31: King, 16-foot jumper from the left baseline. Michigan 67-63. 4:12: Williams, 3-pointer from 22 feet on the right (assist Phelps). Michigan 67-66.
3:07: Phelps, layup off a fastbreak (assist Reese). UNC 68-67.
2:28: UNC TIMEOUT
2:28: Lynch, 4-foot turnaround jumper. UNC 70-67.
1:44: Sullivan, foul (P2T3).
1:18: Rose, foul (P3T4).
1:18: MICHIGAN TIMEOUT
1:15: Howard, foul (P3T5).
1:10: Talley, foul (P1T6).
1:03: Montross, dunk (assist Lynch). UNC 72-67.
0:48: Jackson, 18-foot jumper from the right (assist King). UNC 72-69. 0:46: MICHIGAN TIMEOUT
0:36: Webber, follow shot. UNC 72-71.
0:20: Pelinka, foul (P1T7).
0:20: Sullivan, made 1 of 2 free throws. UNC 73-71.
0:11: MICHIGAN TIMEOUT (TECHNICAL FOUL).
0:11: Williams, made 2 free throws. UNC 75-71.
0:08: Jackson, foul (P5T8).
0:08: Williams, made 2 free throws. UNC 77-71.

FINAL SCORE: UNC 77-71.

SOUTHEAST

Seed	Team	Score
1	Kentucky	96
16	Rider	52
8	Utah	86
9	Pittsburgh	65
5	Wake Forest	81
12	Tenn.-Chatt.	58
4	Iowa	82
13	Northeast La.	69
6	Kansas St.	53
11	Tulane	55
3	Florida State	82
14	Evansville	70
7	Western Kentucky	55
10	Memphis State	52
2	Seton Hall	81
15	Tennessee State	59

Kentucky 83
Utah 62
Memorial Coliseum-Nashville, Tennessee
Wake Forest 84
Iowa 78
Tulane 63
Florida State 94
Orlando Arena-Orlando, Florida
Western Kentucky 72
Seton Hall 68

Kentucky 103
Wake Forest 69
Florida State 81
Western Kentucky 78

Charlotte Coliseum

Kentucky 106
Florida State 81

Kentucky 78

WEST

Seed	Team	Score
1	Michigan	84
16	Coastal Carolina	63
8	Iowa State	70
9	UCLA	81
5	New Mexico	68
12	Geo. Washington	82
4	Georgia Tech	78
13	Southern-B.R.	93
6	Illinois	75
11	Long Beach State	72
3	Vanderbilt	92
14	Boise State	72
7	Temple	75
10	Missourri	61
2	Arizona	61
15	Santa Clara	64

Michigan 86
UCLA OT 84
McKale Center-Tucson, Arizona
Geo. Washington 90
Southern-B.R. 80
Illinois 68
Vanderbilt 85
Jon M. Huntsman Center-Salt Lake City, Utah
Temple 68
Santa Clara 57

Michigan 72
Geo. Washington 64
Vanderbilt 59
Temple 67

Kingdome

Michigan 77
Temple 72

Michigan 81

Louisiana Dome

Michigan

71

Louisiana Dome

North Carolina

Louisiana Dome

77

EAST

Seed	Team	Score
1	North Carolina	85
16	East Carolina	65
8	Rhode Island	74
9	Purdue	68
5	St. John's (NY)	85
12	Texas Tech	67
4	Arkansas	94
13	Holy Cross	64
6	Virginia	78
11	Manhattan	66
3	Massachusetts	54
14	Pennsylvania	50
7	New Mexico State	93
10	Nebraska	79
2	Cincinnati	93
15	Coppin State	66

North Carolina 112
Rhode Island 67
LJVM Coliseum-Winston Salem, North Carolina
St. John's (NY) 74
Arkansas 80
Virginia 71
Massachusetts 56
Carrier Dome-Syracuse, New York
New Mexico State 55
Cincinnati 92

North Carolina 80
Arkansas 74
Virginia 54
Cincinnati 71

Meadowlands Arena

North Carolina 75
Cincinnati 68 OT

North Carolina 78

North Carolina

MIDWEST

Seed	Team	Score
1	Indiana	97
16	Wright State	54
8	New Orleans	55
9	Xavier (Ohio)	73
5	Oklahoma State	74
12	Marquette	62
4	Louisville	76
13	Delaware	70
6	California	66
11	Louisiana State	64
3	Duke	105
14	Southern Illinois	70
7	Brigham Young	80
10	Southern Methodist	71
2	Kansas	94
15	Ball State	72

Indiana 73
Xavier (Ohio) 70
Hoosier Dome-Indianapolis, Indiana
Oklahoma State 63
Louisville 78
California 82
Duke 77
Rosemont Horizon-Chicago, Illinois
Brigham Young 76
Kansas 90

Indiana 82
Louisville 69
California 76
Kansas 93

Saint Louis Arena

Indiana 77
Kansas 83

Kansas 68

Louisiana Dome

FINAL BRACKET

Final Stats For National Champions

PLAYER	G	Field Goal M-A	Pct	Free Throw M-A	Pct	Reb	Avg	A	TO	S	Pf-D	Pts	Avg
Dante Calabria	35	24-52	46.2	7-9	77.8	27	0.8	29	21	9	26-1	64	1.8
Scott Cherry	33	20-33	60.6	25-35	71.4	23	0.7	30	21	9	15-0	69	2.1
Larry Davis	21	14-40	35.0	14-23	60.9	16	0.8	4	5	6	4-0	44	2.1
Ed Geth	21	16-25	64.0	12-17	70.6	28	1.3	0	7	4	14-0	44	2.1
Pearce Landry	1	0-1	00.0	0-0	00.0	1	1.0	1	0	1	1-0	0	0.0
George Lynch	38	235-469	50.1	88-132	66.7	365	9.6	72	89	89	85-3	560	14.7
Eric Montross	38	222-361	61.5	156-228	68.4	290	7.6	28	66	22	113-3	600	15.8
Derrick Phelps	36	111-243	45.7	56-83	67.5	157	4.4	196	110	82	68-1	293	8.1
Brian Reese	35	152-300	50.7	72-104	69.2	125	3.6	83	82	24	34-0	398	11.4
Henrik Rodl	38	58-117	49.6	25-38	65.8	57	1.5	136	60	39	50-0	163	4.3
Kevin Salvadori	38	66-144	45.8	38-54	70.4	138	3.6	12	24	7	79-2	170	4.5
Travis Stephenson	21	5-11	45.5	0-0	00.0	6	0.3	3	4	0	1-0	10	0.5
Pat Sullivan	38	88-170	51.8	60-76	78.9	92	2.4	51	35	26	43-0	245	6.4
Matt Wenstrom	33	34-61	55.7	16-27	59.3	47	1.4	7	13	1	17-0	84	2.5
Donald Williams	37	174-380	45.8	97-117	82.9	71	1.9	46	39	38	52-0	528	14.3
Team						118			5				
UNC TOTALS	38	1219-2407	50.6	666-943	70.6	1561	41.1	698	581	357	602-10	3272	86.1
OPP TOTALS	38	978-2370	41.3	405-603	67.2	1222	32.2	536	686	273	750-20	2596	68.3

DEADBALL REBOUNDS: UNC 148, Opponents 124.
3-POINT FIELD GOALS: Calabria 9-23, 39.1; Cherry 4-8, 50.0; Davis 2-9, 22.2; Lynch 2-11, 18.2; Phelps 15-48, 31.3; Reese 22-60, 36.7; Rodl 22-62, 35.5; Stephenson 0-1, 00.0 Sullivan 9-30, 30.0; Wenstrom, 0-1, 00.0; Williams 83-199, 41.7.

UNC TOTALS: 168-452, 37.2;
OPP TOTALS: 235-716, 32.8.
BLOCKED SHOTS: Calabria 1, Cherry 1, Lynch 21, Montross 47, Phelps 3, Reese 7, Rodl 10, Salvadori 45, Sullivan 2, Wenstrom 6, Williams 2.
UNC TOTALS: 145; **OPP TOTALS:** 138.

RESULTS

(34-4, 14-2 ACC)

Old Dominion	W	119-82	Smith Center	18,807	Dec. 1
*South Carolina	W	108-67	Charlotte Coliseum	17,804	Dec. 4
*Texas	W	104-68	Charlotte Coliseum	16,931	Dec. 5
Virginia Tech	W	78-62	Roanoke Civic Center	8,554	Dec. 9
Houston	W	84-76	Smith Center	20,605	Dec. 13
Butler	W	103-56	Hinkle Fieldhouse	9,951	Dec. 20
Ohio State	W	84-64	St. John Arena	13,276	Dec. 22
**SW Louisiana	W	80-59	Blaisdell Arena	7,634	Dec. 28
**Michigan	L	78-79	Blaisdell Arena	7,640	Dec. 29
**Hawaii	W	101-84	Blaisdell Arena	7,635	Dec. 30
Cornell	W	98-60	Smith Center	18,458	Jan. 4
N.C. State	W	100-67	Reynolds Coliseum	12,400	Jan. 7
Maryland	W	101-73	Smith Center	21,407	Jan. 9
Georgia Tech	W	80-67	Smith Center	21,572	Jan. 13
Clemson	W	82-72	Littlejohn Coliseum	11,000	Jan. 16
Virginia	W	80-58	Smith Center	21,572	Jan. 20
Seton Hall	W	70-66	Meadowlands Arena	20,029	Jan. 24
Florida State	W	82-77	Smith Center	21,572	Jan. 27
Wake Forest	L	62-88	Joel Coliseum	14,475	Jan. 30
Duke	L	67-81	Cameron Ind. Stadium	9,314	Feb. 3
N.C. State	W	104-58	Smith Center	21,572	Feb. 6
Maryland	W	77-63	Cole Field House	14,500	Feb. 9
Georgia Tech	W	77-66	Alexander Coliseum	9,992	Feb. 14
Clemson	W	80-67	Smith Center	21,147	Feb. 17
Virginia	W	78-58	University Hall	8,864	Feb. 21
Notre Dame	W	85-56	Smith Center	21,572	Feb. 23
Florida State	W	86-76	Leon Civic Center	13,251	Feb. 27
Wake Forest	W	83-65	Smith Center	21,572	March 3
Duke	W	83-69	Smith Center	21,572	March 7
***Maryland	W	102-66	Charlotte Coliseum	23,532	March 12
***Virginia	W	74-56	Charlotte Coliseum	23,532	March 13
***Georgia Tech	L	75-77	Charlotte Coliseum	23,532	March 14
$East Carolina	W	85-65	Joel Coliseum	14,366	March 18
$Rhode Island	W	112-67	Joel Coliseum	14,366	March 20
³Arkansas	W	80-74	Meadowlands Arena	19,761	March 26
³Cincinnati	W	75-68 ot	Meadowlands Arena	19,761	March 28
$Kansas	W	78-68	Louisiana Superdome	64,151	April 3
$Michigan	W	77-71	Louisiana Superdome	64,151	April 5

*Diet Pepsi Tournament of Champions, Charlotte. **Rainbow Classic, Honolulu. ***ACC Tournament, Charlotte. $NCAA Tournament, Winston-Salem. ³NCAA Tournament, East Rutherford, N.J. $NCAA Final Four, New Orleans, La.

Sports Illustrated

P R E S E N T S

The Dream Season

A Celebration of North Carolina's
1992–93 National Champions

Sports Illustrated

Nothing Could Be Finer

NORTH CAROLINA TOPS MICHIGAN FOR THE NCAA TITLE

Sports Illustrated

MARCH 8, 1993 · $2.95

Look Who's No.1

It's Brian Reese
And the
North Carolina
Tar Heels

SPORTS

■ Sports
■ Television
■ Comics

Metro
Edition

Williams And Pitino Will Win Eventually

■ Both coaches have the talent and resources for a return to the Final Four

By Paul Attner
THE SPORTING NEWS

NEW ORLEANS

In the past three years, they have totaled three Final Four appearances between them. And no national championships.

Make a list of the best coaches and they would be near the top. Still, no NCAA titles. But here is a prediction: Within the next three years, Kansas' Roy Williams or Kentucky's Rick Pitino will finish atop the college heap.

SPORTS COMMENTARY

"We will be back and we are going to keep knocking on this door, and one day we will knock the sucker down," says Williams, who lost in the title game to Duke two years ago and in a semifinal game to North Carolina last Saturday in New Orleans.

"We've got a very fine program established at the University of Kentucky," says Pitino, whose team fell to Michigan in the other semifinal. "We are going to keep plugging away at our goal."

ROY WILLIAMS

This could have been Pitino's year. Entering the Final Four, his Wildcats were favored to take the title. But the cornerstone of his offensive diversity — the 3-point shot — led to his team's undoing. Kentucky, which made 46 percent of its 3-point attempts during the first four games of the tournament, was seven for 21 against Michigan. Still, it isn't hard to imagine the Wildcats returning to this same event soon and using the 3-pointer to capture the championship. Pitino, one of the shot's leading advocates, certainly isn't going to abandon his faith in the tactic.

RICK PITINO

That time might have been next season, if forward Jamal Mashburn had decided to return for his senior year. With Mashburn, Kentucky would have been the odds-on choice to finish No. 1. But Mashburn is jumping to the National Basketball Association, and Pitino needs to reload without his best player.

BUT EVEN WITHOUT Mashburn, Kentucky will be a title challenger. The Wildcats expect big things from 6-10 Walter McCarty, who sat out this season under Proposition 48. He should move into Mashburn's spot. Guard Dale Brown, the only senior starter, will be replaced by a trio of players, including freshman gunner Tony Delk. Big men Rodney Dent and Andre Riddick matured considerably during the season and freshmen Jared Prickett and Rodrick Rhodes have the potential to be standout forwards.

Pitino also can turn to junior guard Travis Ford, whose leadership and 3-point shooting helped turn Kentucky into an elite squad. Ford's role will be even bigger next season, now that Mashburn is gone.

See BE BACK, Page 18

UNC Wins Title

UNC's Derrick Phelps (right) passes around Michigan's Jimmy King.

AP PHOTO

■ Carolina's strong inside game and Williams' outside shooting give Smith second championship; critical mistake by Michigan's Webber in final seconds seals outcome of 77-71 Tar Heel win

By Bill Cole
JOURNAL REPORTER

NEW ORLEANS

North Carolina held on in a dramatic, nerve-wracking finish to beat Michigan 77-71 at the Louisiana Superdome last night and win the NCAA Tournament championship.

The Tar Heels had to come from four points down in the last 4:14 to give Coach Dean Smith his second national championship. They did it behind guard Donald Williams, who buried 3-pointers and free throws, and with the help of one critical mistake by Chris Webber, the Wolverines' All-America forward.

The Tar Heels closed out the game with a 14-4 run after trailing 67-63. It started when Williams buried a 3-pointer and guard Derrick Phelps scored on a break, giving the Tar Heels the lead for good at 68-67.

After a missed shot by Jimmy King of the Wolverines, the Tar Heels built their lead to 70-67 on a layup by George Lynch. But The Wolverines lost their possession when guard Jalen Rose lost control of the ball in the lane and Williams grabbed it.

The Tar Heels went to a spread, beat the Wolverines' pressure, and Lynch fed center Eric Montross for a dunk that built the lead to 72-67 with one minute left.

UNC's Eric Montross (right) flips a pass over to Donald Williams

AP PHOTO

The Wolverines cut the lead to 72-71 on baskets by Ray Jackson and Webber. They fouled Pat Sullivan with 20 seconds left and sent him to the free-throw line with a one-and-one.

Sullivan, a 79-percent free-throw shooter, made the first to give the Tar Heels a 73-71 lead. But he missed the second, giving the Wolverines life.

But Webber's bad decision followed, ending any chance the Wolverines had of winning.

Webber grabbed the rebound, raced down court, stopped in front of the Michigan bench and called timeout. But the Wolverines had no timeouts left and were called for a technical.

THE CALL GAVE THE TAR HEELS two free throws and the ball with 11 seconds left. It also brought back memories of a similar gaffe in 1982, when the Tar Heels defeated Georgetown 63-62 here and won their first NCAA title under Smith, when Fred Brown threw away the ball in the last seconds.

"Chris said he thought he heard someone holler and call for a timeout," Coach Steve Fisher of Michigan said. "It's an awful way for the season to end. In the heat of the moment, things happen."

Williams buried both free throws to build the lead to 75-71.

Williams was fouled again on the inbounds play with eight seconds left and made two more free throws to end the scoring. He finished with 25 points.

See CHAMPS, Page 18

Wallace's Win Capped Emotional Weekend at Bristol

By Mike Mulhern
JOURNAL REPORTER

BRISTOL, Tenn.

Rusty Wallace kept it all in perspective Sunday: "I don't want this win to stand in the way of the memory of my buddy," he said of Alan Kulwicki after winning the crash-marred Food City 500 in a tight battle with Dale Earnhardt and Kyle Petty.

The pall from Kulwicki's death Thursday night in a plane crash just a few miles from here hung over Bristol Raceway all

weekend. Only that burst of happy emotion from Saturday winner Michael Waltrip in proposing in victory lane to his fiance could break the gloom.

However, emotions of every sort were in evidence Sunday on the track. And it was remarkable that Buddy Parrott, Wallace's crew chief, was able to keep Wallace calm through the three-hour race.

"Emotions were high," Parrott said. "One time Rusty got real uptight on the radio, and we tried to calm him down.

Then he came back on the radio and said 'Hey, my timing is a little high today. Y'all just work with me, and keep me cool.'

"But Bristol brings that out. The guys are so intense. After that race, people said 'Where'd you celebrate?' But riding home in the plane I probably didn't say three words, because I was drained, emotionally, not physically, but mentally. Thinking about the race, and the strategy you have to work with, and of course our good buddy Alan.

"I think every comment I made the first thing I said was 'Alan Kulwicki. . . .'

"Alan was on everybody's minds, from the long prayer we had just before the start of the race till the end.

"After the race, Todd (Parrott, the team's chassis man) said 'Turn the car around.' Rusty said 'What?' 'Turn the car around.' And so Rusty did that 'Polish' victory lap. Emotionally for Todd that

See EMOTIONS, Page 18

OPENING DAY: Baseball Returns to the Field

Greg Maddux, last year's NL Cy Young Award winner with the Cubs, led the Braves to an opening-day win over his old team.

AP PHOTO

THE ASSOCIATED PRESS

With tears in Cleveland and cheers in Miami, baseball returned yesterday.

Jose Canseco started the 1993 season with the first hit, Dwight Gooden pitched the first shutout, Greg Maddux won at Wrigley Field — for Atlanta, not for the Chicago Cubs.

And once again, after a winter of turmoil and turnover, the focus was on the field.

All over, opening day meant new faces in new places, plus a new president throwing out the first ball. New teams, too, and new speed-up rules, although no one was in a hurry on the first day.

The expansion Florida Marlins, in their bright teal uniforms, won at home at Joe Robbie Stadium,

beating Los Angeles 6-3 and setting off a celebration usually reserved for World Series wins.

"I'll never forget it," said Charlie Hough, 45, a Florida native and the Marlins' winning pitcher. "All those years I watched baseball come in the spring and leave. Now, to play for a team that wasn't, in a stadium that wasn't. It's hard to describe the feeling."

The Colorado Rockies, dressed in purple, lost their first game, 3-0 to Gooden and the Mets. For the record, expansion teams are 8-4 in openers since 1961.

The usual festivities found on opening day, how-

See OPENING DAY, Page 18

Braves Blank Cubs in Opener 1-0

■ Maddux returns to Wrigley, beats his old team on five hits

THE ASSOCIATED PRESS

CHICAGO

Greg Maddux pitched another great game at Wrigley Field. Only this time it was against the Chicago Cubs.

Maddux and the Atlanta Braves began their bid to repeat at National League champions in strong fashion, opening the season by beating the Cubs 1-0 yesterday.

Maddux, who left the Cubs as a free agent last winter after winning the Cy Young Award with a 20-11 record, bested Mike Morgan, one of his closest friends. Maddux pitched five-hit ball for 8⅓ innings and left with runners on first and second. Mike Stanton got the last two outs for the save for the Braves, the two-time National League champions.

The Braves led the majors with 24 shutouts last season and hoped that Maddux, signed for five years and $28 million, would make the staff even

See BRAVES, Page 17

1993 Baseball Firsts

Ceremonial Pitch: President Clinton to Baltimore catcher Chris Hoiles at Camden Yards. Clinton threw from in front of the mound, and his pitch to the plate was high.

Official Pitch: A ball. By Rick Sutcliffe of Baltimore to David Hulse of Texas.

Hit: Jose Canseco of Texas. A bloop double.

Run: Brady Anderson of Baltimore.

Home Run: Danny Tartabull of the New York Yankees at Cleveland off Charles Nagy.

RBI: Cal Ripken of Baltimore, on a groundout.

Stolen Base: Delino DeShields of Montreal at Cincinnati.

Strikeout: Don Mattingly of the Yankees against Charles Nagy.

Walk: Juan Gonzalez of Texas against Rick Sutcliffe.

Error: Second baseman Jody Reed of Los Angeles.

Expansion Pitch: Charlie Hough of Florida, who struck out Jose Offerman of Los Angeles.

Expansion Batter: Eric Young of Colorado, thrown out on a bunt attempt by New York Mets catcher Todd Hundley.

Expansion Hit: Bret Barberie of Florida, a single in the first inning off Orel Hershiser.

Appeal: The Yankees, claiming that Carlos Martinez of Cleveland tagged up too early from third base on a fly ball. Home plate umpire Larry Barnett ruled that Martinez was safe.

New York **9**, Cleveland **1**
Texas **7**, Baltimore **4**

Boston **3**, Kansas City **1**
Detroit at Oakland

MONDAY'S GAMES

Cincinnati **2**, Montreal **1**
Florida **6**, Los Angeles **3**

Atlanta **1**, Chicago **0**
Philadelphia **3**, Houston **1**

Sports

1993 FINAL FOUR

DEVIN **STEELE**
Gazette Assistant Sports Editor

Tar Heels answer Fab Five

NEW ORLEANS — North Carolina had an answer for the Fab Five.

One team.

The Tar Heels won their second national championship under Dean Smith and third in history by teaming up to beat Michigan 77-71 Monday night at the Superdome.

It would be easy to write that so-and-so led Carolina to the win, but that would go against everything Smith preaches. For many years, the veteran coach has fed us the ol' total-is-greater-than-the-sum-of-its-parts line.

So, given his track record, how can you argue that point? Particularly when the ink hasn't even dried on the latest installment to that track record.

Smith, the well-worn joke goes, is the only man who can hold Michael Jordan under 20 points. Of course, Smith also won a national championship when His Airness was still in flight school.

STARS do exist in The System. But their individual glimmer is dimmer in Chapel Hill than it would be elsewhere.

But the galaxy as a whole is quite bright.

The biggest asset of Smith-coached teams is the team concept. Never has that been more evident than with this Carolina collection.

Sure, two or three future NBA players brought Smith his second NCAA ring Monday night. But none in particular stands out that much more than the others.

Quick quiz: Name Carolina's five starters. That's easy, right? Right. The names Salvadori, Sullivan and Rodl, probably also come to mind.

You no doubt know that Jimmy Black and Matt Doherty also started with James Worthy, Sam Perkins and Jordan on the '82 team that also clipped the nets.

You remember them individually, but think of them as a whole, too.

THE '93 team won't go down as the most talented in school history, mind you. But it played superbly together and possessed few weaknesses.

The numbers back up that contention. The 1992-93 Tar Heels:

● Won more games (34) than any other Carolina team.

● Won the first 33 of those games by an average margin of 18.2, eclipsing the school's '72 standard of 17.7.

● Pulled down more rebounds (1,532) than any in school history.

● Collected 350 steals, second most among UNC teams.

Yet, in spite of all of these numbers, all of these achievements and, yes, another national championship, Smith will continue to reap criticism.

The new argument: He won *only* two NCAA titles in 30-plus years.

At least another title will help quiet these unwarranted attacks.

Smith has never seemed to let criticism on this point bother him before.

As long as his team is playing as one, he probably won't ever let them bother him.

Finally for Smith, one team equals unparalleled modern-day success.

And, oh yeah, two national championships.

■ **MORE:** Chris Webber's timeout blunder helped give Dean Smith his second NCAA title. More on Carolina. /5C

DEJA BLUE

North Carolina's Eric Montross and Michigan's Chris Webber battle for position Monday night.

Associated Press

MVP

Carolina soph outshines Fab Five

NEW ORLEANS (AP) — Surrounded by two of college basketball's greatest recruiting classes, Donald Williams — the only sophomore on the North Carolina roster — delivered the individual championship for the Tar Heels Monday night.

Williams is the afterthought in the North Carolina lineup, often overlooked in the glow of the other starters. And yet, when there was a championship to be won, it was the slender sophomore from Garner, who made the difference.

When Michigan nosed in front 60-58, Williams went on a run of eight straight points, including his fourth and fifth 3-pointers. That kept the Tar Heels in business, the last 3-pointer narrowing the Wolverine lead to 67-66.

As important as that streak was, Williams then punctuated his effort with a key steal following baskets by Derrick Phelps and George Lynch. That led to a basket by Eric Montross, a member of Carolina's talented junior class, that built a 72-67 lead, an edge the Tar Heels never surrendered.

Williams finished with a game-high 25 points on 8-for-12 from the field, including 5-for-7 one 3-point attempts. The 5-for-7 on 3-pointers mirrored his production in UNC's semifinal victory over Kansas.

Smith's 2nd NCAA crown in Big Easy

NEW ORLEANS (AP) — North Carolina capitalized on a last-second blunder by Michigan and gave Dean Smith his second national championship with a 77-71 victory over the Wolverines on Monday night.

The two titles in Smith's 32 years at North Carolina both came at the Superdome, and this one didn't have to wait for a last-minute jumper by Michael Jordan. That 1982 game also ended on a blunder — by Georgetown.

Tar Heels	77
Wolverines	71

The Tar Heels won with a powerful inside game of Eric Montross and the 3-point shooting of Donald Williams as Michigan's Fab Five lost in the title game for the second consecutive year.

Smith becomes the fourth active coach to win two national championships. Indiana's Bob Knight has won three, while Louisville's Denny Crum and Mike Krzyzewski of Duke have each won two. Only John Wooden with 10 at UCLA, Adolph Rupp of Kentucky with four and Knight have won more than Smith, who was making his ninth appearance in a Final Four.

The Tar Heels (34-4) didn't wrap up the victory until Chris Webber, who had scored 23 points and grabbed 11 rebounds, made the mistake of calling a timeout the Wolverines didn't have.

North Carolina was leading 73-71 when Pat Sullivan missed the second of two free throws with 20 seconds left. Webber grabbed the rebound, charged up court and stopped in front of his bench with 11 seconds left to call a timeout. The Wolverines had already used their allotted three and a technical foul was called.

Williams, who finished with 25 points, made both free throws on the technical and he added two more when he was fouled on the ensuing possession for the final margin.

When the buzzer sounded the Tar Heels charged the court and mobbed Smith, the second-winningest coach of all time who had always been maligned for his Final Four failures.

The Tar Heels got the lead for good when Derrick Phelps scored on a layup with 3:12 left for a 68-67 lead. Jimmy King of Michigan threw up an air ball from 3-point range and the Tar Heels extended the lead to three when George Lynch scored in the

Please see **CHAMPS/5C**

Play ball!

Associated Press
Baltimore catcher Chris Hoiles shakes President Clinton's hand Monday after he threw out the first pitch at Camden Yards.

Baseball back between lines

Eulogies, expansion to Steinbrenner: Baseball takes field

By The Associated Press

With tears in Cleveland and cheers in Miami, baseball was back where it belonged Monday.

Jose Canseco started the 1993 season with the first hit, Dwight Gooden pitched the first shutout, Greg Maddux won at Wrigley Field — for Atlanta, not for the Chicago Cubs.

And once again, following a winter of turmoil and turnover, the focus was on the field.

All over, opening day meant new faces in new places, plus a new president throwing out the first ball. New teams, too, and new speedup rules, although no one was in a hurry on the first day.

The expansion Florida Marlins, in their bright teal uniforms, won at home, beating Los Angeles 6-3 and set-

ting off a celebration usually reserved for World Series wins.

"I'll never forget it," said Florida native Charlie Hough, 45, the Marlins' winning pitcher. "All those years I watched baseball come in the spring and leave. Now, to play for a team that wasn't, in a stadium that wasn't. It's hard to describe the feeling."

The Colorado Rockies, dressed in purple, lost their first game, 3-0 to Gooden and the Mets.

The usual festivities found on opening day, however, were missing in Cleveland, where the Indians began the final season in their old ballpark.

The Indians, their fans and all of baseball still mourning the deaths of

"All those years I watched baseball come in the spring and leave. Now, to play for a team that wasn't, in a stadium that wasn't. I'll never forget it.**"**

Charlie Hough
Florida native and winning pitcher

Steve Olin and Tim Crews in a boating accident during spring training, honored the tearful families of the two pitchers in ceremonies before playing the New York Yankees.

"You have to be thinking about the two pitchers that died," said George Steinbrenner, the Yankees owner who returned to baseball this spring after serving a 2½-year suspension for dealings with a gambler.

While Steinbrenner is back, Cincinnati Reds owner Marge Schott is gone, sort of.

Schott, whose racial and ethnic slurs got her banned for one year, was not allowed to watch the Reds' traditional National League opener from the owner's box.

Red Baron says:
Partly cloudy;
low in 30s.
Wednesday's
high in 60s / **A2**

**Chicks teach
students lesson**
————————— **C1**

**Child abuse
affects many**
————————— **D1**

Bridge/**D6**	Opinion/**A4**
Comics/**D6**	Public Record/**C2**
Classified/**C4**	Puzzles/**C6**
Health-Tech/**D1**	Region/**C1**
Movies/**D4**	Sports/**B1**
Obituaries/**C2**	Television/**D4**

Times-News

Your Freedom
Newspaper

North Carolina whips Wolverines

Tar Heels gain fourth NCAA championship

By ROB LANGRELL
Times-News

➤ Complete NCAA title
coverage / **B1**

NEW ORLEANS -- The University of North Carolina capped a brilliant season by capturing the school's fourth NCAA basketball championship Monday night in the Superdome.

The Tar Heels defeated Michigan 77-71 in front of a sellout crowd of 64,151.

Four free throws by Donald Williams in the game's final 11 seconds — including a pair after a technical foul — helped propel UNC to the title.

Williams scored a game-high 25 points and was named the tournament's Most Outstanding Player.

Joining him on the All-tourney squad were teammates Eric Montross, George Lynch, Michigan's Chris Webber and Kentucky's Jamal Mashburn.

Williams went to the foul line with 11 seconds remaining

after Michigan's Chris Webber was whistled for a technical foul. Webber called a timeout after his Wolverine squad had exhausted its supply.

North Carolina finishes the season with a 34-4 record, the most wins in school history.

The national title is Coach Dean Smith's second.

"I think you have to hand it to our players for our competitive spirit, coming from behind to win against such a good team," Smith said. "This team accomplished the goal we set on day one. It's nice to accomplish something you try so hard all year to reach."

UNC last won the national championship in 1982 with a team led by Michael Jordan and James Worthy. Its other championships came in 1923-1924 and 1956-1957.

Woody Marshall / Times-News
UNC fans in Chapel Hill celebrate the NCAA victory by dancing around a burning sofa in the middle of Franklin Street Monday.

Tar Heel fans take Chapel Hill by storm after win

By MICHAEL L. JACKSON
Times-News

CHAPEL HILL — Within seconds of North Carolina's 77-71 national championship win over Michigan Monday night, the Tar Heel faithful began to hit Franklin Street by the thousands.

As the rain fell and the wind howled, the biggest party this campus had seen in 11 years began to take root in the center of downtown.

The much-heralded freshman class of 1991 had come through for these fans, and it was time for a celebration — one that was long overdue.

"For the past three years, all we've heard about is how good Duke is,"

said UNC senior Brock Page. "As a senior, it's really great to celebrate a national championship.

"It's a pretty good feeling to be the best team in the nation," Page added. "I think we're going to be the best in the nation for several years to come now."

The crowd began to gather early, filling the local bars as early as 1 p.m. Monday. And by the time the game had started, those same bars could not handle any more patrons and had to turn away late arrivals.

"I didn't have to turn people away Saturday night (when Carolina played Kansas) like I am tonight," said Edward Boykin, a 21-year-old student

working at Linda's Downstairs on Franklin Street. "Normally, I wait tables; but tonight, they have me in charge of crowd control."

The fans cheered with every Carolina point and jeered every time Michigan answered. Sometimes they booed legendary Tar Heel coach Dean Smith when he would substitute the likes of Scott Cherry or Matt Wenstrom.

But when the final horn sounded and Smith and won his second national title in 32 years, the fans could do little else but shout, "We're No. 1, we're No. 1."

They hit they streets almost immediately, starting bonfires, climbing trees and street posts, throwing toilet

paper, lighting smoke bombs and bottle rockets, all along chanting "UNC, UNC, UNC."

Yes, they painted this town blue once again, and the wind and the rain didn't matter. All that mattered was that they were no longer in the shadow of rival Duke, the '91 and '92 national champs.

Local merchants boarded up windows in anticipation of the celebration, and many Tar Heel fans took advantage of the space to paint "Duke sucks" where it would do no harm. Others simply painted whatever they wanted wherever they wanted (like a reporter's coat).

Some of these fans, however, didn't

care to be part of the madness taking place in the middle of the road. They simply stood along the sidewalk and watched.

"This is a very exciting victory," said Simone Parker, a junior from Fayetteville. "This is my first experience with something like this, and believe me, it is an experience."

And as the bell from University Methodist Church tolled, signifying the Tar Heels' '93 national championship, someone in the crowd standing shoulder to shoulder on Franklin Street celebrating had but one thing left to say:

"Dick Vitale, you picked the wrong winner tonight, baby!"

Computers stop Discovery launch

The Associated Press
Commander Kenneth Cameron exits the shuttle this morning.

By MARCIA DUNN
The Associated Press

CAPE CANAVERAL, Fla. — Space shuttle Discovery was loaded up and ready to go today on a mission to study the Earth's protective ozone layer, but with only seconds left before liftoff the computers said no.

Computer data indicated a valve had not closed. NASA engineer Stuart McClung said if the shuttle had blasted off with the valve open, hydrogen fuel could have spilled out of the orbiter and ignited, causing an explosion.

He added, however, that engineers think the valve did close properly, despite

the computer readings, and that a bad circuit might be to blame.

This is the second time in two weeks that a shuttle countdown has ended abruptly in the final few seconds before launch. Columbia's main engines shut down three seconds before liftoff on March 22.

Discovery's three main engines were less than five seconds away from igniting this morning when on-board computers detected a problem with the valve in the main propulsion system. The countdown had stopped automatically with 11 seconds to go.

"The system worked just like it was supposed to — again," McClung said.

The four men and one woman aboard

Discovery appeared frustrated and forced smiles as they emerged from the shuttle about 45 minutes after the countdown stopped.

"It was a noble attempt," launch controller James Toohey told the astronauts. "We'll see you another day."

Deputy shuttle director Brewster Shaw said another launch attempt could come as early as Thursday should the problem simply require a change in computer programming.

But if technicians have to enter the engine compartment for repairs, liftoff could be delayed until next week, Shaw said.

"We've had a couple of relatively minor

Please see **LAUNCH** / A2

Zack's restaurant founder dead at 98

By JIM WICKER
Times-News

One of the hardest working men who ever called Burlington home died Monday. Zack Touloupas, founder of Zack's, the downtown restaurant that bears his name, was 98.

"He always worked 18 hours a day," said his son, John Touloupas of Burlington, adding that his late father remained active in the family business until he was around 90 years old.

"Some people say hard

work is bad for you, but it didn't seem to hurt my dad. He was in real good health most of his life," the son recalls.

The late Touloupas grew up in the Greek mountain town of Mega Horion, 100 miles north of Athens. He first came to the United States in 1906, but in 1909 he returned home and served in the Greek Army from 1914-1916.

"After he got out of the army, he went to work for the

Please see **ZACK'S** / A2

A picture from 1939 shows the forerunner of Zack's, Alamance Hot Weinnie Lunch at Front and Worth streets, right, which Zack Touloupas bought in the late 1920s. The restaurant's name was changed to Zack's in 1946.

Times-News

Elon kicks off Centennial bash

By MURRAY GLENN
Times-News

ELON COLLEGE — The town of Elon College officially turns 100 on Wednesday, and town leaders are ready to start celebrating.

At 10 a.m., the town kicks off its Centennial Celebration with a ceremony on the Town Hall lawn. Wednesday's agenda includes a performance by the Western High School Marching Band, introductions by WGHP Piedmont Journalist Roy Ackland, Presentation of the town centennial print,

Please see **BASH** / A2

Times-News

SPORTS

TUESDAY, APRIL 6, 1993
SECTION B
6 PAGES

NCAA FINAL ... B1, B2
BASEBALL ... B3
MARKETS ... B5

Carolina wins it all

Heels top Michigan for NCAA hoop title

By ROB LANGRELL
Times-News

NEW ORLEANS — Strange things happen when North Carolina basketball teams stroll into the Superdome.

Ill-advised passes fly toward the wrong players. Timeouts are called at inadvertent moments. But most importantly, Tar Heel squads win national championships here.

North Carolina claimed the NCAA title with a gut-wrenching 77-71 victory over Michigan Monday night that wasn't secured until Chris Webber called a timeout he'll forever remember with 11 seconds remaining.

The Tar Heels (34-4) were ahead 73-71 when Webber was contained in the corner directly in front of his Michigan bench by a double team from UNC's George Lynch and Derrick Phelps. Webber, sensing the jam he was in, called for a timeout.

The problem was, the Wolverines had exhausted their T.O's with 46 seconds to play. The officials answered Webber's call with a technical, bringing dejection to Michigan's Fab Five and coaching staff.

Donald Williams drilled the two free throws to give Carolina a four-point lead and its first NCAA title since 1982. UNC got the ball back and Williams added two more with eight seconds left to wrap things up.

Williams finished with a game-high 25 points and was named the tournament's Most Outstanding Player. He joined teammates Eric Montross and Lynch on the all-tourney team.

It was a Tar Heel squad 11 years ago that claimed the NCAA's top prize in the very same building. Georgetown's Freddie Brown threw a pass directly to James Worthy that wrapped up Coach Dean Smith's first title.

The site and setting were the same this season for Smith's second. And a boost from yet another strange event helped bring UNC's third overall championship back to Chapel Hill.

"Neither one of those plays neccessarily meant we would win," Smith said of Webber's timeout and Brown's pass. "It's all a part of the game. I've often said you have to be lucky and good."

Webber finished with 23 points and a game-high 11 rebounds to earn a spot on the all-tourney squad, but was openly critical of himself after the contest for calling the timeout.

"That probably cost us the game," Webber said. "There were 20 seconds left and I started to dribble the ball. We were down by two, the ball was on our side of the court and I picked up the dribble and called timeout. If I knew we didn't have any left, then I wouldn't have called for one."

A dejected Michigan squad (31-5) exited the playing floor quickly after the loss, and the Fab Five will head back to Ann Arbor for the second consecutive season as the NCAA's bridesmaids.

"It hurts to lose two national titles in a row, but you have to be proud of yourself," said Michigan's Juwan Howard. "Our team has been through a long road and great times and great games. We can hold our heads up proudly."

The hex that Carolina basketball teams apply to opponents in this building can't be explained.

Please see HEELS / B2

The Associated Press
Mammoth Eric Montross and his teammates had plenty to celebrate in beating Michigan.

Webber's mistake earns place in hall of shame

By BERNIE LINCICOME
Knight-Ridder News Service

NEW ORLEANS — Dumb.

In the end, Michigan wasn't better than North Carolina, just dumber.

Whatever Michigan's Chris Webber does from here, his life will always be defined by one thoughtless bit of stupidity with 11 seconds to play in the national title game. Webber called time out when Michigan had none to call.

"If I knew we didn't have any timeouts left," Webber said, "I wouldn't have called one. I cost

our team the game."

No argument here.

This is one of the great blunders in sports, large because the Final Four has become so large. It will stand with Roy Reigels wrong-way run and Bill Buckner's error and Jackie Smith's dropped pass and Johnny Pesky holding the ball. Garo Yepremian. Fred Merkel. Lonnie Smith.

Fairly or unfairly, in the blink of an eye, young Chris Webber is keeping legendary company.

This may very well be the single most obvious foulup in the history of basketball. And it happened to a college sophomore.

"It hurts to lose," said Michigan coach Steve Fisher. "It cuts to the quick when it happens this way."

Maybe this is the way North Carolina has to win its national titles. It won its last when Georgetown's Fred Brown threw a pass to North Carolina's James Worthy when the Hoyas had a chance to win. And that one was not as dunderheaded as this one.

"The final score stands," said North Carolina coach Dean Smith.

So it does, 77-71, with the last four points coming after Webber's lapse.

"We had (Webber) double-teamed and in a tough situation," Smith said. "Even if the timeout hadn't occurred, we might have won."

It would be easier to be generous to Webber, to all the Michigan players, if they had not spent their brief careers so obviously ignoring their coach. This is what you get for not listening.

Did you say the words, Fisher was asked, "We do not have any timeouts left?"

"I said those words," Fisher said.

Then, what happened?

"Obviously," Fisher said, "we weren't point

Please see SHAME / B2

Donald Williams steals show

Hot-shooting sophomore named most outstanding player

By ROB LANGRELL
Times-News

NEW ORLEANS — It's generally the older, more mature players who dominate on the basketball court at North Carolina.

Don't tell Donald Williams.

Sophomores aren't supposed to win the Most Outstanding Player in the NCAA championship.

Williams isn't listening.

Not only did Williams do both Monday night as the Tar Heels won the national title, he made himself a part of history.

Williams scored 25 points, the most of any player on the floor of the Superdome. And with guys like Chris Webber, Jalen Rose, George Lynch and Eric Montross running around you, that's a special accomplishment.

"Donald's run in these last four games has been outstanding," said UNC coach Dean Smith. "When he's on a streak, we screen for him and look for him. I'm impressed with him.

"He is in a different zone," Smith added. "I thought he was going to make it every time he

UNC parties at Kenan Stadium

Times-News

NEW ORLEANS — A celebration honoring the 1993 national championship team from the University of North Carolina will be held at Kenan Stadium in Chapel Hill today at 5 p.m.

Fans are encouraged not to try to meet the team at the airport, but rather to go directly to the stadium.

put it up."

The soft-spoken sophomore from Garner didn't see much playing time a year ago. Then again, not many Carolina freshmen do.

Williams was selected the North Carolina High School Player of the Year after his senior season in 1990-91. His rewards for signing with the Tar Heels

were a good spot on the bench and a great teacher.

He saw time in 29 games last year, averaging 2.2 points. His season-high output was 11 points against Cornell.

Fast forward to the 1992-93 season and Donald Williams is a different person.

"I have been just trying to move as quickly as I can without the ball to get to good, open spots on the floor," Williams said. "I take myself out when I get tired. I try to stay fresh at the end."

That's all a part of Smith's system. It doesn't neccessarily accomodate the flashy freshmen who come to UNC, but Monday night it proved it can win a national championship.

Williams set three Final Four records for 3-point proficiency.

His 10 treys in the two games bettered the old mark of nine shared by Indiana's Steve Alford and UNLV's Anderson Hunt.

Williams' 5 for 7 shooting in each of the games were single-game bests, and his 10 for 14 effort (71.4 percent) established a standard for two games.

The Associated Press
Donald Williams, left, set a Final Four record by connecting on 10 3-pointers.

UNC's Basketball Family

If you have to ask why comments from former UNC players would be included in a book about the 1993 national champions, and why we would go to the trouble of including the names of all of Dean Smith's lettermen, then you don't understand Carolina basketball.

True, this championship was won by the 1993 players, but in Dean Smith's extended Carolina basketball family, each man who played under his direction had a hand in it. The former players still feel a part of the program and the team, and therein lies the beauty of Carolina basketball.

So in addition to the 1993 players, here are the rest of the members of the championship "team" and what some of them have to say about the season.

MICHAEL JORDAN, 1985
Player, Chicago Bulls, Chicago

"The fundemental part of the game, the education part of it, is what Coach Smith taught me. A lot of people thought he held me back (offensively), but I think what he did was teach me other aspects of the game. Coming out of high school, the first thing you know how to do is score and shoot the ball and whatever. But Coach Smith taught me defense. He taught me how to prepare for the games. He taught me how to prepare myself for life. He taught me how to prepare myself for life after basketball."

Peppy Callahan 1962
Manager, McDonnell Douglas Space Systems Co., Kennedy Space Center, Fla.

"It was really great to be able to be there for the games in New Orleans. I did go to the Final Four this year, and I saw a lot of the former players, and even the 1957 (UNC national championship) guys. This was my third Final Four. I saw us lose to UCLA in 1968 and to Indiana in 1981. You really appreciate how great it was for them to win. This year's team was particularly close. They really liked each other. This team looked like it was a close team and the players looked liked a great group of kids who played well together.

"I really think Coach Smith has the ability to bring these kids up to another level. Some of these kids who were good players developed into great players under Coach Smith. They've come up two or three levels. What Coach Smith has done with Donald Williams, as far as giving him the confidence to shoot off the dribble, is impressive, and Donald became such a great offensive threat. Coaching definitely won that national championship game because there were great players on both sides. In the wins against Cincinnati, Kansas and Michigan, coaching was the extra edge."

Donnie Walsh 1962
President, Indiana Pacers, Indianapolis.

"It confirms to me that a fine man like Dean Smith, who I think treats the players in a very balanced, overall manner and still wins a championship, should be a college coach. Men like Dean Smith should be college coaches. I've always felt that way about Dean Smith. He's the perfect college coach because he presents athletics on a college level in the right way to the athletes he's involved with.

"Coach Smith's few critics don't have anything else to say now because he has outflanked them in every other area. I know that he runs the best program in the United States, and I don't think he puts pressure on his players to win national championships. He tries to get them to do their best every year, and if you look at his record, I don't think anybody else in the country can stand up to it. Winning the national championship just nails down another statistic that shows what a great program Dean Smith has."

Richard Vinroot 1963
Attorney and Mayor, Charlotte, N.C.

"I'm happy for everyone associated with our program--Bill Guthridge, Phil Ford, the staff and players, our fans and alumni. But most of all, I'm happy for Coach Smith, whose entire career has been one of 'championship' caliber in all the ways that really matter--his relationship with players and staff; his emphasis on things other than winning; his loyalty to players long after their playing days are over; and the first-class way in which he has conducted his life on and off the court.

"To me, Coach Smith is a quality human being who's been 'winning big ones' throughout his life, not just in 1982 and 1993."

Bob Bennett 1966
Attorney, Los Angeles.

"Very few people realize how hard it is to get to the Final Four once, to have a real good season and take a team out of nowhere and rise to the top. But it's something else to keep yourself up there for 25 or 30 years, performing every single year, which is what Coach Smith has done. The problem is that people get used to it, they just assume that you're going to have a great team every year, and even when you win the national championship, you're not Coach of the Year.

"We've reached parity in college basketball, and Michigan, Kentucky, Indiana, Kansas, those teams were loaded with talent. There were missing ingredients on this Tar Heel team. It didn't have everything and it had some injuries and setbacks. And yet, they won the thing. When they do that, people say, 'Oh, yeah, business as usual in Chapel Hill.' But they don't give enough credit to Coach Smith. We won when I was there, even ranked for a while in the Top 10, with not much talent. That's the kind of coach Dean Smith is."

Bob Lewis 1967
Stage Management, Kennedy Center, Washington, D.C.

"I'm very happy for Coach Smith. I was with him at the beginning when he was still a young man. We won his first ACC championship in

1967 and that was his first trip to the Final Four. It's hard to believe that it was more than 25 years ago. That fact that he's been to the Final Four so many times and has now won two national championships is just fantastic. I'm happy for him.

"Coach Smith has always been the same, though I think he's learned a lot through the years. He's such a fine man and he deserves all the credit that he gets. He is out for his team, his players, and that doesn't change. This was a great team this year. It makes you proud to be a Carolina guy."

Larry Miller 1968
Owner, Larry Miller and Associates, Raleigh, N.C.

"My blood is Carolina Blue all the way and it gets worse every year. Of course, I couldn't be happier for Coach Smith and the staff. I'm ecstatic for Carolina. I wanted Carolina to win so badly. That made my whole year. Anybody who knows or played for Coach Smith roots for him tremendously.

"I didn't sit during the whole tournament. I stood the whole time. But I must admit, I was not worried that we wouldn't win it. Even in the closing minutes against Michigan, when we were down by a few points, I just felt secure. I don't know why. I just felt that this group was so well-prepared and focused on what they were doing. I just wasn't worried.

"I think Coach Smith's place in history is secured as probably the greatest coach."

Rusty Clark 1969
Surgeon, Fayetteville, N.C.

"It certainly gave all of us former players a lot of pride to see Coach Smith win another national championship. A group of us went down to New Orleans and we were sitting there at courtside during the game, and it was a great thrill. I was real happy for Coach Smith, and happy for everybody associated with the program.

"You could tell early on that this team got along real well. You could tell they kind of liked each other and they played well together, and they are great athletes. I was not surprised they won it. I picked Carolina going all the way, so it didn't surprise me."

Bobby Jones 1974
Athletic Director, Head Basketball Coach, Charlotte Christian School, Charlotte, N.C.

"I recall back when they won it in 1982, and I was in a hotel in Milwaukee when I was still in the NBA. It's the same feeling. You can barely stand to watch it. Every possession, you just sort of live it. I coach high school and I played in in the pros and in college. I never get nervous, except when I watch Carolina play in the NCAA tournament. I want it so much for Coach Smith.

"Coach Smith likes to pour his life into other people, and he's done that through his players. I'm so appreciative of the seniors, especially George Lynch, because those guys just willed that win (over Michigan). I'm grateful because they did something that so many of us could not do, and that's win the championship. That's a special feeling."

Jimmy Black 1982
Assistant Basketball Coach, Notre Dame University, South Bend, Ind.

"It was a great experience being part of the Carolina program. We put in a lot of hard work, and when I returned to the Final Four, I felt the same kind of feeling. As a player, you don't really participate in the atmosphere. But this year, I had a chance to be a part of it, and it was incredible. I had the utmost confidence that Carolina would win. I knew that the team would be very well prepared, just like we were in '82. And I knew who would win if it came down to coaching.

"After being part of the program and then leaving, I really found out Final Four weekend that my heart is still in Chapel Hill. I know now that it is the best place in the country. This championship is really a source of pride for myself and all those who love Carolina basketball and Coach Smith."

Matt Doherty 1984
Assistant Basketball Coach, University of Kansas, Lawrence.

"I was up in the stands jumping up and down. I went to their hotel after the game to celebrate with the Carolina group. I couldn't help but say 'we,' from time-to-time to include myself in the Carolina family.

I went up to Coach Smith in the hotel after the game and I just wanted to shake his hand and congratulate him. He deserves to win it every year, in my opinion. But you have to be lucky and you can't be lucky every year. You have to be lucky and injuries play a large part of that.

"Coach Smith cares more about his players than he does about his own success. If he cared about his own success, he would have talked James Worthy and Michael Jordan into staying their senior years (instead of going early to the NBA). If Michael had been on that team in '85, it would have been difficult for any team to beat North Carolina.

"Coach Smith has been unselfish with the way he's handled his team. He has the best interests of his players, not himself."

Kenny Smith 1987
Player, Houston Rockets, Houston.

"This team really deserved it. This is a group of guys who worked extremely hard. When I was back in Chapel Hill last summer, these guys were putting in the extra minutes. It was clear to me they were willing to work for what they wanted. In talking to Coach Smith during the year, I could tell the team was coming together, working hard. That's how you do it.

"I was right there in the Superdome and it was a great year. I'm really glad for the team and for Coach that they won. It was exciting and emotional afterwards. I was getting up to walk out and the fans in the Carolina section gave me a standing ovation. I couldn't believe it. People were coming up to me and hugging me. Some were crying. Really, it was an unbelievable scene and shows how much it meant to us all.

"It was good for Coach Smith that they won, but it doesn't change anything about what kind of coach he is. People who have criticized him for the number of national titles he's won simply don't understand the game of basketball. Coach Smith creates the environment where you can get your degree at a great university, you can be the best basketball player you can be, and you can be the best person you can be. I know this, I wouldn't want to play for anyone else."

Jeff Lebo 1989
Assistant Basketball Coach, University of South Carolina, Columbia.

"Being there and watching it, it was probably tougher for me watching Coach Smith and the Carolina team play in the national championship than it was watching our own team play at Vanderbilt (where Lebo coached during the 1992-93 season). (South Carolina head) Coach (Eddie) Fogler (the former head coach at Vanderbilt who is also a former UNC basketball letterman) and I were more nervous for that game than we were for any of our own games, and we wanted Coach Smith to win so badly, and we probably would have been really, really down if he had lost.

"It was exciting. I'm happy for Coach Smith. He deserved to win it, and he deserves to win more than the two national championships he has won. He's given his life to the University of North Carolina, his players, and to basketball in general, and to see him win another one at this time in his life was tremendously gratifying to all of us who have been around him and know the type of person he is."

Charles Shaffer 1964
Attorney, 1996 Olympic Organizing Committee Member, Atlanta.

"I have never wanted a Carolina team to win as much as I did this 1993 team in the Final Four. That's because of my great respect for Coach Smith. In my view, he coached the perfect basketball game against Michigan in the final. Throughout his career, he has reached perfection in coaching on a number of occasions. I can remember when I was playing in the early '60s, we beat Kentucky in Lexington, and I thought at that time that he had coached the perfect game. And there have been a number of other instances of that throughout his career.

"Because of the excellence that he has achieved in coaching, he deserved, more than anybody, to win another national championship. To me, it's fascinating that he earned that second national championship against Michigan by reaching, once again, the perfection level of coaching. Not only did he get what he deserved, but he earned it in that very game with an incredible coaching performance. I'm thrilled for him."

Brad Daugherty 1986
Player, Cleveland Cavaliers, Richfield, Ohio.

"I knew that it was just a matter of time before Coach Smith would win another national championship, and the same goes from here on out. He'll probably win another one, too. He's just a tremendous basketball coach and a tremendous person. He's extremely dedicated to the University of North Carolina, and I'm very happy for him. He deserves it.

"He had a lot to do with where I am today, on and off the court. He is a great role model, and being with him was a great growing and learning experience."

Steve Previs 1972
Investment Banker, Jeffries International Ltd., London, England.

"This was actually Coach Smith's third national title, because I consider the NIT championship we won in 1971 a major victory, because the NIT meant a great deal back then.

"I'm really very, very happy for Coach Smith and the team. I couldn't be happier for him. He is the top coach forever and ever for basketball in the world. You think about it, he is the best in his profession globally, and this is just one more to add to his list of many accomplishments. I was very happy for them to win, and especially the way they did it, which was first class."

Charlie Scott 1970
National Promotions Representative, Champion Products, Atlanta.

"It's a great thrill. I was talking to Scott Montross (father of UNC center Eric Montross) and I told him that when you play basketball at Carolina, it's just like a family. It's a very special feeling to see those kids win. I feel very happy for them. I feel very good for the team and for Coach Smith. This is very good for the Carolina tradition. I really felt like I was part of it, even though I was in the stands. I'm very excited for the school and the program.

"Coach Smith is a very special person. He cares about his players as people and he really cares about the school. There's a tradition at Carolina that can't be matched anywhere else in the country. It all starts with Coach Smith and his character. He's the one who made the whole program what it is today. He's been successful because he makes people believe that they can be successful."

Dave Chadwick 1971
Senior Pastor, Forest Hill Presbyterian Church, Charlotte, N.C.

"It is such a wonderful feeling to see Coach Smith win his second national championship. There were always detractors who felt like he hadn't won 'the big one' enough, but those of us who know him and his program know that throughout the years he has won the big one, and now all the detractors must remain silent and he can be truly recognized as one of, if not the most outstanding collegiate coach ever.

"For those of us who have been a part of the Carolina basketball family, we feel such a kindred spirit among ourselves, but mostly because of the one to whom we've looked for all these years has achieved a level of greatness unsurpassed by others. We think that this is the crowning blow to Coach Smith's accomplishments, and will probably forebode perhaps others in the future, which will only continually recognize how great a man Coach Smith truly is."

Bill Chamberlain 1972
Director of Agency Safety, N.C. Department of Justice, Raleigh, N.C.

"It really was a very, very happy feeling watching them win, especially with the kind of team these guys had this year. I wrote Coach Smith shortly after the national championship and indicated to him that I was never prouder of a team than this team, and that includes teams I played on at Carolina.

"These guys played together and they exemplified Coach Smith's philosophy. They worked hard and they were unselfish, and they played hard defense. I was just really proud of the fact that they were selfless and they did a super job, and of course, things came together and they won the whole thing."

Mike O'Koren 1980
Broadcaster, New Jersey Nets, East Rutherford, N.J.

"I thought that this Carolina team was good all season, and was probably the most consistent team throughout the NCAA tournament, and also in the regular season. The best team won the national championship this year. As the season progressed, Carolina was the most consistent team, and going into the NCAA tournament, they were the

team to beat. Personally, I was very confident that they'd get to the Final Four, and once you get to the Final Four, anything can happen.

"All of us former players were rooting for Coach Smith to win that national championship again, and it was satisfying for me to see him win another title. We're the ones who fight the critics more than Coach Smith does. Put it finally to rest. He's one of the best to ever coach the game, if not the best."

Larry Brown 1963
Head Coach, Indiana Pacers, Indianapolis.

"Obviously, Carolina has meant a lot to me. One of my daughters graduated from there and another daughter is there now, and of course, I went there, too. Playing there and being a part of that program was one of the most significant things that has ever happened to me. I've been fortunate to have some good things happen to me in the sport, but watching Coach Smith this year was the highlight of my basketball career. He's been so important in my life and so important to so many people.

"That moment, watching him win another national championship, gave me the greatest feeling in the world, and anybody who has ever been connected with him would have the same response. I know he'd be mad at me for saying that 'he' won another national championship, because he thinks of his players first. Watching Carolina win didn't bring back memories of our championship at Kansas (in 1988), but more than anything, my feeling for Coach Smith stood out in my mind. I never would have been in a position to be part of a national championship had it not been for him."

John Kuester 1977
Assistant Coach, Boston Celtics, Boston.

"One of the things that Coach Smith has always instilled in all of us is how a team can do anything it if stays focused and concentrates on doing the little things, and that's what this year's Carolina basketball team did. They stayed focused and I was very much impressed with how they played defense.

"To me, Coach Smith is the pinnacle of what coaches ought to be in college today. If you have someone whom you're very fond of win another national championship, it is extremely special. I know all the Carolina guys who played in my era were so pleased because we think so much of the man. When Carolina won it all, it brought us all great joy and great satisfaction for Coach Smith. But as Coach is, he doesn't take any of that credit. He always gives it to his team."

Steve Hale 1986
Pediatrician, Burlington, Vt.

"I was very excited that Coach Smith won another national championship. I think what pleased me most was the way that he won the championship. I felt like this group of players that he had this year understood his philosophy of a team perhaps better than any other. They were willing to put the team ahead of themselves. Each one of them accepted a role on the team and was willing to stick to that role and have the success of the team outshine individual success.

"It is also a great comfort to see sportsmanship and teamwork occur in athletics today, which I think is becoming more and more rare. That is a tribute to Coach Smith in the way that he develops people as well as players."

Al Wood 1981
Marketing Consultant, Youth Minister, Monroe, N.C.

"For me personally, I was just elated for Coach Smith and the players. Coach Smith had received some flak about not winning more than one national championship before, but a lot of his better players have been separated by classes. He's never really had a lot of great players there at the same time. He's had a real good freshman and a real good senior, or a good junior and a good freshman, so he's never really had the great players there at the same time. Guys have matured at different times.

"He's gotten older and wiser, and it is good to see him do so well in his later years. People tend to remember the last things that you do in a career. I don't know how much longer he's going to coach, but he seems to be getting better and better with time. He's always been a great coach, but he's getting better with age."

DEAN SMITH'S FORMER PLAYERS AT NORTH CAROLNA

Dean Smith has been winning basketball games and graduating student-athletes for 32 years at the University of North Carolina. Here is a list of Coach Smith's former players and what they are doing now.

Class of 1962

PEPPY CALLAHAN Degree: B.A. Mathematics Education; M.A.T. Mathematics Education, 1964
Present Position: Payload Manager, McDonnell Douglas Space Systems Co., Kennedy Space Center Fla.,

HUGH DONOHUE Degree: B.A. History, Education
Present Position: Safety Director and Security Investigator, Queens Surface Co., Flushing, N.Y.

JIM HUDOCK Degree: B.S. Industrial Relations; D.D.S., 1968
Present Position: Dentist, Kinston, N.C.

HARRY JONES Degree: B.A. Philosophy, M.A. Philosophy, 1963
Present Position: Teacher, Lansing, N.C.

DONNIE WALSH Degree: B.A. Political Science; J.D., 1965
Present Position: President, Indiana Pacers, NBA, Indianapolis, Ind.

Class of 1963

LARRY BROWN Degree: B.A. History
Present Position: Head Coach, Indiana Pacers, NBA, Indianapolis, Ind.

CHARLES BURNS Degree: B.A. Sociology
Present Position: Sales Representative, Levi Strauss, Lexington, Ky.

DIETER KRAUSE Degree: B.A. Recreation Administration
Present Position: Lt. Colonel, U.S. Army, Colonial Heights, Va.

YOGI POTEET Degree: B.A. Sociology; M.A.T. Sociology, 1965
Present Position: School Dean, U.S. Army, Logistics Management College, Fort Lee, Va.

RICHARD VINROOT Degree: B.S. Business Administration; J.D., 1966
Present Position: Attorney, Mayor, Charlotte, N.C.

Class of 1964

BRUCE BOWERS Degree: B.A. History
Present Position: Senior Trust & Investment Officer, Quincy Savings Bank, Quincy, Mass.

MIKE COOKE Degree: B.A. English
Present Position: Owner, Apparel Brokers, Myrtle Beach, S.C.

ART KATZ Degree: B.A. Education; M.A.T. Education, 1967
Present Position: High School Teacher, Health Specialist, Wayne, N.J.

BRYAN McSWEENEY Degree: B.A. Political Science; M.B.A. Professional Management, 1975
Present Position: Vice President, Branch Manager, Fitzgerald, Dearman & Roberts, Irvine, Calif.

CHARLES SHAFFER Degree: B.A. History; J.D., 1967
Present Position: Attorney, Member of Atlanta 1996 Olympic Committee, Atlanta, Ga.

Class of 1965

BILL BROWN Degree: B.A. History; J.D., 1968
Present Position: Attorney, Atlanta, Ga.

BILLY CUNNINGHAM Degree: B.A. History
Present Position: Executive Vice President, Paddick Press, Philadelphia, Pa.; Partner, Miami Heat, NBA, Miami, Fla.

BILL GALANTAI Degree: B.A. History; M.A. Education, 1972; Ph.D. Education, 1976
Present Position: Administrator, New York City Schools, Baldwin Harbor, N.Y.

PUD HASSELL Degree: B.A. History; J.D., 1968
Present Position: Attorney, Raleigh, N.C.

RAY RESPESS Degree: B.S. Industrial Relations
Present Position: Director of Administrative Services, Caswell Training Center, Kinston, N.C.

TERRY RONNER Degree: B.S. Business Administration
Present Position: Vice President, Carolina Treet Inc., Wilmington, N.C.

MIKE SMITH Degree: B.S. Mathematics
Present Position: Manager, Indiana Bell, Indianapolis, Ind.

Class of 1966

BOB BENNETT Degree: B.A. Political Science; J.D., 1969
Present Position: Attorney, Los Angeles, Calif.

MIKE CONTE Degree: B.A. English; M.A., English 1967
Present Position: Numismatist, Sharon Hills, Pa.

BILL HARRISON Degree: B.A. Economics; M.B.A., 1967; S.M.P., 1979
Present Position: Vice Chairman, Chemical Bank, New York, N.Y.

RAY HASSELL Degree: B.A. History Present Position: Financial Counselor, Registered Investment Advisor, Cigna Financial Services, Charlotte, N.C.

EARL JOHNSON Degree: B.S. Political Science; D.D.S., 1970
Present Position: Dentist, Raleigh, N.C.

JIM MOORE Degree: B.A. Psychology; M.A., Psychology 1967
Present Position: Insurance Executive, Wilmington, N.C.

JIM SMITHWICK Degree: B.S. Chemistry; M.D., 1970
Present Position: Pediatrician, Laurinburg, N.C.

JOHN YOKLEY Degree: B.S. Industrial Relations
Present Position: Vice President, Universal Furniture Industries Inc., High Point, N.C.

Class of 1967

TOM GAUNTLETT Degree: B.A. Political Science
Present Position: President, Chief Executive Officer, Payne Precision Color, Dallas, Pa.

BOB LEWIS Degree: B.A. Recreation Administration
Present Position: Stage Management, John F. Kennedy Center, Washington, D.C.

MARK MIRKEN Degree: B.A. Political Science; J.D., 1970
Present Position: Executive Vice President, KSL Sports Inc., New York, N.Y.

DONNIE MOE Degree: B.S. Business Administration; M.B.A., 1973 Present Position: Vice President, Martin-Marietta Aggregates, Greensboro, N.C.

IAN MORRISON Degree: B.S. Education; M.S.W., 1974
Present Position: High School Teacher, Coach, Marshall, Mich.

Class of 1968

GREG CAMPBELL Degree: B.S. Business Administration
Present Position: Vice President, Financial Services, Rex Hospital, Raleigh, N.C.

RALPH FLETCHER Degree: B.S. Business Administration; M.B.A., 1969
Present Position: Investment Banker, Saloman Brothers, New York, N.Y. (retired)

JIM FRYE Degree: B.A. Psychology; M.A. Education, 1980
Present Position: High School Dean of Students, Orland Park, Ill.

DICKSON GRIBBLE JR. Degree: B.A. Chemistry; M.B.A., 1978
Present Position: Colonel, Commander, 704th Military Intelligence Brigade, U.S. Army, Fort Meade, Md.

LARRY MILLER Degree: B.S. Business Administration
Present Position: President, Larry Miller & Associates Real Estate, Raleigh, N.C.

Class of 1969

JIM BOSTICK Degree: A.L., B.A.; M.S. Biomedical Engineering, 1981
Present Position: Coordinator of Academic Computing, Coach, N.C. School of Science and Mathematics, Durham, N.C.

JOE BROWN Degree: B.S. Business Administration
Present Position: Vice President, Mortgage Loans and Real Estate, Durham Life, Raleigh, N.C.

BILL BUNTING Degree: B.A. Education
Present Position: Banker, First Federal Savings & Loan Association, Raleigh, N.C.

RUSTY CLARK Degree: B.A. Zoology; M.D., 1973
Present Position: Vice President, Lithotripters Inc., Fayetteville, N.C.

DICK GRUBAR Degree: B.S. Business Administration
Present Position: President, Weaver Properties, Greensboro, N.C.

GERALD TUTTLE Degree: B.A. Physical Education
Present Position: President, Classic Leather Inc., Hickory, N.C.

Class of 1970

JIM DELANY Degree: B.A. Political Science; J.D., 1973
Present Position: Commissioner, Big 10 Conference, Schaumburg, Ill.

EDDIE FOGLER Degree: B.A. Mathematics; M.A.T., 1972
Present Position: Head Basketball Coach, University of South Carolina, Columbia, S.C.

CHARLIE SCOTT Degree: B.A. History
Present Position: National Promotions Representative, Champion Products, Atlanta, Ga.

RICKY WEBB Degree: B.A. Chemistry; D.D.S., 1973
Present Position: Periodontist, Real Estate, New Bern, N.C.

GRA WHITEHEAD Degree: B.S. Business Administration
Present Position: President, Grasunan Farm, Scotland Neck, N.C.

Class of 1971

DAVE CHADWICK Degree: B.A. Radio, Television, Motion Pictures; Ed.S., 1976; D.Min., 1980
Present Position: Senior Pastor, Forest Hill Presbyterian Church, Charlotte, N.C.

LEE DEDMON Degree: B.A. Recreation Administration; M.A. Education, 1976
Present Position: Principal, Cherryville High School, Cherryville, N.C.

DON EGGLESTON Degree: B.A. Political Science; J.D., 1974
Present Position: Attorney, Greensboro, N.C.

DALE GIPPLE Degree: B.A. Political Science
Present Position: Sales Representative, Nike Shoe Co., Raleigh, N.C.

RICHARD TUTTLE Degree: B.S. Recreation Administration
Present Position: Assistant Director, City Parks and Recreation, Gastonia, N.C.

Class of 1972

BILL CHAMBERLAIN Degree: B.A. General Studies
Present Position: Director of Agency Safety, N.C. Department of Justice, Raleigh, N.C.

BILLY CHAMBERS Degree: B.A. Chemistry; D.D.S., 1976; M.S., 1979 Present Position: Pediatric Dental Specialist, Asheville, N.C.

CRAIG CORSON Degree: B.A. Psychology; M.B.A., 1983
Present Position: Working on Ph.D., Winston-Salem, N.C.

MIKE EAREY Degree: B.S. Business Administration
Present Position: Officer, Central Carolina Bank, Wilmington, N.C.

KIM HUBAND Degree: B.A. English; M.S. Recreation Administration, 1976
Present Position: Parks and Recreation Planner, N.C. Department of Natural Resources and Community Development, Raleigh, N.C.

STEVE PREVIS Degree: B.A. Radio, Television, Motion Pictures
Present Position: Investment Banker, Jeffries International Ltd., London, England

DENNIS WUYCIK Degree: B.A. Economics
Present Position: President, DMW Enterprises, Chapel Hill, N.C.

Class of 1973

JOHN AUSTIN Degree: B.S. Industrial Relations
DECEASED

JOHN COX Degree: B.A. Psychology; M.E.D. Education, 1975
Present Position: Teacher, Businessman, Durham, N.C.

DONN JOHNSTON Degree: B.A. Political Science; J.D., 1980
Present Position: Attorney, Philadelphia, Pa.

GEORGE KARL Degree: B.S. Political Science
Present Position: Head Coach, Seattle SuperSonics, NBA, Seattle, Wash.

ROBERT McADOO Degree: B.S. Sociology
Present Position: Professional Basketball Player, Flori, Italy

Class of 1974

DARRELL ELSTON Degree: B.A. History
Present Position: Material Management, GM/Delco Inc., Kokomo, Ind.

RAY HITE Degree: B.S. Education; M.E., 1975
Present Position: Vice President, Commercial Leasing, Carey Winston Realtors, Chevy Chase, Md.

BOBBY JONES Degree: B.A. Psychology
Present Position: Director of Development, Athletic Director, Head Basketball Coach, Charlotte Christian School, Charlotte, N.C.

JOHN O'DONNELL Degree: B.A. Psychology, Political Science; M.D., 1980
Present Position: Orthopedic Surgeon, Baltimore, Md.

Class of 1975

MICKEY BELL Degree: B.S. Business Administration
Present Position: Executive Vice President, Converse Inc., North Reading, Mass.

RAY HARRISON Degree: B.A. Recreation Administration
Present Position: Olympic Chemical Co., Greensboro, N.C.

BRAD HOFFMAN Degree: B.S. Business Administration
Present Position: National Sales Representative, Classic Leather/St. Timothy Chair Co., Hickory, N.C.

ED STAHL Degree: B.S. Business Administration
Present Position: Account Executive, IH Service Inc., Raleigh, N.C.

CHARLES WADDELL Degree: B.S. Industrial Relations; M.B.A., 1984 Present Position: Assistant Commissioner, Big 10 Conference, Schaumburg, Ill..

DONALD WASHINGTON Degree: B.A. Studio Art
Present Position: President, The Washington Corp., Upper Marlboro, Md.

Class of 1976

BILL CHAMBERS Degree: B.A. Psychology
Present Position: Head Basketball Coach, N.C. Wesleyan College, Rocky Mount, N.C.

DAVE HANNERS Degree: B.A. Education; M.A. Education, 1978
Present Position: Assistant Basketball Coach, University of North Carolina, Chapel Hill, N.C.

MITCH KUPCHAK Degree: B.A. Political Science, Psychology; M.B.A., 1987
Present Position: Assistant General Manager, Los Angeles Lakers, NBA, Inglewood, Calif.

TONY SHAVER Degree: B.S. Business Administration; M.A.T. Social Studies, 1981
Present Position: Head Basketball Coach, Hampden-Sydney College, Hampden-Sydney, Va.

Class of 1977

BRUCE BUCKLEY Degree: B.A. Mathematics; J.D., 1981
Present Position: Attorney, Charlotte, N.C.

WOODY COLEY Degree: B.A. Economics
Present Position: Real Estate Developer, Trammell Crow Co., Orlando, Fla.

WALTER DAVIS Degree: B.A. Recreation Administration
Present Position: Front Office Administrator, Broadcaster, Denver Nuggets, NBA, Denver, Colo.

ERIC HARRY Degree: A.S. Computer Science
Present Position: Software Consultant, Durham, N.C.

JOHN KUESTER Degree: B.A. Education
Present Position: Assistant Coach, Scout, Boston Celtics, NBA, Boston, Mass.

TOMMY LAGARDE Degree: B.A. Economics
Present Position: Investment Consultant, New York, N.Y.

JAMES SMITH
Degree: B.A. Humanities; M.A. Education, 1979
DECEASED

Class of 1978

GEFF CROMPTON Degree: B.A. Recreation Administration
Present Position: Management, Pizza Hut Corp., Tallahassee, Fla.

PHIL FORD Degree: B.A. Business Administration
Present Position: Assistant Basketball Coach, University of North Carolina, Chapel Hill, N.C.

TOM ZALIAGIRIS Degree: B.A. Education
Present Position: President, Taylor-King Furniture Inc., Taylorsville, N.C.

Class of 1979

DUDLEY BRADLEY Degree: B.A. Sociology, Recreation Administration
Present Position: Player, Coach, CBA, Oklahoma City, Okla.

GED DOUGHTON Degree: B.A. Political Science
Present Position: Vice President, Trading, First Union Securities Inc., Charlotte, N.C.

LOREN LUTZ Degree: B.A. Physical Education
Present Position: Teacher, Head Basketball Coach, Falcon High School, Colorado Springs, Colo.

KEITH VALENTINE Degree: B.A. Recreation Administration
Present Position: Computer Operator, Heilig-Meyers, Richmond, Va.

RANDY WIEL Degree: B.A. Education; M.S. Education, 1987

Present Position: Head Basketball Coach, University of North Carolina at Asheville, Asheville, N.C.

Class of 1980

DAVE COLESCOTT Degree: B.A. Education
Present Position: Regional Director of Sales, Hanes Corp., Chicago, Ill.

MIKE O'KOREN Degree: B.A. Recreation Administration Present Position: Broadcaster, New Jersey Nets, NBA, East Rutherford, N.J.; Owner, Custom Specialtees, Washington Township, N.J.

STEVE KRAFCISIN Degree: B.S. Recreation Administration; M.E.,1982
Present Position: Assistant Basketball Coach, Iowa State University, Ames, Iowa

JOHN VIRGIL Degree: B.A. Recreation Administration
Present Position: Owner, OMS Courier, Decatur, Ga.

JEFF WOLF Degree: B.A. Political Science Present Position: Marketing Manager, Accutech Computer System Ltd., Sheboygan, Wis.

RICH YONAKOR Degree: B.A. Recreation Administration
Present Position: Assistant Basketball Coach, Southwest Baptist University, Bolivar, Mo.

Class of 1981

PETE BUDKO Degree: B.A. Physics
Present Position: Investment Banker, NationsBank, Charlotte, N.C.

ERIC KENNY Degree: B.A. Chemistry; M.D., 1985
Present Position: Rheumatologist, Lynchburg, Va.

MIKE PEPPER Degree: B.A. Industrial Relations
Present Position: Vice President, CB Commercial Real Estate, Oakton, Va.

AL WOOD Degree: B.A. Recreation Administration
Present Position: Marketing Consultant, Youth Minister, Monroe, N.C.

Class of 1982

JEB BARLOW Degree: B.S. Business Administration
Present Position: Sales, Standard Oxygen Service, Little Rock, Ark.

JIMMY BLACK Degree: B.A. Radio, Television, Motion Pictures Present Position: Assistant Basketball Coach, Notre Dame University, South Bend, Ind.

CHRIS BRUST Degree: B.A. Recreation Administration
Present Position: Assistant Women's Basketball Coach, Marshall University, Huntington, W.Va.

Class of 1983

JIM BRADDOCK Degree: B.A. Psychology
Present Position: Teacher, Coach, St. Matthews School, Jacksonville, Fla.

JAMES WORTHY Degree: B.A. Recreation Administration
Present Position: Player, Los Angeles Lakers, NBA, Inglewood, Calif.

Class of 1984

MATT DOHERTY Degree: B.S. Business Administration
Present Position: Assistant Basketball Coach, University of Kansas, Lawrence, Kan.

CECIL EXUM Degree: B.A. Recreation Administration
Present Position: Professional Basketball Player, Victoria, Australia

TIMO MAKKONEN Degree: B.S. Business Administration; M.B.A., 1986
Present Position: Chief Financial Officer, Fusion Investment Co. Ltd., Budapest, Hungary

SAM PERKINS Degree: B.A. Radio, Television, Motion Pictures Present Position: Player, Seattle SuperSonics, NBA, Seattle, Wash.

Class of 1985

MICHAEL JORDAN Degree: B.A. Geography
Present Position: Player, Chicago Bulls, NBA, Chicago, Ill.

CLIFF MORRIS Degree: B.S. Biology; M.D., 1989 Present Position: Physician, Medical College of Virginia, Richmond, Va.

BUZZ PETERSON Degree: B.A. Geography
Present Position: Assistant Basketball Coach, Vanderbilt University, Nashville, Tenn.

LYNWOOD ROBINSON Degree: B.S. Communications
Present Position: Student, Film Directing Program,
Winston-Salem, N.C.

GARY ROPER Degree: B.A. Chemistry; M.D., 1989
Present Position: Physician, Andrews, N.C.

DEAN SHAFFER Degree: B.S. Social Sciences
Present Position: Sales Representative, Kenan Transport Co.,
Tampa, Fla.

Class of 1986

JOHN BROWNLEE Degree: B.A. Psychology
Present Position: Brokerage Services, BEI Management Inc.,
Dallas, Texas

BRAD DAUGHERTY Degree: B.A. Radio, Television, Motion Pictures
Present Position: Player, Cleveland Cavaliers, NBA, Richfield, Ohio

JAMES DAYE Degree: B.A. Education, English
Present Position: Assistant Basketball Coach, Niagara University, Niagara, N.Y.

STEVE HALE Degree: B.A. Biology; M.D., 1991
Present Position: Pediatrician, The Medical Center Hospital of Vermont, Burlington, Vt.

WARREN MARTIN Degree: B.A. History, Geography
Present Position: Teacher, Basketball Coach, Lee County High School, Sanford, N.C.

Class of 1987

CURTIS HUNTER Degree: B.A. African Studies
Present Position: Girls' Basketball Coach, N.C. School of Science & Mathematics, Durham, N.C.

MICHAEL NORWOOD Degree: B.A. Economics
Present Position: Broker, Merrill Lynch, Richmond, Va.

DAVE POPSON Degree: B.A. Geography
Present Position: Sales Representative, Plains, Pa.

KENNY SMITH Degree: B.A. Industrial Relations
Present Position: Player, Houston Rockets, NBA, Houston, Texas

JOE WOLF Degree: B.A. Industrial Relations
Present Position: Player, Portland Trail Blazers, NBA, Portland, Ore

Class of 1988

JOE JENKINS Degree: B.A. Biology
Present Position: Student, Graduate School, University of North Carolina, Chapel Hill, N.C.

RANZINO SMITH Degree: B.A. Afro-American Studies
Present Position: Intern, WCHL Radio, Chapel Hill, N.C.

Class of 1989

STEVE BUCKNALL Degree: B.A. Radio, Television, Motion Pictures
Present Position: Professional Basketball Player,
Villeurbanne, France

JEFF LEBO Degree: B.S. Business Administration
Present Position: Assistant Basketball Coach, University of South Carolina, Columbia, S.C.

DAVID MAY Degree: B.S. Chemistry
Present Position: Student, School of Medicine, University of North Carolina, Chapel Hill, N.C.

Class of 1990

JEFF DENNY Degree: B.A. Industrial Relations
Present Position: Investment Representative, Edward D. Jones & Co., Roxboro, N.C.

JOHN GREENE Degree: B.A. Industrial Relations
Present Position: Sales Representative, Ferguson Enterprise, Greenville, N.C.

MARTY HENSLEY Degree: B.A. Industrial Relations
Present Position: Investment Representative, Edward D. Jones & Co., Greensboro, N.C.

RODNEY HYATT Degree: B.A. History
Present Position: Coach, Teacher, Wadesboro Middle School, Wadesboro, N.C.

KEVIN MADDEN Degree: B.A. Geography
Present Position: Professional Basketball Player, CBA, Rapid City, S.D.

J.R. REID Degree: B.A. Radio, Television, Motion Pictures
Present Position: Player, San Antonio Spurs, NBA, San Antonio, Texas

SCOTT WILLIAMS Degree: B.A. Radio, Television, Motion Pictures
Present Position: Player, Chicago Bulls, NBA, Chicago, Ill.

Class of 1991

PETE CHILCUTT Degree: B.A. Industrial Relations, Psychology
Present Position: Player, Sacramento Kings, NBA, Sacramento, Calif.

DOUG ELSTUN Degree: B.A. Economics
Present Position: Business and Management Consultant, William Larmer and Associates, Kansas City, Mo.

RICK FOX Degree: B.A. Radio, Television, Motion Pictures
Present Position: Player, Boston Celtics, NBA, Boston, Mass.

KING RICE Degree: B.A. Radio, Television, Motion Pictures
Present Position: Assistant Basketball Coach, University of Oregon, Eugene, Ore.

Class of 1992

JASON BURGESS Degree: B.S. Biology
Present Position: Student, School of Medicine, University of North Carolina, Chapel Hill, N.C.

HUBERT DAVIS Degree: B.S. Administrative Criminal Justice
Present Position: Player, New York Knicks, NBA, New York, N.Y.

Class of 1993

SCOTT CHERRY
Degree: B.S. Business Administration

GEORGE LYNCH
Degree: B.A. Afro-American Studies

HENRIK RODL
Degree: B.S. Biology

TRAVIS STEPHENSON
Degree: B.A. Political Science

MATT WENSTROM
Degree: B.A. Political Science

The Future

Less than a week after North Carolina won the 1992-93 NCAA basketball championship, talk began about next season. The so-called experts said that the Tar Heels would be favorites to repeat.

Carolina coach Dean Smith knows that he has problems to face in building his 1993-94 team, and one of his chief challenges will be to get his team to ignore all the talk about how good it is.

That won't be easy.

Carolina returns Derrick Phelps at point guard, Donald Williams at big guard, Brian Reese at small forward and Eric Montross at center. Missing from that lineup is George Lynch, the leader of the championship team, and maybe the best offensive rebounder that Carolina has ever had. Lynch will be missed, there is no doubt about that, but there are qualified players to step forward.

The only other player in Carolina's top eight from last season who doesn't return is Henrik Rodl, who ended the season backing up Williams at big guard and Phelps at the point. Top reserves Kevin Salvadori, 7-0, and Pat Sullivan, 6-8, return.

The Tar Heels have other players on the bench who are eager to win playing time. Dante Calabria, 6-4, a freshman on last year's team, played a good bit early in the season before he lost confidence and therefore playing time. Calabria can play point guard, big guard or small forward. He is one of the team's best passers and outside shooters.

Larry Davis, 6-3, who will be a sophomore in 1993-94, is one of the most gifted athletes ever signed by Dean Smith. He has quickness, strength and jumping ability. Davis is versatile enough to play at big guard or small forward. His basketball skills improved last season, but he still has a ways to go.

Another freshman on last year's team, Ed Geth, 6-9, started the season out of shape, but as he lost weight and increased his strength and endurance, he displayed rebounding skills that will one day make him a fine ACC player.

Carolina held freshman Serge Zwikker, 7-3, out last season to give him a year to mature physically. Zwikker is still a little frail to stand up to the beating big men take in the ACC, but he has fine shooting skills.

That would be a formidable team in itself. But Smith and assistant coaches Bill Guthridge and Phil Ford went out and had one of the finest recruiting years in the entire nation.

The first to sign with the Tar Heels was Jerry Stackhouse, 6-6, Kinston, N.C., who played last year at Oak Hill Academy in Mouth of Wilson, Va. Stackhouse is a strong and explosive player, a quick and powerful leaper who has the skills to play inside and outside.

Stackhouse, who went to Oak Hill after playing his first two high school seasons at Kinston High, averaged 26 points and seven rebounds last season, while shooting an impressive 59 percent from the field.

Stackhouse was named the MVP and slam dunk champion of the McDonald's All-America game last April.

The second player to sign with the Tar Heels is Jeff McInnis, 6-4, a point guard from Charlotte, who played for two seasons at Oak Hill Academy. McInnis, who played his sophomore season for state 4-A champion West Charlotte High School, also played AAU ball with Stackhouse.

"I love (McInnis) because he's just like me as far as wanting to win," Stackhouse said. "We hate to lose."

The two experienced no losing last season. Oak Hill Academy went 36-0. McInnis, a true point guard, had a sparkling season. He averaged 17 points a game, broke his own season record when he picked up 373 assists, and shot 81 percent from the foul line. McInnis, who played in the McDonald's All-America game, is a rangy player who has the potential to be outstanding on defense. Playing a year behind Phelps should benefit him greatly over the course of his college career.

McInnis is nicknamed "Touche," because he spent time as a youngster watching the cartoon, "Touche the Turtle."

Rasheed Wallace, 6-11, of Philadelphia, made his official visit to Carolina on March 7, the day that Carolina closed out its regular season with a 14-point victory over Duke on Seniors' Day in the Smith Center. Stackhouse and McInnis were also at that game.

Wallace wasn't talking much after that game about which school he would choose, but he told some Carolina players that he was pretty sure that it was between Carolina and Villanova. Two days after getting a visit in his home from Dean Smith and Phil Ford, Wallace held a news conference at his school and said he was going to become a Tar Heel.

Wallace led Simon Gratz High School in Philadelphia to a 31-0 record last season, and the team was listed No. 1 in the nation by USA Today. In his 32 seasons of coaching basketball at North Carolina, Smith has never had a true shot-blocker. Wallace could be his first. He was an outstanding shot-blocker and rebounder in high school, and he is considered versatile enough to play center or power forward.

Wallace played on the same McDonald's All-America team with Stackhouse and McInnis. On one sequence, McInnis passed to Stackhouse, who fed Wallace for the jam. The three ran back down the court smiling and talking about "the Carolina connection."

As has been well documented throughout these pages, team chemistry was the strength of Carolina's championship team. UNC should again get excellent senior leadership from Phelps, Montross, Reese, Sullivan and Salvadori. The only junior on the roster will be Donald Williams, so again the Tar Heels will blend experience with youthful enthusiasm.

Smith is excellent at finding roles for his players and building team togetherness. He's also been gifted at persuading his teams to ignore outside expectations.

Coaching talent is not easy. But Smith has done it many times before, and in 1993-94, he will face an interesting challenge indeed.

1993-94
UNC BASKETBALL ROSTER

ERIC MONTROSS

DERRICK PHELPS

BRIAN REESE

DONALD WILLIAMS

PAT SULLIVAN

KEVIN SALVADORI

NAME	POS	HT/WT	YR	HOMETOWN
Dante Calabria	G	6-4, 186	SO	Beaver Falls, PA
Larry Davis	G	6-3, 184	SO	Denmark, SC
Ed Geth	F	6-9, 250	SO	Norfolk, VA
Jeff McInnis	G	6-4, 175	FR	Charlotte, NC
Eric Montross	C	7-0, 270	SR	Indianapolis, IN
Derrick Phelps	PG	6-4, 181	SR	East Elmhurst, NY
Brian Reese	F	6-6, 215	SR	Bronx, NY
Kevin Salvadori	F/C	7-0, 224	SR	Pittsburgh, PA
Jerry Stackhouse	F	6-6, 190	FR	Kinston, NC
Pat Sullivan	F	6-8, 216	SR	Bogota, NJ
Rasheed Wallace	C	6-11, 220	FR	Philadelphia, PA
Donald Williams	G	6-4, 194	JR	Garner, NC
Serge Zwikker	C	7-3, 245	FR*	Maassluis, HOLLAND

HEAD COACH: *Dean Smith, 33rd season*
ASSISTANT COACHES: *Bill Guthridge, Phil Ford, Dave Hanners*
REDSHIRTED 1992-93 season

EPILOGUE

The mission complete, the dream a reality, the airplane carrying North Carolina's national championship basketball team arrived at Raleigh-Durham Airport shortly after 4 p.m. on April 6.

The players boarded a bus that was waiting at the airport and took the 25-minute ride to Chapel Hill. The bus pulled into the Smith Center parking lot at 4:47 p.m. and backed into the tunnel on the ground floor. The players got out of the bus and headed to their locker room, where they unloaded their gear.

Then, as they had done as a team many times before, they walked about 100 yards and stood at the entrance to the arena. An estimated 20,000 fans were there to greet the NCAA champions. They cheered and shouted and the band played the school fight song. The cheers reached epic proportions when Pat Sullivan led the team into the arena.

Serge Zwikker, 7-3, was much a part of this team, even though he redshirted his freshman season. He was on the bench dressed in street clothes for each game, and when a Carolina player took a 3-point shot, Zwikker always stood while the ball was in the air, his arms extended over his head, giving the 3-point signal. "I'd like to thank the town for coming out," Zwikker said. "I hope to see you next year when we do it again."

Matt Wenstrom, senior, broke down on stage when he tried to talk about his career. An emotional and moving moment.

Sophomore Donald Williams, the MVP of the Final Four, is a young man of few words. "There's not much left to be said," Williams said, "but we are number one."

One by one the players went to the microphone. Sometimes youth overwhelmed logic. "I've had my ups and downs this year," said freshman Ed Geth, "but with the help of the coaches and you fans, I hope we can be champions for the next four or five years."

Derrick Phelps thanked fans for sending him get well cards, and he added: "The coaches did a great job with this team. I really appreciate it. I hope next year we can do the same thing."

Wenstrom and Eric Montross shot video cameras to record the moment. There are times when you want the hands on the clock to stop, and this was one of them. "Dean Smith can no longer be challenged by critics for not winning national championships," Montross said.

"I hope this silences the critics," said Scott Cherry, "but if it doesn't, they can look at the big, fat championship ring on my finger."

The last player to speak was George Lynch. Anticipating it, the crowd roared: "George, George, George..."

Lynch thanked the coaching staff, his teammates, and spoke of his own happiness. Then he looked into the rafters where 13 former UNC players have their jerseys retired. One of those jerseys is No. 12, worn by the great Phil Ford, an assistant coach on this team.

"(Coach Ford) has his jersey hanging up there," Lynch said, looking at Ford. "But I have something that he doesn't have; I have a national championship banner going up."

Ford delighted the crowd by going to the podium and bowing to Lynch.

Missing from this grand homecoming was Dean Smith. When the Tar Heels won the national championship in 1982, some 25,000 fans turned out at Kenan Stadium to welcome that team home. Not far away, Smith had taken young daughter Kristen for a quiet walk. It was announced at the 1993 celebration that Smith was on a re-

cruiting trip. Smith does not covet adulation and is uncomfortable around it. Once again he left the stage lights to his players and spent the afternoon with his family.

Pat Sullivan, the junior who had weathered the wrath of the critics and contributed in many ways to the championship, told the crowd that he wanted to share a little something with them. Then he reached into his pocket and pulled out part of the netting that the team had cut down in the Superdome the night before.

"We have a family atmosphere on this team," Sullivan said. "This is one of the greatest moments."

The very next day, Wednesday, April 7, Dean Smith and Phil Ford went to Philadelphia and visited in the home of Rasheed Wallace, 6-11, one of the nation's most highly recruited high school basketball players. Before the week was out, Wallace called a press conference and announced that he was going to become a Tar Heel.

Carolina was not resting on its laurels.

Dean Smith's last radio call-in show of the season was also on that Wednesday night. Bill Guthridge substituted on air while Smith was recruiting. The show didn't begin until 7 p.m., but callers couldn't wait. The four lines used to take calls were all filled by 6 p.m.

In the days after, Carolina's basketball office was busier than a New York subway at rush hour. Fans wanted autographs and photos and a chance to meet the players. Dean Smith was invited to just about every event planned in the state of North Carolina for the next few months. The office telephones would not stop ringing and the mail bag overflowed.

Smith played in the pro-am of the K-Mart Greater Greensboro golf tournament 10 days later, and fans cheered his name and swarmed him for autographs. Davis Love III, who attended UNC and is one of the world's great golfers, was Smith's pro partner that day. He told friends that he was so nervous about the prospects of playing with Smith that he hadn't been able to sleep the night before.

The Tar Heels were busy. They visited the White House on April 27 and met President Clinton. After Smith made his remarks in the White House Rose Garden, he was supposed to have introduced Lynch. Smith forgot and Clinton began talking. Then Smith remembered, went to the podium and interrupted the President so Lynch could present him with a Carolina basketball jersey. An embarrassed Smith couldn't believe that he had done it, interrupted the President of the United States.

"That's okay," someone said to Smith later. "Lynch had a better year than the President."

Carolina's graduation ceremonies were held on May 9. The five seniors on the basketball team received their degrees. They graduated in four years.

Now these five young men will go their separate ways. Henrik Rodl and wife Susan are in Germany, where Rodl has signed a lucrative contract to play professional basketball in that country. Lynch was the first-round choice of the Los Angeles Lakers in the June 30th NBA draft. Matt Wenstrom hopes to play professional basketball, if not in this country, then in Europe. Scott Cherry also hopes to play more basketball overseas. Travis Stephenson will start his career.

But no matter where life takes them, they have a common denominator, a bond that will remain strong. The 1993 national championship is their legacy to college basketball's top program.

The underclassmen, meanwhile, will see if next year they can match the grit and determination of their five senior leaders. The 1993 North Carolina team learned how strong it could become when everyone sacrificed for the good of the whole.

In the process, the team wrote its own chapter in the rich history of Carolina basketball. No matter how long basketball is played in Chapel Hill, the 1993 Tar Heels will be known as a special team, one of the greatest in the school's history. ●

UMI Publications publishes the ACC, Big Eight, Big 10, PAC 10, SEC and Big East Basketball Handbook magazines. For subscription information, phone 704-374-0420.